THE ENGLISH
CIVIL WARS

THE ENGLISH
CIVIL WARS
1642 – 1660

BOB CARRUTHERS

CASSELL&CO

It is a pleasure to dedicate this book to Dave Ryan of Caliver Books whose unceasing work in the field of English Civil War publishing allowed me to answer at least some of the questions in the early days.

Thanks too must go to Stuart Reid who provided much of the original text in script form and Dr Les Prince for his thought provoking interviews.

First published in 2000 by
Cassell & Co
Wellington House, 125 Strand
London WC2R 0BB

Designed and produced by Cromwell Productions Limited
Copyright © Cromwell Productions Ltd 2000

British Library Cataloguing-in-Publication Data
A catalogue record for this book is available from the British Library

ISBN 0-304-35390-6

Distributed in the USA by
Sterling Publishing Co. Inc.,
387 Park Avenue South
New York, NY 10016-8810

Printed and bound in Spain by
Graficas Estella

Half-title page: Attack on Baggage Train at Edgehill by Richard Beavis
Opposite title page: Portrait of King Charles I amid the pomp and splendour of his court, painted by the Royalist artist Sir Anthony van Dyck c.1637-38
Title page: Oliver Cromwell by R. Walker c.1649

CONTENTS

King Charles I and Queen Henrietta Maria, with the future King Charles II at his knee and Princess Mary in the Queen's arms. This was one of the first of many portraits of the royal family painted by Sir Anthony van Dyck, the Dutch court painter appointed by Charles.

THE WAR BEGINS

A pro-Royalist cartoon shows the great Royal Oak being toppled by the forces of revolution. Oliver Cromwell is on the left of the engraving.

'Brother, what I feared is proved too true, which is your being against the King; give me leave to tell you in my opinion 'tis most unhandsomely done, and it grieves my heart to think that my father already and I, who so dearly love and esteem you, should be bound to be your enemy. I hear 'tis a great grief to my father'.

Edmund to his elder brother, Ralph Verney MP

During the early years of the seventeenth century, the quiet shires and peaceful towns of England were enjoying a long period of peace. This happy state of affairs had stretched unbroken, from the battle of Flodden in 1513, during the time of Henry VIII, through Queen Elizabeth's long rule, throughout the reign of King James I and into the time of his son, Charles I.

This long peace was finally shattered by an unparalleled conflict in the three kingdoms of Britain which first took the form of armed conflict in 1639. Although these disturbances are generally known as the English Civil Wars, the sparks for this great conflagration were first kindled in Scotland and by the time the fighting ended twenty years later, men had died on battlefields in all three kingdoms.

It is notoriously difficult to attribute the outbreak of a war to a single clear cut cause. History is not a precise science in any event, and once vested interests and differing interpretations cloud the issue, it

A contemporary cartoon showing the two sides at each other's throats. Note how the Royalists are shown as long haired dandies in riding boots while the Parliamentarians are more soberly dressed for walking. It is interesting to note also that the terms 'cavalier' and 'roundhead' were already in use as terms of abuse.

can be almost impossible to trace the roots of conflict in our own century. The events of nearly four centuries ago are obscured, not just by the passing of time, but also by the activities of propagandists on both sides, right up to the present day.

We can be fairly certain though that the causes of the war which led Englishmen to fight against other Englishmen in the bitter conflict which erupted into life in 1642, stemmed from the disruptive process of evolution. In this case, the evolution of the Church and Constitution from a medieval society to a modern nation state.

The accelerating pace of progress during the long peace of the sixteenth and seventeenth centuries had imposed intolerable strains on the feudal structures by which the people of England were governed.

In the fields of art, science, theology and commerce, old boundaries were constantly being pushed back. The process of renaissance, the rediscovery, which had dragged Europe out of the Middle Ages, was by now almost complete and England was a peaceful and prosperous nation.

Almost every day, it seemed new advances in trade and industry created an increasingly sophisticated society and many Englishmen felt this new society needed new forms of government to reflect this bold new world. As the merchant classes expanded, increasingly they demanded a voice in their own affairs. More ominously, they also continued to explore new forms of religious worship.

Among those who sought change, the precise nature of what this new society needed had yet to be defined. Throughout the nation there was a heated debate on matters of government, commerce and religion which would eventually form into two distinct parties.

For some Englishmen, constitutional change was uppermost. To others, freedom of trade was the great issue of the day. For the mass of the population, however, religious reform mattered most. It was this factor which lay at the root of the polarisation which took place in English society during the late 1630's and early 1640's.

Richard Baxter was a moderately puritan Anglican preacher at the time of the outbreak of the civil war. In his memoirs of the period, first published in 1696, Baxter leaves us in no doubt that there was a clear division along the lines of those who could be described as being of a puritan persuasion, and the remainder of English society.

"But though it must be confessed, that the public safety and liberty wrought very much with most, especially with the nobility and gentry, who adhered to the Parliament, yet was it principally the differences about religious matters that filled up the Parliament's armies, and put the resolution and valour into their soldiers, which carried them on in another manner that mercenary soldiers are carried on. Not that the matter of "Bishops or no Bishops" was the main thing (for thousands that wished for good bishops were on the Parliament's side) though many called it Bellum Episcopale (and with the Scots that was a greater part of the controversy). But the generality of the people through the land (I say not all

THE CAVALIERS

A contemporary cartoon attacking the merchants with the monopoly on the distribution of wine.

Initially a derogatory term applied to the supporters of King Charles in the Civil War, it became almost a badge of pride associated with desperate men in a desperate, romantic cause.

Generally these men were drawn from the ranks of those who favoured the status quo in matters of politics and religion.

They were by no means exclusively drawn from the ranks of the gentry and in fact, at the time of the civil war, the majority of the Lords supported Parliament.

In matters of religion the Cavaliers were generally in favour of the Anglican settlement as proposed by Laud. They included in their ranks the relatively small number of Catholic gentry in England at the time.

They were united in their opposition to the Puritans whom they labelled with the derogatory term 'Roundhead'.

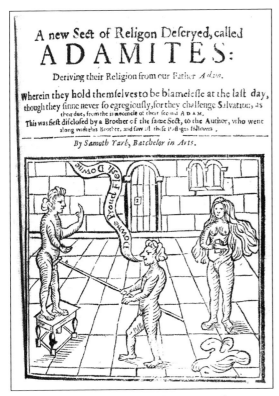

Religious pamphlets were issued both in support of new sects and against them, as is the case with this tract attacking the Adamites.

King James I, father of Charles I. It was from James that Charles inherited the Scottish and English thrones.

who were happy to embrace at least some of the more earthly delights.

"And on the other side, the gentry that were not so precise and strict against an oath, or gaming, or plays, or drinking, nor troubled themselves so much about the matters of God and the world to come, and the ministers and people that were for the King's Book, for dancing and recreations on the Lord's days; and those that made not so great a matter of every sin, but went to church and heard Common Prayer, and were strictness and precise-ness in religion, and this strict observation of the Lord's day, and following sermons and praying extempore, and talking so much of scripture and the matters of salvation, and those that hated and derided them that take these courses, the main body of these were against the Parliament. Not but that some such for money, or a landlord's pleasure, served them, as some few of the stricter sort were against them, or not for them (being neuters) but I speak of the notable division through the land..."

There was clearly a division throughout the land, but it was by no means an equal division. According to Baxter, Parliament enjoyed the bulk of the

or every one) who were then called Puritans, Precisions, religious persons that used to talk of God and heaven and scripture and holiness, and to follow sermons and read books of devotion and pray in their families and spent the Lord's day in religious exercises, and plead for mortifi-cation and serious devotion, and strict obedience to God, and speak against swearing, cursing, drunkenness, profaneness, etc. I say, the main body of this sort of men, both preachers and people, adhered to the Parliament."

Baxter emphasised the division between the puritans and the less zealous elements of the population which were, in the main, to provide the bulk of the king's supporters. Although Baxter appears to have been broadly in accord with the puritan faction, in his writing he displays a rare tolerance for those who did not conform exactly with his own views. Nonetheless, we are left with a very clear picture of a society which was being torn apart by the conflicting views of those who wanted religion to occupy the dominant position and those

Prince Henry, James I's eldest son, was passionate about the arts and was an outstanding young man by all accounts. Unfortunately, he died tragically young at the age of nineteen of typhoid fever, and so left the succession of the crown to Prince Charles.

'The Plea for Unity', a rare attempt to try and reconcile both sides in the run up to the Civil Wars.

support from the ordinary mass of the population and the Royalist cause was better represented among the middle and upper classes. In rural areas, there was a greater representation of support for the royalists at grass roots level and most of the great cities tended to be solidly behind Parliament. This meant that the bulk of the population would fall into the parliamentarian camp, and once again this phenomenon was noted by Baxter.

"But as to the generality, they went so unanimously the other way, that upon my knowledge many that were not wise enough to understand the truth about the case of the King and Parliament, did yet run into the Parliament's armies, or taking their part (as sheep go together for company) moved by this argument, "Sure God will not suffer almost all his most religious servants to err in so great a matter". And "if all these should perish what will become of religion". But these were insufficient grounds to go upon. And abundance of the ignorant sort of the country, who were civil, did flock into the Parliament, and filled up their armies afterward, merely because they heard men swear for the Common Prayer (Book) and bishops and heard others pray that were against them; and because they heard the King's soldiers with horrid oaths abuse the name of God, and saw them live in debauchery, and the Parliament's soldiers flock to

sermons, and talking of religion, and praying and singing psalms, together on their guards. And all the sober men that I was acquainted with, who were against the Parliament, were wont to say, "The King has the better cause, but the Parliament has the better men."

The issues which concerned each of these groups were not entirely separate matters and there was some overlap between them, but any move towards reform would inevitably come into collision with the person of the King, Charles I.

KING CHARLES I

Charles' father, James VI of Scotland, had ascended the empty throne of England left by the childless Elizabeth I and so became both James VI of Scotland and James I of England. When he succeeded his father, Charles was therefore the second King to rule both Kingdoms of Scotland and England, which were still separate countries in every legal and economic sense.

King Charles was a man of great principle and conviction, but he was a man totally opposed to the kind of change towards which large sections of his people were gravitating.

Although he was born in Scotland and spoke with a trace of the Scots accent which he had inherited from his father, Charles largely turned his back on that country. His slight speech impediment meant that he lacked a certain presence but this was more than made up for by his earnest, sincere faith and the serious manner in which he accepted the burden of Kingship. Charles was studious, dedicated and absolutely resolute in any cause in which he firmly believed. He was particularly staunch in his desire to uphold the ancient laws and structures of England - as he interpreted them. If there was one major manifestation of the stubborn streak which was to prove his undoing it lay in his attitude to Parliament.

Charles distrusted Parliaments absolutely and had in fact governed the country for long periods without recourse to one. At that time Parliament was not an essential requirement for the government of England. The King could effectively govern the country without one. Charles' failure to call a

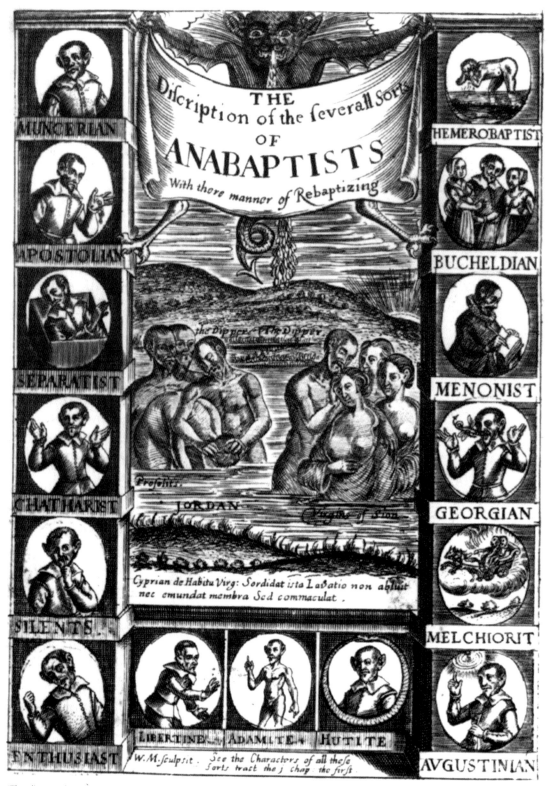

'The dippers dipped'. A savage attack on the various Baptist sects which grew into prominence in the years leading up to the Civil Wars.

Parliament, however, meant that there was no effective platform for national debate, as the unrest fermenting beneath the surface of English society had no real outlet.

Without this safety valve, pressure continued to build. This was to have disastrous consequences for Charles when he was eventually forced by events to re-call Parliament. In the meantime, he continued to exercise what, he felt, was literally his God given right to rule as he saw fit.

Charles himself clearly articulated the imminent role of the sovereign in his view.

"A good king acknowledges himself ordained by God for his people. He receives from God the burden of government for which he must be accountable. But a king must rule his people like a father and, like a father, his authority is founded on the immutable decrees of Almighty God. His subjects must therefore respect the sovereign like a father.

I alone must answer to God for our exercise of the authority he has vested in me. It is for me to decide how our nation is to be governed, how my subjects are to be ruled and above all how the Church shall be established under the rule of law.

These are the Divine Rights of Kings and are ordained by the Almighty. It is not the place of the subject to question the royal prerogative. I shall endeavour to uphold the liberties of the country, but my authority is absolute and may not be questioned. You may rest assured that I have no other intention but to honour God and to procure the good of my people."

With his inflexible views on the role of the sovereign coupled with an equally intransigent stance on the central role of the Church of England, the King and his party represented a common obstacle to change in all of the main spheres where many of his subjects demanded reform. Inevitably the King's supporters would come to be viewed as the common enemy for those who sought to change society in some way or another. In the seventeenth century there was still a great deal of reverence for the position of the sovereign and even his severest opponents stopped short of actual hostility to the King's

THE ROUNDHEADS

Roundhead was the popular collective name which was applied to the enemies of Charles I by his supporters.

In reality, this all-embracing term covered a number of separate factions who were opposed to the King, either in matters of politics, religion or both. By no means all were the sober, black-dressed killjoys of popular imagination. Most wore their hair fashionably long and even Cromwell himself could dress with colour and flamboyance when the mood took him.

In politics the Roundheads had come to oppose the King on matters such as arbitrary taxation and the King's right to raise and control the army.

In religion, they were uniformly opposed to the Anglican church which Charles sought to impose upon them. They included in their ranks Presbyterians, Independents, Anabaptists, Baptists and a large number of other persuasions.

Broadly these groups were labelled as Puritans, though they covered a wide spectrum of beliefs from the thoroughly reasonable to the almost fanatical.

Although they believed in a number of different religious solutions they were united in their hatred of Catholicism in all its forms.

Thomas Wentworth, Earl of Strafford, from a portrait painted around 1635.

person. They were in dispute, they claimed, not with the King, but with his "evil counsellors". Chief among them was Charles' close friend and confidant, Thomas Wentworth, Earl of Strafford.

Eventually the various groups seeking to change English society would coalesce from a range of separate interests into a single party directly opposed to the King's party. These zealous groups became generally known as Puritans. But this process took some time and in order to understand how the Parliamentarians could draw a unified strength from a range of disparate issues, we first need to look closer at the great issues of the day.

RELIGIOUS ISSUES

Viewed from an increasingly secular society where the influence of the Church wanes with every year that passes, it is barely possible for us to understand the fundamental role which religion occupied in seventeenth century life.

English society at that time was profoundly and sincerely religious. People attended church and felt the influence of God in everyday events. They were also deeply concerned over the form and manner in which God's worship was observed. Religion and religious debate occupied a central place in the lives of seventeenth century men and women, to such an extent that it is almost impossible for us, the products of a less Godly age, even to begin to comprehend. This was the age of the Puritan revolution.

The term Puritan was the collective name for the various Protestant sects which thrived in England and the New World from the early 1600's. They were the disciples of Jean Calvin and Martin Luther.

In 1530 when he made the Augsburg Confession, Luther had begun the radical period of religious reform which led to the birth of a Protestant Church. Protestants rejected the old Roman Catholic Church in favour of a new reformed religion, based more closely upon what they considered to be the preaching of the word of God as set forth in the bible.

The old Catholic church had relied for centuries on a Latin mass which included a prescribed form of religious worship. This took the form of a ritual procedure which was scrupulously observed throughout the entire Roman Catholic community, with specific ceremonies performed on certain days.

To Luther, the observance of these rituals had become more important than the preaching of the word of God. More importantly, he could identify no specific passage in the scriptures to justify the existence of the Pope. In consequence, the new Protestant followers viewed the Pope with hostility, but events moved quickly and before long he had become a bogeyman, the manifestation of all the evil which stemmed from the Catholic Church. Added to this debatable conclusion was the undeniable and widespread corruption coupled with abuse of power which had become endemic in the Church of Rome.

The new Protestant religion quickly took root and by 1630 Protestant Churches were firmly established throughout northern Europe and the official state religions in Scotland, England, Switzerland, Northern Germany and Scandinavia

(Continued on page 19)

RELIGIOUS ASPECTS

Archbishop Laud,
leader of the Anglican Church.

ANGLICANISM

The established state religion in England, at the time of the civil wars, was the Anglican Church of England. Under the Archbishop Laud, there was a steady move to reintroduce many of the practices which had formerly been outlawed because of their association with the Church of Rome.

These included the wearing of surplices for the clergy, the burning of incense and the lighting of candles in church. Under Archbishop Laud and King Charles, it was clear that the church would be driven by the importance of the altar and the sacraments, rather than the preacher and the pulpit, favoured by the Puritans. For many Anglicans, too much ritual had overtones of the hated Catholic religion and consequently the Anglican Church of England had many dissenters even within the ranks of its supporters.

Among its enemies, the church was viewed as being not only dangerously close to Rome, but also as an instrument for state control over religious worship.

It was these independent thinkers who were to become the main religious opponents to the Church of England. Together with the Presbyterians, they made up the Puritan party which came to a breach with Charles in 1642.

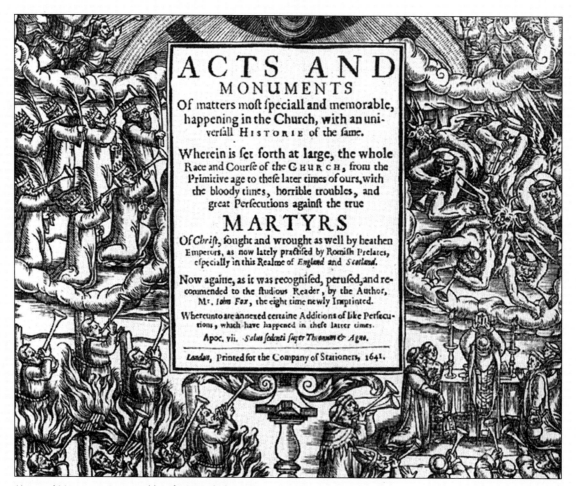

'Acts and Monuments', a pamphlet of 1641, which sought to highlight the injustices endured by the many members of the puritan population who were dubbed as martyrs to the cause.

THE INDEPENDENTS

The Independents were those who disagreed with the Anglican ideal of a single state church, but who had no fixed view on what should replace it.

In practice, they were not a single faction but encompassed a whole range of religious viewpoints including Baptists, who believed that the number of sacraments should be reduced to Baptism and Marriage only, and the Fifth Monarchists, like Thomas Harrison, who believed that after the four Kings of the Old Testament book of Revelation, the next new King would be King Jesus.

Besides these, there were various other sects including Anabaptists, Quakers and Brownists.

They were united in their opposition to King Charles because at the heart of each of these beliefs was the necessity to be free from a state controlled religion.

Oliver Cromwell, Henry Ireton and Thomas Fairfax were the leading Independents in the later years of the Civil War. In the early years, the torch had been carried by the likes of Hampden and Pym. The outcome of these two short and relatively bloodless wars proved to be an unmitigated military disaster for King Charles. The victorious Scots army easily defeated the English forces hastily thrown against them at the battle of Newburn before going on to occupy Newcastle.

The Arch-Prelate of St Andrewes in Scotland reading the new Service-booke in his pontificalibus assaulted by men & women, with Crickets stooles Stickes and Stones.

The famous incident in St Giles Cathedral Edinburgh, which saw prayer stools thrown at the first clergyman to employ the new book of prayer.

PRESBYTERIANISM

The Presbyterians believed that there was no place in an organised religion for Bishops or any other form of church hierarchy, other than the national assembly which met annually. The church was effectively governed at local level through parishes, formed into Presbyteries.

They believed in a very simple liturgy which was heavily concentrated on the preaching and expounding of the scriptures.

Presbyterianism was the established religion in Scotland and had a great many supporters in England. Among them were the Earl of Essex, Sir William Waller and General Massey.

When Charles attempted to impose the Anglican Book of Common Prayer on the Scots he provided the spark which was to flare into the English Civil War.

So resolute were the Scots in their desire to defend their religion that they were ready to take the field against Charles and did so in the Bishops' wars of 1639 and 1640.

The Scots also managed to extract a promise from John Pym to introduce Presbyterianism as the official religion of England as the price of their entry into the Civil War in 1644.

For a time it looked as if this state of affairs might come to pass but in the power struggles between the Independents and the Presbyterians during 1644, it was the Independents who would emerge victorious. Thereafter, the influence of the Presbyterians waned rapidly. With it went the possibility of Presbyterianism being introduced into England.

During the struggle for power between the army and Parliament in 1647, it was again the Independent faction which would emerge victorious. Led by Oliver Cromwell, the Independents had the support of the army over Parliament which favoured the Presbyterians.

The execution of Charles I outraged the Scots Presbyterians. There was no biblical reference in the Old Testament to a republic and the Presbyterians defended their right to depose wicked Kings. They used the example of Samuel, however, who replaced Saul with another King, David, not with a republic.

They were therefore prepared to fight on the side of the Royalists in the second civil war and supported Charles II in 1649.

Queen Henrietta Maria, the Catholic wife of King Charles. Her religion played a significant part in the events leading up to the Civil Wars.

CATHOLICISM

The Catholic religion, based on the rigid principles of a prescribed worship and a hierarchical church with the Pope at its head, had been the only Christian religion in England until the time of the Reformation.

In the intervening years, Catholicism had come to be viewed with suspicion boarding on paranoia, a national whipping boy and the root cause of all evils in the land. Although the vast majority of Englishmen were Protestants, the hatred and suspicion with which they viewed Catholicism was out of all proportion to the possibility of a re-imposition of the Catholic faith in England.

The population as a whole were so opposed to Catholicism and, in many cases, so wrapped up in religious debate, there was not the faintest possibility of their ever embracing Rome.

At the time of the Civil War, Catholics were naturally in the minority. Those few Catholic gentlemen, such as Thomas Tildsley and the Marquis of Winchester who were active in the civil war, invariably turned out on the side of the King.

Master PYM

HIS SPEECH

In *Parliament*, on *Wednesday*, the fifth of *January*, 1641,

Concerning the Vote of the House of *Commons*, for his discharge upon the Accusation of High Treason, exhibited against himselfe, and the Lord *Kimbolton*, Mr. *Iohn Hampden*, Sr. *Arthur Haslerig*, Mr. *Strowd*, M. *Hollis*, by his Maiesty,

The true Effigies of Mr. Iohn Pym, Esquire

London Printed for I. W, 1641.

One of the many political pamphlets published at the time recording the events of Parliament as they occurred. Both parties were active in promoting their own particular cause and pamphlets like this took the place of newspapers in our own society.

(Continued from page 14)

were all Protestant. The process of worship for the godly now centred fully upon the Word of God.

But the process of reformation had not ended in the 1500's. By the time of the English Civil Wars, the reformation was still continuing and there was much heated debate over the form and manner of Church organisation and worship.

At the very heart of the Protestant faith lies the concept of Predestination.

Unlike the Catholic Church, where it is acknowledged that a soul can be saved by the simple process of confessing sin, Luther argued that God foreknows and forewills all things, otherwise we could never accept the promises he makes to us of the certainty of heavenly salvation.

The argument then ran, that as the events of all our lives are pre-ordained by God, a portion of mankind must already be destined for salvation.

These were the elect - those touched by Divine Grace, who would be saved. But it was not just in the next world that the elect would become aware of their fate. They knew of it in this world. They were aware of having been chosen for salvation and this made them work consciously throughout their lives to glorify God.

Calvin took the doctrine of Predestination a step further when he argued that our lives were not just pre-ordained, but that God had knowable purposes with which we could co-operate, in complete security of mind.

This was the concept of Divine Providence, the protective hand of God in man's affairs. For Calvin, ignorance of God's Providence was the "greatest of all miseries" and knowledge of it "the highest happiness".

The net effect of these doctrines in the 1640's was to produce a section of society who confidently believed themselves to have been pre-ordained for salvation and who would therefore work tirelessly to glorify God by physical effort and moral energy; a concept which lay at the heart of what was to become known as the Protestant work ethic.

For the committed Calvinist, his faith revealed itself in the work of a man's life. Calvin argued that the elect could be judged by the quality of their work on earth, just as trees may be judged by their fruits.

What this effectively meant was that the Puritan movement produced a society committed to hard work and effort. They were cheerfully dedicated to producing good works, safe in the knowledge that God had chosen them for salvation.

The passing of time has painted these Puritan groups as being somehow oppressively dull, joyless and sober minded. In reality, almost the exact opposite was true. Although they eschewed more frivolous earthly pastimes, their assurance of salvation gave them a very real feeling of inner satisfaction, an inner glow which told them they were in communion with God. Often this spiritual warmth was described as a feeling of great joy which stayed with them for life.

Cromwell himself was to express this joy on many occasions. Very importantly, this overriding

The execution of the Earl of Strafford was in many respects the straw which broke the camel's back for Charles. Although he stood by and allowed the execution to proceed, the loss of his friend was a great blow to the King.

faith in the Lord also gave the Puritans a sense of freedom, which helped them to deal with the external difficulties of earthly life and face the greater adversity with hope and courage.

On the whole, Calvinism was most eagerly accepted by men who led active lives. They were full of vigour and readily shouldered their duty to work hard and produce good works.

Such men, it has been noted, "who have the assurance that they are to inherit heaven, have a way of presently taking possession of the earth."

THE CHURCH OF ENGLAND

In direct opposition to both the Catholic Church and the new protestant sects introduced by the puritans, stood the Church of England.

The official Church of England, as presided over by King Charles, was rigidly and efficiently organised. Under Archbishop William Laud, many practices were reintroduced which had been swept away at the time of the reformation which the people associated with Catholicism.

The lighting of candles, the burning of incense, making the sign of the cross, bowing at the name of Jesus, images of the Virgin Mary, surplices and vestments for the clergy had all made a return to the Anglican Church during Charles' reign. Many were now officially recognised as a part of the prescribed service for the Church of England.

Naturally the Puritans, with their desire for an even more stern form of Protestant worship, were outraged by these changes.

In an age where a man's religious conscience could lead him to endure any form of suffering to defend the particular strain of religion in which he believed, there were many who were prepared to die in the fight against what they saw as the return of papacy. The Catholic religion was vilified and loathed with an unforgiving passion in seventeenth century England.

The English were overwhelmingly Protestant, so most Englishmen would not therefore recognise Papal authority, nor would they indulge in the more elaborate Catholic rituals for which there was no apparent scriptural justification. If the English people, however, were agreed on the aspects of religion which they would not accept, there was still considerable discussion as to what was the correct form of worship in a reformed Protestant church.

Many Englishmen favoured the adoption of the Scottish Presbyterian system which was based on the Calvinist model of a reformed church organised into Presbyteries. Under this model, the church was effectively governed at a Parish level with major issues decided at an annual General

A contemporary engraving of the council of war held by Charles in preparation for the Bishops' wars.

S.R. GARDINER ON THE ENGLISH CIVIL WAR

'The English Gentleman' from a contemporary engraving from the 1630's.

"The Civil War was rendered inevitable by the inadequacy of the methods of the day to effect a reconciliation between opposing moral and social forces which derived their strength from the past development of the nation. The personal characters of the leaders might do much to shorten or prolong the time of open warfare, but no permanent restoration of harmony would be possible till some compromise, which would give security, had been not only thought out by the few, but generally accepted by the many.

On both sides the religious difficulty was complicated by a political difficulty."

A contemporary engraving of King Charles with the Parliament of 1625. Charles' distrust of Parliament was one of the root causes of the Civil Wars. Although the institution of Parliament was very different from its modern descendant, Charles could not reconcile himself with the concept of even limited participation in Government.

Assembly. Significantly, there was no place for a formal hierarchy with Bishops and Archbishops.

Others were Baptists who sought the freedom to worship God in the manner they saw fit. Others were not actually Presbyterians, but still felt that a Protestant church had no place for Bishops or Archbishops and clamoured for their removal. Gradually, these various Protestant sects began to group together under the banner of Parliament.

HENRIETTA MARIA

Into this complex morass of religious issues, we should also introduce the often neglected role played by the Catholic religion of Henrietta Maria, the King's French wife. Henrietta was allowed to maintain her own private priests, but even this low profile arrangement had its critics. As Catholicism was held in such deep suspicion, the fact that the Queen of England was herself a Catholic, was a source of considerable unease for the more extreme factions of the population who saw a papist plot lurking behind every new development in the religious landscape. There was the constant, and given the circumstances, not altogether groundless fear, that Charles might at some stage be converted to the Catholic faith. King Charles himself went to great lengths to demonstrate his adherence to the principles of Protestantism, but the fact that his wife was allowed to embrace, and privately celebrate, the despised Catholic mass, was always going to work against him in the hothouse climate of the 1630's and early 1640's.

As the forces of puritanism began to gain the upper hand, physical signs which might be associated with Catholicism were decreed to be eradicated by order of Parliament. Everywhere, stained-glass windows, village crosses and religious imagery disappeared as zealous mobs continued the work of the Reformation as they interpreted it. It was not all one way traffic, however, particularly in the more rural regions where the fondness for their beautiful and in some cases ancient church fittings, caused some congregations to rally in the defence of their own local heritage.

In Kidderminster, Richard Baxter recalled how he had narrowly escaped death, as a consequence of the turbulent national debate over religion:

'The Shepherds Oracle', a puritan tract which depicts King Charles I as the enemy of the state.

"About that time the Parliament sent down an order for demolishing all statues and images of any of the three persons in the blessed Trinity, or of the Virgin Mary, which should be found in churches, or on the crosses in churchyards. My judgment was for the obeying of this order, thinking it came from just authority; but I meddled not in it, but left the churchwarden to do what he thought good. The churchwarden (an honest, sober, quiet man) seeing a crucifix upon the cross in the churchyard, set up a ladder to have reached it, but it proved too short. Whilst he was gone to seek another, a crew of the drunken riotous party of the town (poor journey-men and servants) took the alarm, and ran alto-gether with weapons to defend the crucifix, and the church images (of which there were divers left since

the time of popery). The report was among them that I was the actor and it was me they sought, but I was walking almost a mile out of town, or else I suppose I would have there ended my days. When they missed me and the churchwarden both, they went raving about the streets to seek us. Two neighbours that dwelt in other parishes, hearing that they sought my life, ran in among them to see whether I were there, and they knocked them both down in the streets, and both them are since dead, and I think never perfectly recovered that hurt. When they had roamed about half an hour, and met with none of us, and were newly housed, I came in from my walk, and hearing the people cursing at me in their doors, I wondered what the matter was, but quickly found how fairly I had escaped. The next Lord's Day, I dealt plainly with them, and laid open to them the quality of that action, and told them, seeing they so requited me as to seek my blood, I was willing to leave them, and save them from that guilt. But the poor sots were so amazed and ashamed that they took on sorrily and were loth to part with me.

About this time the King's Decisions were read in our market-place, and the reader (a violent country gentleman) seeing me pass the streets, stopped and said, "There goes a traitor", without ever giving a syllable of reason for it.

And the Commission of Array was set afoot (for the Parliament meddled not with the militia of that county, the Lord Howard their Lieutenant not appearing). Then the rage of the rioters grew greater than before! And in preparation to the war they had got the word among them "Down with the Roundheads!" Insomuch that if a stranger passed in many places that had short hair and a civil habit, the rabble presently cried "Down with the Roundheads!" and some they knocked down in the open streets."

Faced with the prospect of death at the hands of his own parishioners, Baxter fled Kidderminster for what he hoped would be a safe haven at Worcester; but Worcester was still very much in the Royalist heartland and pro-Royalist mobs accosted strangers to check for Roundhead sympathies. Baxter was nervous that there would be a repeat of the scenes which he had witnessed in Kidderminster. He therefore moved on to Gloucester which was a Puritan town, later to play a major role in the course of the civil war. In this God-fearing town Baxter noted how the calming influence of the pious faith of the inhabitants contrasted with the riotous scenes he had witnessed elsewhere. When he finally considered it safe, Baxter once more returned to Kidderminster, but the manifestations of a disturbed society still haunted the town.

"When I came home I found the beggarly drunken rout in a very tumultuating disposition, and the superiors that were for the King did animate them, and the people of the place who were accounted religious were called Roundheads and openly reviled and threatened as the King's enemies (who had never meddled in any cause against the King). Every drunken sot that met any of them in the streets would tell them, "we shall take an order with the Puritans ere long." And just as at their shows and wakes and stage-plays, when the drink and the spirit of riot did work together in their heads, and the crowd encouraged one another, so was it with them now. They were like tied mastiffs newly loosed, and fled in the face of all that was religious, yea, or civil, which came in their way. It was the undoing of the King and Bishops that this party was encouraged by the leaders in the country against the civil religious party. Yet after the Lord's day when they had heard the sermon they would awhile be calmed, till they came to the alehouse again, or heard any of their leaders hiss them on, or heard a rabble cry. "Down with the Roundheads!" And when the wars began almost all these drunkards went into the King's Army, and were quickly killed, so that scarce a man of them came home again and survived the war."

The earnest supporters of the various Protestant sects became generally known as Puritans and despite their many differences they did share one thing in common. King Charles would not yield to any of their requests for change, unless they fitted precisely with his own view of how religious worship should be governed.

When the time did eventually come to fight, more than half of the King's subjects could be said to be of a Puritan persuasion to some degree or other.

THE BISHOPS' WARS

Although religion was the major factor in the escalation of national unrest, it was economic issues which would finally light the fuse and plunge the country into civil war. Once again, however, religion would play its part, even in the secular world of finance.

Not content with imposing a rigid form of worship on the Church of England, Charles sought to extend his reforms to the Church of Scotland. In doing so, he committed a fatal error. Charles attempted to impose a new Anglican Book of Common Prayer on the Presbyterian Church of Scotland. From its first introduction there were riots and unrest culminating in the famous incident where a stool was thrown at the first Bishop to introduce the new form of worship. It seemed as if the whole Scots nation was incensed, and they signed a national covenant in defence of their own fiercely Protestant religion which led them into open conflict with the King.

The Scots were fully aware of the potential consequences of their actions and they bound themselves together by a National Covenant, under which every able-bodied man and woman in the Kingdom vowed to protect their religious liberties. They then proceeded to raise an army of the covenant.

King Charles naturally responded to this threat by mobilising his own army, but in order to find the money to pay and equip them he was reluctantly forced to recall a Parliament, the first since 1628. It was to prove a disastrous step.

In two short wars in 1639 and 1640 Charles was defeated and humiliated by the Scots Covenanters in two almost farcical conflicts which were to become known to posterity as the Bishops' Wars. Charles' father, James I, using great skill, had managed to achieve the seemingly impossible; he had successfully re-introduced Bishops into the Scottish Presbyterian system. It was no mean feat, given that Presbyterianism even today is diametrically opposed to the Episcopalian principle. Charles,

The trial and subsequent execution of Thomas Wentworth, Earl of Strafford, was one of the key events leading up to the Civil Wars. This contemporary engraving conveys a sense of both the significance and the intense public interest in the trial.

THE ROUNDHEADS

JOHN PYM

Born in Somerset in 1583, John Pym was at the very heart of the English revolution.

It has frequently been argued that the whole morass of political and religious issues could be boiled down to a simple choice of whether England should be ruled by King Charles or by King Pym.

John Pym was a sober, God-fearing and devout Protestant. He was bitterly opposed to Catholicism in all its forms and pushed hard for his own cause at the expense of anything which was tainted by popery.

He was suspected of dealing with the Scots in their wars against King Charles in 1639 and 1640 and when the Long Parliament met in November 1640, Pym assumed the leadership of the Parliamentary party opposed to the King in the House of Commons.

He employed great political skill in the impeachment and subsequent execution of Stafford. Neither was he above using the London mob to make his political points for him. The apprentices were often incited to riot by the subtle machinations of King Pym.

In 1642, after the fated attempt by the King to arrest the five members, the committee of safety was established to govern during the King's absence. Naturally, Pym was a leading figure on that committee. Nearly sixty when the war commenced, Pym was too old for active service but remained at Westminster where he acted effectively as Prime Minister of the territory under the control of Parliament.

Pym played a leading role in bringing the Scottish Covenantor Army into war on the side of Parliament. By a sleight of hand, he managed to give the impression that Presbyterianism would be established in England, in return for their aid.

The introduction of the Scots into the war was to be Pym's last great act. He died on 8th December 1643, worn out by years of overwork, strain and political turmoil. Although the Royalists, who hated Pym, suggested that the cause of his death was syphilis, it is more likely to have been cancer of the bowel.

with his high-handed attitude, managed to undo all of his father's achievements. Incensed, the Scots now threw out these Bishops and took up arms. The outcome of these two short and relatively bloodless wars proved to be an unmitigated military disaster for King Charles. The victorious Scots army easily defeated the English forces hastily thrown against them at the Battle of Newburn and then marched on to occupy Newcastle.

Charles had been confident of an easy victory and all of the historical precedents pointed to the certainty of an English victory, but it was the Scots who were successful in their armed struggle. For the first time in a thousand years of cross-border warfare, the city of Newcastle-Upon-Tyne fell into Scottish hands, and it was they who dictated surrender terms to the King.

With the hostile Scots army before him and an increasingly unruly Parliament at his back, Charles recognised that, although for the moment at least, he could not bend Scotland to his will by force, he was still their King. With the pigheadedness which was to typify Charles' rule, he performed an amazing about-turn and travelled to Edinburgh in a forlorn attempt to court Scots assistance. Charles was now on the verge of a Civil War with his own Parliament. He needed their help to curb the growing power of his English Parliament, which was proving to be not just unhelpful but positively opposed to the politics of King Charles. In the meantime John Pym had constructed and pushed through Parliament an ingenious piece of legislation protecting this Parliament from being disbanded.

The King's attempt to win over his erstwhile enemies in Scotland was to prove futile. His visit to Scotland was a complete failure. The Scots would not support their monarch, who had so recently attempted to deprive them of their religious liberties, but for the time being at least they would not oppose him either. When the war in

This contemporary engraving depicts the leaders of the English and Scots Armies agreeing the peace at the conclusion of the Bishops' Wars. It was these disastrous affairs which set Charles on the road to civil war.

Surprise raids and insurrections were a feature of the rebellion in Ireland. This European engraving from approximately the same period gives a flavour of how these events were depicted at the time.

England eventually did come, the Scots stood menacingly on the sidelines and waited to see the outcome.

THE ECONOMIC COST

Militarily the Bishops' Wars had been a shambles but worse still for Charles was the financial cost of waging war.

For eleven years he had been governing the country without recourse to Parliament. Charles mistrusted Parliament and whenever possible sought to rule the country without one. In order to raise the money to govern the country without the backing of Parliament he had twisted and manipulated the laws governing taxation and took full advantage of the sovereign's right to grant monopolies.

In so doing, he had created huge unrest among the merchant classes. They objected to royal monopolies being granted on, among other things, the manufacture of soap and salt. The reintroduction and extension of dormant taxes like ship money further fanned the flames of revolt, although the revenues they raised were insufficient to keep the King's coffers in order, far less finance a war. Since 1639 little has changed in that respect. The prospect of waging war was, even then, the single biggest financial burden which could be placed upon the exchequer of any nation.

Forced to call a Parliament so that it could vote him the funds to finance his Scottish wars, Charles found that he had unleashed a pent-up force which would not be easily contained.

The Parliament of 1639 refused to vote Charles any funds until its own grievances had first been dealt with. In a fury Charles dismissed this short-lived Parliament, but he was soon forced to call another, the so called "Long Parliament" of 1640, which was even more hostile in its demands.

Skilfully marshalled by the arch-politician John Pym, Parliament introduced legislation which effectively meant that it could not be disbanded until its grievances had been dealt with.

Critics of Pym have noted that the MP's had

immunity from prosecution for debts as long as Parliament remained sitting and with the parlous financial stratum which Pym and other MPs found themselves in following the collapse of business interests in the West Indies, there was a strong suspicion of self interest. In any event the move proved to be an inspired piece of political machination, safe from the threat of abolition. Parliament presented King Charles with a list of grievances which were known as the "Grand Remonstrance" and further challenged the authority of royal control by claiming that Parliament, not the King, should have the right to raise and control the army. Once again Pym had chosen his movement with supreme political skill.

THE IRISH REBELLION

For a country which had been so long at peace, this move would in itself have presented an insurmountable obstacle, but there was to be a major development in the military and political landscape.

In 1641 Ireland exploded into rebellion, and the question of who controlled the armed forces was more pressing than ever. To an already volatile situation there was now added the need to raise and equip an army to suppress the Irish rebellion. Clearly both sides had one eye on this force in the event that civil war might come to England as well. The control of the armed forces had become a vital issue.

A continental engraving from the 1660's depicts scenes of pillage and violence. Images like these were used to fan the flames of outrage over the events in Ireland.

King Charles at the time of his failed attempts to enlist the support of the Scots. Charles is shown en route to Edinburgh to court the favour of his errant Scottish subjects.

Charles demanding the imprisonment of the five impeached MPs, painted by the American artist John Singleton Copley in 1785.

Under the able leadership of John Pym, the Long Parliament increasingly used the Irish situation and other domestic arguments to bring into question Charles' right and his personal suitability to govern. Using great political skill, Pym moved for the impeachment of Strafford, Charles' great friend and advisor, who was tried and executed. For Charles, this was the last straw; always hostile towards his Parliaments, he gradually lost patience and decided to act with force if necessary.

The two factions finally came to an all-out declaration of war after a failed attempt by Charles to seize the leaders of the party acting in opposition to him. With his failure to arrest the five members, Pym, Holles, Hampden, Haselrigg and Strode, the King had played his last card. He had attempted to over-rule the rights and privileges of Parliament by a coup d'etat. The London mob took to the streets in support of Parliament and there was no turning back.

Unrest in society now took the form of increasingly open conflict. Soon riots and brawls became more serious and the first shots were fired in anger. Faced with the outright hostility of the Commons and the populace of London, the King fled north to York. From there he attempted to seize arms and ammunition stored at Hull but was refused entry by the governor, Sir John Hotham, on St George's Day 1642.

Desperately short of arms and ammunition, Charles spent the next four months gathering the beginnings of an army. When he felt strong enough he raised his standard at Nottingham and the genteel pretences were cast aside. Civil war had begun in earnest.

THE ARMIES

A Victorian view of the Roundhead armies. It is now widely believed that the musketeer on the right would not have been equipped with the cavalry style helmet.

'I would rather have a plain russet-coated captain that knows what he fights for, and loves what he knows, than that which you call a gentleman and is nothing else.'

Cromwell, 1643

There is no doubt that the Parliamentarian leader, the Earl of Essex, began recruiting much earlier than the King. Robert Devereux, the Earl of Essex, went into the eastern association counties, to the east and south of London, and began to build a substantial field army. So by the time the King began to take this threat seriously, Parliament had a very considerable head start.

Even when the King did begin to recruit, having raised his standard at Nottingham in late August of 1642, Charles was very disappointed by the initial reaction. Three thousand militia had been paraded for his delectation on that occasion, but despite the best harangues of the King and his ministers, only three hundred agreed to take service. Charles, having to be

content with this, disarmed the remainder, put all their weapons in his wagons and moved away hoping to recruit the rest of his army somewhere else.

At this juncture, there was some feeling among the Parliamentarians that the King might not have the ability to raise an army, considering the depth of feeling in the country as a whole. Throughout the period of the Civil Wars the King's army was always smaller than that of Parliament, but there was never the real possibility that he might not be able to raise at least one significant field army. To his enemies' dismay he, at length, succeeded in finding sufficient men to take the field, though many were very poorly armed and were described by one contemporary as "poor Welsh vermin".

In the ranks of the Royalist armies, there were many gentlemen who were there out of a sense of duty. They did so despite their own reservations about being in the company of the Catholic gentry, who, almost without exception, joined the King.

Spencer was one who would not take up arms against the Crown, but like most Protestant Englishmen of the time, he was anti-Catholic, and it was galling for him to be in the company of Catholic gentry. In his surviving letters written in September 1641, he candidly shared his views with his wife.

"My dearest Heart,

The King's condition is much improved of late; his force increases daily, which increases the insolence of the papists. How much I am unsatisfied with the proceedings here, I have at large expressed in several letters. Neither is there wanting, daily, handsome occasion to retire, were it not for gaining honour. For let occasion be never so handsome, unless a man were resolved to fight on the Parliament side, which for my part, I had rather be hanged, it will be said without doubt that a man is afraid to fight. If there could be an expedient found, to salve the punctilio of honour, I would not continue here an hour. The discontent that I and many other honest men, receive daily, is beyond expression. People are much divided; the King is of late very much averse to peace...it is likewise conceived that the King has taken a resolution not to do anything in that way before the Queen comes...nevertheless honest men will take all occasions to procure an accommodation. I fear the papists' threats have a much greater influence upon the King...What the King's intentions are, to those that I converse with are altogether unknown, some say he will hazard a battle very quickly, others say he thinks of wintering, which as it is suspected, so if it were generally believed, Sunderland and many others would make no scruple to retire, for I think it as far from gallant, either to starve with the King, or to do worse, as to avoid fighting. It is said the King goes on Friday toward Chester, for a day or two, leaving his forces here; which are six thousand foot, fifteen hundred dragoons, and above two thousand horse. There are four thousand foot more raised, they say two thousand by Lord Strange, one thousand by Sir Thomas Salisbury, and twelve hundred by Sir Edward Stradling, all which will be here within a very few days. This a Lightning before Death."

Nonetheless, Parliament had certainly managed to raise the more sizeable army. A large part of these men were drawn from the regiments which had been recruited to suppress the rebellion in Ireland.

London was then a hotbed of puritanism; large numbers of Londoners therefore joined the army and the popular Earl of Essex was appointed to command it. Unfortunately he was to prove a more able politician than a soldier.

This German engraving from the 1660's gives a sense of the savagery of hand-to-hand fighting.

THE SOLDIERS - MUSKETEERS

Infantry regiments of the Civil War period were made up of two quite different types of soldier: musketeers and pikemen. In action the pikemen were grouped together in the centre of each battalion forming a forest of pike shafts with a wing of musketeers on each side.

A detail from Callot's etchings of the misery of war, showing a group of musketeers from the 1630's.

The musketeers were mainly armed with matchlock muskets. These were simple muzzle-loading weapons with a slow burning fuse or match which was used to fire them. An experienced soldier could load and fire within thirty seconds, but there were few enough of those when the war began.

Because it took so long to fire and reload a musket, regiments were drawn up six deep and only one rank fired at a time.The first rank would fire their inaccurate muskets in the general direction of the enemy, aiming as best as they could, then move smartly to the rear to reload while the second rank moved up into their place.

Part of the drill for loading and firing a musket.

A musketeer from an engraving of the 1630's. The bandolier around his chest was for storing gunpowder; each wooden container held sufficient gunpowder for one charge. The bag under his left arm contains musket balls. His match and powder flask are also suspended from the bandolier on his left. In his right hand he holds the slow-burning match.

By the time all the ranks had fired, the first would have finished the cumbersome reloading process and would have moved back up to the front ready to start the cycle afresh.

In order to load his musket the soldier had first to level it waist-high, and pour some gunpowder into the flashpan at the bottom of the barrel.

He then placed the butt of his musket on the ground and poured the main powder charge down it, followed by the musket ball and some wadding.

After ramming down with his scouring stick, the soldier had to look to his match. At this time the widespread introduction of the flintlock still lay in the future and firelock muskets were actually fired by a lighted match being plunged into the gunpowder in the pan.

Once loaded, the musketeer therefore needed to fix his match to the lock of his musket and make sure that it was burning properly. He was now ready to fire.

THE SOLDIERS - PIKEMEN

For every two musketeers in the regiment there would ideally be one pikeman. The pikemen had once been the more important element of an infantry regiment and had formed two thirds of the regiments in Elizabeth's time, but by the time of the Civil War they were in decline, eclipsed by the more versatile and deadly musketeers.

A pikeman in the 1630's. The elaborate feather crest would probably not survive too long on campaign.

Pikeman in armour from a Victorian source. For the rank and file the sword is far too long and would have actually been a short weapon known as a 'tuck.'

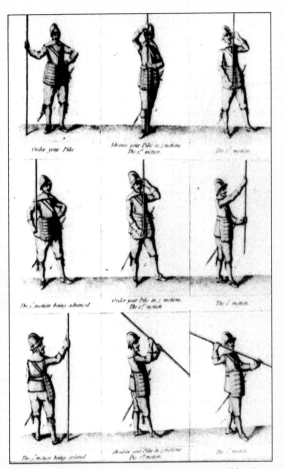

The postures of a pikeman, from a contemporary drill book.

Fewer and fewer of them now wore the armour shown in the elegantly illustrated drill books but they still had an important role to play, especially in using their long pikes to fend off enemy cavalrymen.

They could also be called upon to deliver the decisive blow by moving forward with their pikes levelled at the charge. Usually the threat of coming to grips with the pike was enough to cause one side or the other to break and run, but if both parties were resolute it came to push of pike with both parties contending, locked in mortal combat as one observer put it, "like bulls trying to bear the other down".

Pikemen in typical formation at the battle of Naseby, from a contemporary engraving by Streeter.

THE SOLDIERS - CAVALRY

Cavalry were of two kinds; the heavy cuirassiers, clad in armour from head to toe like medieval knights, and the light cavalrymen called harquebusiers who wore only helmets and either a breast-plate or a heavy buff leather coat.

Cuirassiers and harquebusiers are used to illustrate the correct methods for marching and pistol drill, from a contemporary drill book.

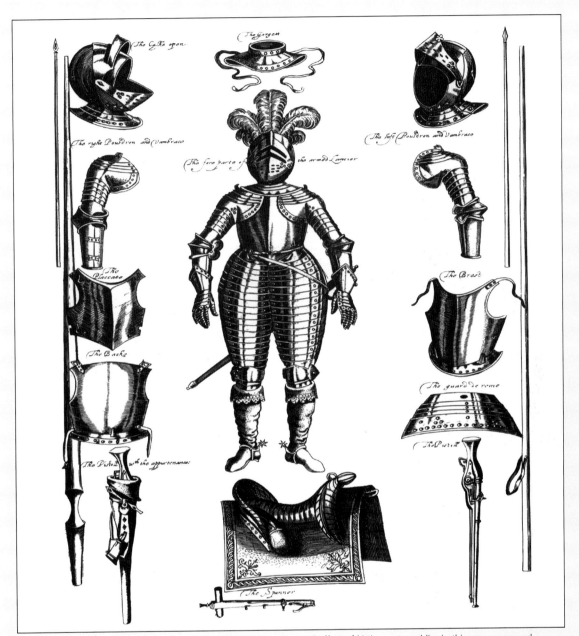

Various elements of cuirassier armour and weaponry. The expense and effort of kitting out a soldier in this manner proved prohibitive and very few cuirassier regiments saw action. Individual men of means could and did afford this elaborate gear.

The cuirassiers were intended to charge home, while the harquebusiers were skirmishers, trained to fight with firearms rather than close with the sword.

In the England of 1642 both the armour for cuirassiers and horses fit to bear them were hard to find, but Prince Rupert, the King's flamboyant young nephew, appointed to command the Royalist company, ignored convention and trained his lightly armed troopers to charge home as if they were cuirassiers.

No such stroke of imagination was to be seen on the other side. Parliament could muster only three troops of cuirassiers, but the rest of their cavalry were trained to rely on their firearms rather than the sword.

THE SOLDIERS - ARTILLERY

Civil war cannons ranged from small bore pieces not much larger than muskets to large siege guns firing 24lb balls.

The role of field artillery in the Civil Wars is a subject which can be tackled only with some difficulty as detailed information is rather sketchy. Writing in his book, "Civil War England", even a respected authority of the stature of Brigadier Young has little more to say on the subject than:

"The rate of fire was slow, for the loading drill was complicated, and the provision of ammunition was but small...."

Given the lack of good contemporary references to artillery in the field, it is not altogether surprising that the modern consensus is largely with the belief that the artillery train of Civil War times was useful only in siege warfare. Monluc, a veteran of the Italian Wars of the preceding century, summed up what was to become the modern view when he observed:

"Il fait plus de peur, que du mal."
(It frightens more than it wounds.)

Artillery nevertheless exhibited a strange kind of charisma of its own; it is one of those curious groups of inanimate objects which seem to develop a living persona. Even into the Civil War period the practice of naming individual guns like ships continued.

The menacing form of lethal twenty four pounders might be graced with the title of 'Sweet Lips', 'Roaring Meg', or, more ominously, 'Kill Cow'.

Despite the obvious fondness of the armies for their field guns they were relatively ineffective. For evidence we need look no further than the earliest accounts of artillery in action – for example in Bolton, late 1642.

"A demi-cannon fired most of the night and

the following day.... the greatest execution it did.... a bullet out of it entered into a house and burst the bottom of a frying pan."

At this early stage of the struggle, even trained gunners would be little more than civilians. In many cases, they would be full of the terror and excitement of a new experience and certainly not the hardened professionals produced by continued exposure to the horror of a grim war. A similar ineptitude to Bolton's kitchenware despoilers was displayed by the Scots gunners fighting in one of the earliest engagements for the Covenanting Armies in England, Bolden Hill in March 1644.

"....their cannon played all the while upon the Lord Marquis with so little success as is not easily imagined".

Given that these references are to gunners at the very outset of their own wars, it is not surprising that accuracy was so limited, both from lack of experience and certainly much more importantly, from the uncertainty with which they regarded the actions of their new comrades in arms.

An army new to the field, regardless of its commitment and zeal, requires time to knit together and gel into a cohesive whole where the different component parts feel confident of the reliability and steadfastness of their comrades. There can be little doubt this settling in period was particularly important for seventeenth century gunners.

Having fired their particular cannon, the gunners would immediately undergo a period of extreme anxiety, effectively defenceless until the lengthy re-loading process was complete. If the crew had faith in the surrounding infantry to protect their position at the time, it is reasonable to assume that the difficult art of measuring the charge, re-laying the piece and cooling and sponging out the barrel of the gun before the next shot could be aimed, would be carried out with a reasonable degree of composure.

If on the other hand, the crew harboured doubts as to the steadiness of nearby units or their position looked shaky, the complicated firing drill would suffer from the hasty actions

Various stages of firing a cannon. The gunner in the top picture is 'giving fire', the crew in the middle are going through the motions of loading while the bottom team are draping the gun with cloths to cool the piece and prevent premature firing during reloading.

of men with one eye to the front and one eye on a route of escape. Being armed with a sword, at best, close combat was to be avoided; consequently the flight of the gunners would often precede other units of the army. That is, if they could be made to man the guns in the first place. Writing of his own gunners at the battle of Newbury, Henry Foster had this to say:

"Our gunners dealt very ill with us, delaying to come up to us. Our noble Colonel Tucker fired one piece of ordinance against the enemy, and aiming to give fire the second time was shot in the head with a cannon bullet from the enemy."

Of course this failure to provide support and assistance was not restricted to the gunners themselves. Armies of both sides during the war were notoriously fickle and it did not necessarily

A Victorian image of artillery at work in a Civil War siege.

require many casualties to precipitate the flight of some part of a force. Occasionally, the infantry would be the villains; for example at Cropredy Bridge where fifteen pieces of ordnance were captured by the Royalists before they were subsequently recovered by Parliamentary action.

"....We recovered three pieces of our ordnance which we had lost, some half a dozen small pieces besides, which were unadvisedly drawn over before the foot were ready to march along them...."

Atkyns at Roundway Down made this observation of the Roundhead gunners:

"....by reason of our sudden charge we were about them at both ends. The cannoneers seeing our resolution did not fire their cannon."

Despite this apparently damning evidence on their lack of effectiveness, both sides invested considerable resources, money and man-power in maintaining, servicing and transporting what were obviously field pieces, designed for service in battle and too light for the demands of a

protracted siege. According to Hexham in "Diagrams of cannon and their equipment", the number of horses required to pull a "fired piece" was thirteen, with a similar number required to draw powder, shot, tools and equipment. The train of artillery not only used up scarce resources, it also considerably hampered mobility to an extent that it is most unlikely that its presence would have been maintained without some tangible military benefit.

There is, however, evidence from a number of key engagements to suggest that field artillery did play at least some part in many of the major actions. The artillery played its part with differing levels of effectiveness at Edgehill. At the first battle of Newbury, the Parliamentarian Henry Foster recalled his actions:

"The enemies cannon did play most against the Red Regiment of trained bands; they did some execution amongst us at first and were somewhat dreadful when men's bowels and brains flew in our faces."

Due to the protective nature of the enclosed terrain over which the battle was fought, artillery played an unusually important role in the action. From the opposite end of the guns, Captain Gwyn recalled the gruesome effects of the Royalist artillery fire on that very regiment:

"Near unto this field, lay a whole file of men, with their heads struck off with one cannon shot of ours."

Where co-operation between infantry and artillery was good, where each had faith in the other's determination, artillery could be used with deadly efficiency. In these cases the gunners and infantry each enjoyed the other's mutual support to produce a clinical force of studied violence, as here in the prelude to Cropredy Bridge.

Firing mortars was a very dangerous occupation, as both the fuses of the bomb and the mortar had to be lit. If the bomb fuse ignited, but the charge did not, it would explode, destroying both the mortar and the crew.

THE SOULDIERS Pocket Bible :

Containing the moſt(if not all)thoſe places contained in holy Scripture, which doe ſhew the qualifications of his inner man, that is a fir Souldier to fight the Lords Battels, both before he fight, in the fight, and after the fight ;

Which Scriptures are reduced to ſeverall heads, and fitly applyed to the Souldiers ſeverall occaſions, and ſo may ſupply the want of the whole Bible; which a Souldier cannot conveniently carry about him :

And may bee alſo uſefull for any Chriſtian to meditate upon, now in this miſerable time of Warre.

Imprimatur,   *Edm. Calamy*:

Joſ.18. This Book of the Law ſhall not depart out of thy mouth,but thou ſhalt meditate therein day and night, that thou maiſt obſerve to doe according to all that is written therein, for then thou ſhalt make thy way proſperous, and have good ſucceſſe.

Printed at *London* by *G.B.* and *R.W.* for *Aug*:3ᵈ *G.C.* 1643.

'The soldier's catechism'; the armies on both sides, had, in their ranks, a large number of devout believers. The advent of cheap mass printing allowed soldiers to carry the word of God into the field.

"But His Majesties commanders being intelligent on all occasions, and sent two more small pieces of six pound bullet and a demi-cannon to secure the bridge and put some foot into a mill adjoining, to defend the ford which they maintained with much courage and discretion, that the rebels were repulsed with both musket and ordnance playing hot upon them by which a great many rebels were slain and the rest beat off."

We are fortunate that at both Newbury and Cropredy Bridge we have been left accounts of the actions of the ordnance by both sides. A Parliamentarian on the receiving end of His Majesty's guns at Cropredy left us this account:

"Col. Adam had his arm shot off with a bullet of twenty-four pounds weight. Lt. Matthews and divers others were hurt and wounded."

At Marston Moor a witness recalls the grisly fate of the Royalist Thomas Danby, who was shot to death with a cannon bullet and cut in two as he had been locked or tied into his saddle that very day.

The *Poſtures*, as afore-ſaid, were firſt done with the *Muſquettiers* in the *Front*, the *Pikes* at the ſame inſtant performing their *Poſtures* in the *Reer* of the *Muſquettiers*; the *Body* then ſtanding as the *Figure* under A. When the *Muſquettiers* gave fire they ſtood as *Figure* under B. When the *Pikes* did their *Poſtures* in the *Van*, then the *Body* ſtood as *Figure* under C.

Music for the postures of muskets and pikes from Barriffe's drill book.

Cromwell himself gives us an indication of the fact that this was not the only effective artillery activity at Marston Moor. Writing in what must be one of the most brutal letters of "condolence" ever written, he addressed his brother-in-law thus:

"Sir, God has taken away your eldest son by a cannon shot. It break his leg. We were necessitate to have to cut it off, whereof he died."

The awful nature of wounds like this are mirrored in many other recollections from the period. Hopton, for example, has this to say of Cheriton.

"....their Chief commander doing his duty like a worthy person had his leg shot off to the ankle by grape shot, whereof he died."

It is perhaps an indication of the importance placed upon the artillery by commanders of the day, that a respected figure of the status of Hopton later assumed command of the Royalist artillery whilst seeming not to lose face.

Supported by infantry and firing grape shot, field guns could, of course, be devastatingly efficient against cavalry. Byron, this time on the first Newbury....

"....and charged the enemy, who entertained us with a great salvo of musket shot, and discharged two drakes upon us laden with case shot which killed some and hurt many, so that we were forced to wheel off and could not meet them at the charge."

A similar effective deployment of artillery in the field was demonstrated in other smaller struggles such as Braddock Down, where Royalist artillery caused heavy casualties among Sir John Cell's Parliamentary pikemen, or at the little known engagement at Southam Green.

"Lord Brooke started the engagement by ordering his guns to open fire. It is recorded that the first shot ploughed through a file of five horsemen and blew the wheel off a gun... the parliamentarians were also equipped with some light guns which opened up the grape shot on the unfortunate Royalist foot, who in this engagement soon broke and ran...."

The experience of the Red Regiment at Newbury is clearly not an isolated case, but the aftermath is an indication of the vicious power of properly utilised artillery operated by gunners secure in the support of their comrades in arms.

"This 20th September we lost about sixty or seventy men in our Red Regiment of the trained bands, besides wounded men, we having the hottest charge from the enemies cannon of any regiment in the army. Also that very wealthy and valiant gentleman Captain Hunt was slain in this battle, whose death is much lamented. These two regiments were the very objects of the enemy's battery that day and have since made a boast of it."

CIVIL WAR COLOURS

Colonel

Lieutenant Colonel

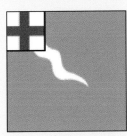

Major

1st Captain

2nd Captain

3rd Captain

4th Captain

5th Captain

6th Captain

7th Captain

EARL OF ESSEX (PARLIAMENT)

The Regiments of the Civil War period were theoretically divided into ten companies. Many regiments, particularly Royalist, never reached the full ten, while several Parliamentarian units had more. Each company had its own colour which provided a rallying point in battle and also a clearly recognisable position for regimental formation.

After the Civil War, Captain Thomas Venn provided a description of the various flags. Venn described the Colonels' colour as a plain background, the Lieutenant Colonels' as a plain background and a St. George's cross. The Majors' was differentiated by a stream blazent. Each of the companies was then marked with a device according to the seniority of its officers from a first Captain to a seventh Captain.

This system of differentiation has become known as the Venn system and is illustrated here by the flags of the Earl of Essex's Regiment.

Venn himself wrote:

"The Colonels Colours in the first place is of a pure and clean colour, without any mixture. The Lieutenant Colonels only with a Saint George Armies in the upper corner next the staff; The Major's the same; but in the lower and outermost corner with a little stream Blazent, and every Captain with Saint George Armies alone, but with so many spots of several Devices as pertain to the dignity of their respective places."

In an age with very high levels of illiteracy the use of a visual device was essential in order to train and discipline inexperienced and raw troops. The men would quickly come to recognise their own colour, which served as the forming up point for parades and marches. Carried by an ensign, the colours were prized as battle trophies and from the outset of the Civil Wars the magnitude of a victory was measured by the number of colours captured.

Colonel

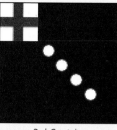

3rd Captain

Lieutenant Colonel

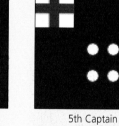

4th Captain

Major

5th Captain

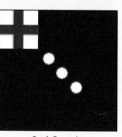

1st Captain

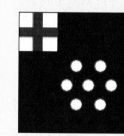

6th Captain

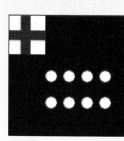

2nd Captain

7th Captain

THE BLUE REGIMENT. THE LONDON TRAINED BANDS (PARLIAMENT)

To confuse matters the use of a stream blazent as the device to differentiate the Major's colour as described by Venn did not become universally accepted until after 1660.

In the meantime, and throughout the Civil War period, another system existed alongside the Venn system to differentiate the banners of the different companies in which a single device of the regimental pattern was used for the Major's company. This was equally popular during the Civil War. In this system the First Captain would have two devices, the Second Captain, three and so on.

An engraving of the Civil War period depicts the ensign with his colours. Ensigns were chosen for their personal bravery and were expected to die before relinquishing the colours.

PRINCE RUPERT'S REGIMENT OF FOOT

Without doubt, one of the most bizarre designs for a Civil War Standard was that of Prince Rupert's Foot. It is also unique and bears no relation to any other regiment. From the fragmentary evidence that survives, a conjectural reconstruction of the first four colours in the Regiment would look like this. The mind boggles to visualise the progression through to its logical conclusion.

CHARLES GERARD'S REGIMENT (ROYALIST)

In this example of what has become known as the Gyronny system, an increasingly elaborate geometrical programme was incorporated into the design. It is not difficult to imagine the result of this design taken to its logical extent. No examples beyond this number, however, appear to have survived. It is also possible that in some of the smaller Royalist regiments, the full number of companies was never actually reached.

1st Captain

4th Captain

Colonel

1st Captain

2nd Captain

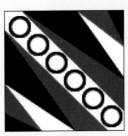

6th Captain

Lieutenant Colonel

2nd Captain

A harquebusier fires a wheellock carbine. His bullet pouch and powder flask hang from his belt off his right hand side.

Major

3rd Captain

TOWER HAMLETS REGIMENT OF TRAINED BANDS · 1643 (PARLIAMENT)

This Stand of colours was unusual among infantry colours in that they carried a written legend. This was the usual practice among the cavalry but almost completely absent from infantry colours. The various companies of the regiment are differentiated by the white roundels on the flags.

Colonel

1st Captain

Lieutenant Colonel

2nd Captain

Major

3rd Captain

KING'S LIFEGUARD (ROYALIST)

Based on a Stand of the King's regiment captured at Naseby, we must assume that the Tudor Rose theme would be carried on throughout the other companies of foot, although only six colours actually survive.

If the scheme was carried through to its logical conclusion, we would expect the sixth captain's colour to carry either six or seven roses, depending on which system was used for differentiation.

STRIPED COLOURS

This pattern was popular during the Elizabethan period, and amongst Trained Band units during the 1630's. Whilst it is not impossible that field units of either side carried colours of such an obsolete design, it is probable that such flags belonged to Trained Bands or other local units. Unfortunately, no records of a complete set of striped flags have survived and this reconstruction is conjectural.

Colonel

1st Captain

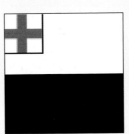
Major

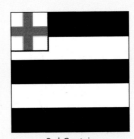
3rd Captain

Lieutenant Colonel

2nd Captain

1st Captain

4th Captain

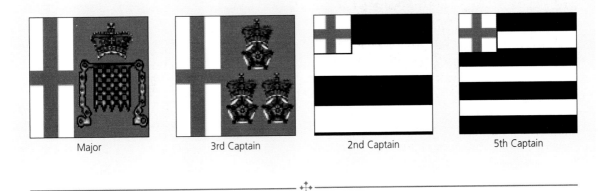
Major

3rd Captain

2nd Captain

5th Captain

SCOTS COVENANTERS

The vast majority of the Scots regiments that comprised all of the armies of the Covenant based their colours on the national flag. The Scots were unusual in that they used conventional arabic numbers to differentiate the companies in some regiments. A great deal of variation in colours outside of the traditional dark blue were to be seen. The Scots Standard featured red, yellow, green and black background in addition to the traditional blue. The cross itself was also used in a variety of other colours apart from the usual white.

CAVALRY CORNETS

Each troop within a cavalry regiment carried a different flag, or Cornet. There was often no unifying system within the set, other than having the same background colour, or Field. Each Captain was free to choose his own cartoon, political slogan, family motto or religious message. They came in an enormous variety, as can be seen from these illustrations.

Standard of
Kings Lifeguard
(Scots Army 1648)

Scot's Covenanter 1644

Standard of Captain
Owen Cambridge
(Parliamentary)

Standard of
Captain Brown
(Parliamentary)

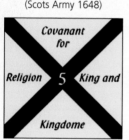

Scot's Covenanter 1644

Scot's Covenanter 1648

Standard of
Sir Arthur Haselrigg
(Parliamentary)

Unidentified Royalist
Standard, captured at
Marston Moor

A French engraving of a soldiers' camp during the Thirty Years War. Scenes like this would have been common throughout England during the Civil Wars.

THE ROAD TO EDGEHILL

Royalist troops as the Victorians imagined they would have looked. While some of the figures correspond accurately to paintings of the period, others are slightly more fanciful, in particular the headgear and equipment of the pike.

"My Lords and Gentlemen here present, if this day shine prosperously for us we shall be happy in a glorious victory... come life, come death, your King will bear you company, and ever keep this full, this place, and this day's service in his grateful remembrance"

Charles I at Edgehill

During the summer and early autumn of 1642, the two sides jockeyed for position in the Midlands of England, which was to become the cockpit of the Civil Wars for the next four years.

In support of the King, the Earl of Northampton seized the initiative and besieged Warwick Castle, but this bungled affair had all the hallmarks of amateurs learning a professional trade.

The brief siege of the castle was raised by the Parliamentary garrison with very little bloodshed,

but the precedent had been set and throughout the towns and villages of the North and Midlands, ugly little skirmishes were being fought, and they were steadily rising in scale.

At Southam on 22nd August 1642, the Parliamentarian forces of Lord Brooke defeated a small Royalist army, leaving the fields and the little River Itchen choked with corpses.

As these events were being played out, the real Parliamentary field army, under Essex, was growing in strength. In its ranks was one Nehemiah Wharton, a London apprentice, whose colourful letters to his master in London have left us one of the few primary sources from the ranks of Civil War armies.

"Worthy Sir,

Aylesbury, August the 16th, 1642.

On Monday, August the 8th, we marched to Acton, but being the Sixth Company, we were late, and many of our soldiers were constrained to lodge in beds whose feathers were above yard long. Tuesday, early in the morning, several of our soldiers inhabiting the out parts of the town sallied out unto the house of one Penruddock, a papist, and being basely affronted by him and his dog, entered his house, and pillaged him to the purpose. This day, also the soldiers got into the church, defaced the ancient and sacred glassed picture and burned the holy rails. Wednesday, Mr Lower gave us a famous sermon this day; also, the soldiers brought the holy rails from Chiswick and burned them in our town. At Chiswick they also intended to pillage the Lord of Portland's house, and also Dr Duck's, but by our commanders, they were prevented.

This day our soldiers generally manifested their dislike, of our Lieutenant-Colonel, who is a Godamme blade, and doubtless hatched in hell, and we all desire that either the Parliament would depose him or God convert him, or the Devil fetch him away quick. This day, towards even, our regiment marched to Uxbridge, but I was left behind, to bring up thirty men with ammunition the next morning. Thursday I marched toward Uxbridge, and at Hillingdon, one mile from Uxbridge, the rails being gone, we got the surplice, to make us handcherchers, and one of our soldiers wore it to Uxbridge.

This day the railings of Uxbridge, formerly removed, was with the service book, burned. This even Mr Harding gave us a worthy sermon. Friday, I with three other commanders, were sent with one hundred musketeers to bring the ammunition to Amersham in Buckinghamshire, which is the sweetest country that ever I saw, and as is country so also is the people... Every day our soldiers by stealth do visit papists' houses, and constrain from them both meat and money. They give them whole great loaves and cheeses, which they triumphantly carry away upon the points of their swords. I humbly entreat you, as you desire the success of our just and honourable cause, that

An 18th century depiction of the events outside the city of Hull when the forces of King Charles called upon the Governor to surrender.

A rather fanciful depiction of the Royalist Cavalry, led by Prince Rupert at the Battle of Edgehill. It is highly unlikely that the Royalist Cavalry would have had such a uniform appearance.

you would endeavour to root out our Lieutenant Colonel; for if we march further under his command, we fear, upon sufficient grounds, we are all but dead men."

It was only a matter of time before the small scale affairs which were witnessed by Wharton gave way to the first big battle of the war, and the key players in the coming struggle were already beginning to move into place.

King Charles placed a great deal of faith in his nephew, Prince Rupert of the Rhine, whom he appointed to lead the cavalry. The young Prince brought a much needed sense of energy and purpose to his command. He was to become the epitome of the dashing cavalier, and was followed everywhere by his faithful dog named 'Boye', yapping and barking around the hooves of his horse.

On the 23rd September cavalry detachments of Rupert's command met the Roundhead cavalry at Powick Bridge, outside Worcester. Neither side had realised that the other was close at hand but the Royalists were the first to recover from the shock of discovery and in the short fight which followed, Prince Rupert's Cavaliers were victorious.

Of itself, the skirmish was unimportant, but significantly, it began the myth that the Cavalier Horse were invincible, a belief which the Parliamentarians would need some time to destroy.

EDGEHILL

A month after the skirmish at Powick, the first major battle of the Civil War was fought at Edgehill in the Vale of the Red Horse in Warwickshire.

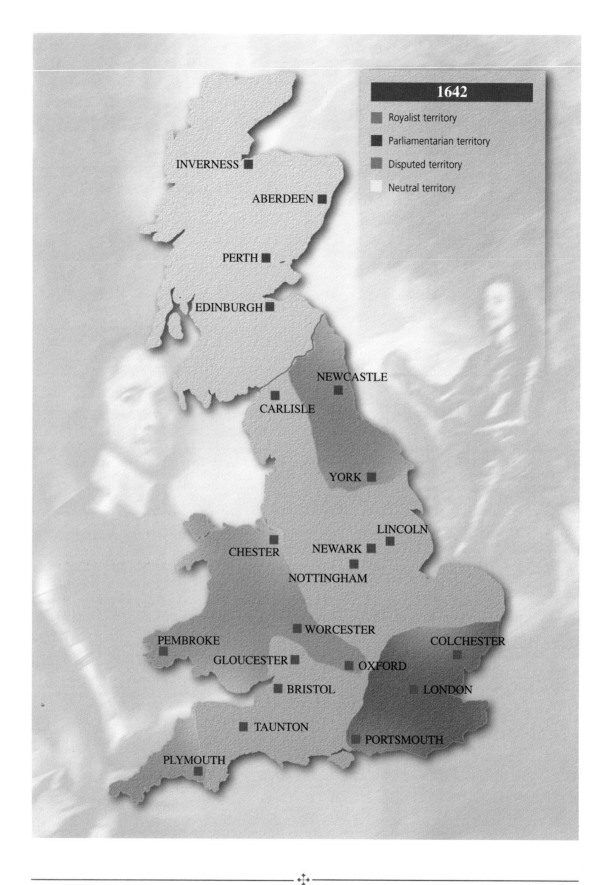

1642

Royalist territory

Parliamentarian territory

Disputed territory

Neutral territory

INVERNESS

ABERDEEN

PERTH

EDINBURGH

NEWCASTLE

CARLISLE

YORK

LINCOLN

CHESTER

NEWARK

NOTTINGHAM

WORCESTER

COLCHESTER

PEMBROKE

GLOUCESTER

OXFORD

BRISTOL

LONDON

TAUNTON

PORTSMOUTH

PLYMOUTH

As a commander, Essex was to develop an unfortunate reputation for allowing his opponent to interpose between him and his home base. The Edgehill campaign was the first example of this dangerous tendency. Essex had been out-manoeuvred by the King. His army therefore formed up with the Royalist forces between him and his base at London.

Before the battle, the Royalist engineer, De Gomme, had sufficient time to sketch the disposition of the armies on the field, for it seems neither side wished to start the battle which would precipitate the war, and there was a lengthy stand-off. As the Roundheads could not be tempted to attack the favourable Royalist positions on the hill itself, the King's men moved off the hill and moved down onto the forward slope looking from Radway

(Continued on page 58)

Robert Rich, Earl of Warwick, was the Parliamentarian Admiral in command of the fleet.

S.R. GARDINER ON THE ENGLISH CIVIL WAR

Another contemporary engraving of Essex, probably executed during the time of the Civil Wars.

"When Essex drew up his troops at some little distance from the foot of the hill, the Royal army had no choice but to descend. It was in the midst of a hostile population, and with Banbury fortified in its rear and the Parliamentary army in front, it would hardly escape starvation.

Whether these considerations presented themselves to Charles is more than doubtful. In his camp victory was regarded as a certainty. It was fully believed that Essex had but a turbulent mob under his orders, and that most of his soldiers and many of his officers would refuse to fight against the King now that they knew that he had taken the field in person.

Full of spirit as the Royalists were, they had to contend against one fatal disadvantage. Charles had himself undertaken the direction of the campaign."

THE ROUNDHEADS

Robert Devereux, 3rd Earl of Essex, from an engraving made at the time of the Civil Wars. Beneath the horse's hoof we can see a reference to the Edgehill battle which was fought outside Kineton.

ROBERT DEVEREUX, THIRD EARL OF ESSEX

Born in 1591, Robert Devereux, Third Earl of Essex, was to be Parliament's main commander in the field during the early years of the war. Although he gave sterling service to Parliament, he did have an unnerving habit of allowing enemies to get between him and his base at London, as happened at Edgehill, 1st Newbury and Lostwithiel.

Nonetheless, it was Essex who was able to inspire and motivate the army of Parliament successfully to take the field against Charles in 1642.

They gave a good account of themselves at Edgehill and in early 1643, he successfully captured Reading. Later in that year, Essex marched to the relief of Gloucester and fought his way past the King's blocking position at 1st Newbury.

In the military campaign of 1644, Essex was to be disastrously defeated by King Charles at Lostwithiel, although Essex himself escaped to London. Essex was removed from his position of command in the army by the Self-Denying Ordinance of 1645. As a Presbyterian, Essex had many supporters in the Parliamentary camp but ultimately the Independents were to win the religious debates.

Away from the field of battle, he caught an ague while out hunting in Windsor Great Park and died in September 1646, only three months after the end of the war.

THE CAVALIERS

Prince Rupert is one of
the legendary figures from
the period. A dashing and
flamboyant cavalry leader, he
has come to epitomise the image
of the dashing cavalier.

PRINCE RUPERT

Prince Rupert of the Rhine, the nephew of King Charles, was the epitome of the dashing cavalier. Joining the King at the beginning of the war, he was present from the first cavalry skirmish at Powick Bridge, through Edgehill, Bristol, Chalgrove, Marston Moor, and Naseby, until his fall from grace and departure for exile after his failure to hold Bristol against the Roundheads. His uncanny ability to avoid injury, despite constantly being in the thick of the battle, led his opponents to claim that he was in league with the Devil.

His failure to hold Bristol in 1645, led to a breach with the King. The Prince was dismissed and despite a rapprochement with the King, went into exile in 1646. Rupert's Achilles heel was his inability to rally his men after a successful charge and it was this failure which quite possibly cost the King victory at Edgehill and Naseby.

Prince Rupert survived the Civil War and on the restoration, accepted a position from Charles II and became a naval Admiral. He died in 1682. Prince Rupert never married, but true to the modern meaning of the word 'cavalier' he appears to have enjoyed various affairs and assignations. He left behind at least one illegitimate son, and a daughter, Ruperta.

Judge Mallet, Archbishop Williams and Thomas Lunsford, enemies of the Church and State to Parliamentarian eyes (from a contemporary engraving).

(Continued from page 55)

towards the village of Kineton, in the hope that the Roundheads would strike the first blow.

The King's nephew Prince Rupert commanded the cavalry on the right wing and Lord Wilmot, a professional soldier turned courtier, commanded the left. In the centre the infantry formed five brigades with three in the front line and the two others in support. The dragoons were deployed on the flanks of the cavalry.

In total it is estimated that the Royalists fielded nearly three thousand cavalry, one thousand dragoons and just over ten thousand infantry.

The Earl of Essex's army, waiting for them at the foot of the hill, was drawn up in much the same way.

The Parliamentarians had twelve thousand infantry but less than three thousand cavalry and dragoons.

With the King between him and his base, a major defeat in the battle would have been disastrous for Essex. To compound matters, many of Essex's soldiers were scattered in farms and villages where they had been finding shelter from the cold October nights, and they were still hurrying to the field when hostilities began. In order to instil some heart into the ranks of nervous men, many of whom were about to experience combat for the time, *"King Charles 'rode to every Brigade of Horse, and to all the Regiments of Foot, to encourage them to their Duty'... and... 'spoke to them with great courage and cheerfulness, which caused Huzza's thro' the whole Army."* as Captain Kightly, a Royalist eyewitness, remembered.

Another Royalist, Sir Richard Bulstrode, who served in the Earl of Northampton's troop in the Prince of Wales' regiment of horse, also left a detailed account of the battle. His recollection is remarkably detailed, right down to the positions of the regiments at the various combats.

"Our whole army was drawn up in a body, the horse three deep in each wing, and the foot in the centre six deep. The Prince of Wales' regiment was on the right wing, which was commanded by Prince Rupert, and Colonel Washington was with his dragoons upon our right. In the centre was the infantry, commanded in chief by General Ruthven, and under him, by Sir Jacob Astley. The Earl of Lindsey marched on foot, in the head of the regiment of the royal foot guards, with his son, the Lord Willoughby, and Sir Edmund Verney carried the Royal Standard. The left wing of our horse was commanded by Commissary-General Wilmot, with Lieutenant-Colonel Edward Fielding and some other principal officers, and Lieutenant-Colonel George Lisle, with Lieutenant-Colonel John Ennis were in the left wing, with a regiment of dragoons

to defend the briars on that side, and we had a body of reserve of six hundred horse, commanded by the Earl of Carnarvon. When our army was drawn up at the foot of the hill and ready to march, all the generals went to the King (who intended to march with the army) and desired he would retire to a rising ground, some distance from thence, on the right, with the Prince of Wales and the Duke of York (having his guard of Pensioners on horseback with him) from whence he might see the issue of the battle and he out of danger, and that otherwise the army would not advance towards the enemy. To which the King (very unwilling) was at last persuaded."

THE BATTLE COMMENCES

It may be that the King's address and the storm of cheering, guaranteed it provoked Essex's men to open fire.

The fact that the Parliamentarians opened fire first is well documented and is not disputed by either side. The Parliamentarian Ludlow is the best source on that issue.

"My Lord General did give the first charge, presenting them with pieces of ordnance, which killed many of their men, and then the enemy did shoot one to us, which fell twenty yards short in ploughed land and did no harm.

Our general having commanded to fire upon the enemy, it was done twice upon that part of the army wherein, as it was reported, the King was. The grape shot was exchanged on both sides for the space of an hour or thereabouts."

Lord Wharton, also on the Parliament side, later compared the effects of the artillery of the two sides. He came down decisively on the side of his own gunners.

"Their cannon did not kill even twenty men, while we gave them two shoots for one, and their ordnance did scarcely any hurt at all, whereas we scarcely discharged away a bullet in vaine..."

This superior effectiveness is certainly plausible; with at least ten more guns than the King, the Parliamentarians should certainly have been able to inflict greater casualties. Much has been lost with the passing centuries but, curiously enough, the name of the very first casualty of the battle is known. He was Lieutenant Francis Bowles of Fielding's Regiment, who was standing near the centre of the Royalist line when he was killed by a cannonball. This would certainly appear to support the claims of Wharton and Ludlow.

The Parliamentarians could therefore arguably have got the best of the early exchanges but, it was now time for the Royalist cavalry to make their move. This was very much the trump card in the Royalist deck.

"Just before we began our march, Prince Rupert passed from one wing to the other, giving positive orders to the Horse, to march as close as was possible, keeping their ranks with sword in hand, to receive the enemy's shot, without firing either cabin or pistol, till we broke in amongst the enemy, and then to make use of our fire-arms as need should require; which order was punctually observed."

The Royalist horse, three deep, began to move forward, gaining speed as they advanced.

At first it looked as though the cavaliers might end the war in an afternoon. Led by the fiery Prince Rupert, the Royalist cavalry swept all before them. As the Royalists advanced upon the Parliamentary cavalry, the Roundheads, who opened fire with their carbines, expected the Royalists to respond in kind. Instead the cavaliers came on at a furious charge and the Parliamentarians, panicking, fled away, pursued clear of the battlefield by the jubilant Royalist cavalry who thought the day won.

Charles' second son, the future King James II's description of this charge has survived:

"The Royalists march'd up with all the gallantry and resolution imaginable, especially the right wing led by Prince Rupert; while they advanced, the enemy's cannon continually played upon them, as did the small divisions of their Foot which were placed in the intervals betwixt their squadrons, neither of which did in the least discompose them so much as to mend their pace. Thus they continued moving, till they came up close to the enemy's cavalry, which immediately turn'd their backs, the Royalists pursuing them with great eagerness."

(Continued on page 62)

THE ENGLISH CIVIL WARS

THE FIELD ARMIES - PARLIAMENTARIAN

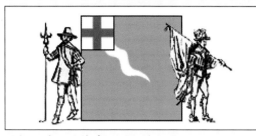

Major's colour, Earl of Essex's Regiment

ESSEX'S ARMY

The principle Parliamentarian field army for much of the war until the formation of the New Model Army. Much of its strength came from the London trained bands who were reluctant to campaign away from home for too long. As a consequence Essex always had an Achilles heel.

Nonetheless, the troops marched and fought well at Edgehill, Reading and 1st Newbury. The last independent army commanded by Essex was totally destroyed in the debacle at Lostwithiel in 1644.

Following on from Edgehill and Naseby, this was the third consecutive major engagement in which the Earl had allowed King Charles to interpose himself between Essex's army and their base at London. The third time was to prove unlucky for Essex.

Opposite is a soldier of the Earl of Essex's army in the orange/tawny coats which marked them out from the other armies of the period.

Listed below is a selection of regiments who served at various times:

Foot
- Earl of Essex
- Lord Rochford
- Sir Henry Cholmley
- Col. Randall Mainwaring
- Sir Phillip Skippon
- Lord Robarts
- Col. John Venn
- Col. Cunningham

Horse
- Earl of Essex
- Col. Arthur Goodwin
- Col. Edwyn Sandys
- Col. William Balfour

THE FIELD ARMIES - ROYALIST

THE OXFORD ARMY

The Oxford Army under the direct control of King Charles I was to fight in some of the most significant battles of the Civil War.

They were present at Edgehill, Bristol, 1st Newbury, Lostwithiel, 2nd Newbury, Cropredy Bridge and Naseby.

Constantly plagued by shortages of arms and ammunition, the cavalier army was nonetheless able to give as good as it got, despite its cataclysmic defeat at Naseby. The King's nephew, Prince Rupert, would frequently lead large detachments from Oxford on raids and mini-campaigns, such as his march to the relief of York in 1644 and his lightning campaign through the Midlands in the prelude to Naseby in 1645.

Opposite is a musketeer from Prince Rupert's Blue Coats. These unfortunate soldiers were issued with uniforms for their Oxford status in 1643. Either red or blue was issued, with Rupert's regiment apparently receiving blue.

Listed below is a selection of the regiments who served at various times:

Foot
- The King's Lifeguard
- The Queen's Lifeguard
- The Duke of York
- Col. Sir Henry Bard
- Prince Rupert
- Lord Hopton
- Col. Henry Tillier
- Sir Thomas Tyldesley
- Sir John Owen
- Col. Charles Gerard
- Sir Marmaduke Rawdon
- Col. Francis Garnel

Horse
- Lord George Goring
- Sir Francis Mackworth
- Col. Ralph Mylott
- Prince Rupert
- Prince Maurice
- Lord Molyneaux

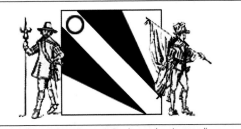

Major's colour, Prince Rupert's Regiment (conjectured).

THE ENGLISH CIVIL WARS

(Continued from page 59)

After a brief resistance, Rupert's furious charge had routed Ramsey's entire wing of Parliamentarian cavalry and left the cavaliers 'Masters of their Cannon'. No doubt, the victors of Powick Bridge had been confident of victory, but even they could not have expected it to be so sudden and complete.

In the ranks of the Royalist cavalry, Bulstrode witnessed the brief struggle and recalled just how swiftly the Parliamentarians were brushed aside.

"The enemy stayed to receive us in the same posture as was formerly declared; and when we came within cannon shot of the enemy; they discharged at us three pieces of cannon from their left wing, commanded by Sir James Ramsey; which cannon mounted over our troops without doing any hurt, except that their second shot killed a quartermaster in the rear of the Duke of York's troop. We soon after engaged each other, and our dragoons on our right beat the enemy from the briars, and Prince Rupert led on our right wing so furiously, that after a small resistance, we forced their left wing, and were masters of their cannon; and the Prince being extremely eager of this advantage (which he better knew how to take than to keep) was not content with their cannon, and keeping their ground, but eagerly pursued the enemy, who fled on the other side of Kineton towards Warwick. And we of the Prince of Wales' regiment (who were all scattered) pursued also till we met with two foot regiments of Hampden and Holles, and with a regiment of horse coming from Warwick to their army, which made us hasten as fast back as we had pursued."

The Parliamentarian cavalry may have given in easily, but the Foot was made of sterner stuff. A little way behind Ramsey's men stood Holles' Regiment whose colonel now saw the fleeing mass of his own cavalry, with the Royalist horse at their heels come rushing pell-mell down upon his regiment and break through it.

"Undaunted, he went and planted himself just in the way, and did what possibly he could do to make them stand; and at last prevailed with three troops to wheel a little about, and rally..."

This small force of cavalry was to prove invaluable later in the battle.

Despite the exhortations of Prince Rupert, his cavalry swept on in great disorder to Kineton. When they reached the town they found a new prize: the carts and wagons of Essex's Army. All sorts of prizes came their way: Essex's coach, Sir Samuel Luke's commission, and the personal baggage belonging to the six Parliamentarian commanders.

On the other wing, Lord Wilmot had a more difficult task than Rupert, for he had 'to charge in worse cavalry ground, amongst hedges, and through gaps and ditches, which were lined with musketeers'. But Wilmot led his men forward with as much determination as Rupert.

Although Wilmot's force was much weaker than Rupert's, he still outnumbered the Roundhead cavalry under Fielding by nearly three to one. The direct result of this discrepancy in matters was that the unfortunate Fielding was swept from the field with, if anything, even less resistance than Ramsey's men. The Foot regiment of Sir William Fairfax ran too, and none faster than Lieutenant Thomas Whitney, who we are told found himself a horse and galloped posthaste all the way to London crying the news of Parliament's defeat.

Whitney could be forgiven his mistake with the Parliamentarian horse being swept aside.

An interesting engraving from the 19th century which has the participants in the Civil Wars dressed in the fashions that were prevalent at least one hundred years after the events they described.

It was now time for the Royalist Foot to decide the day. If they could gain a similar success to the cavalry, the battle and, probably the war, would be won for the King in a single day.

It was now that the third Sir Jacob Astley, at the head of the Royalists, is reported to have made his famous prayer:

"O Lord! Thou knowest how busy I must be this day. If I forget Thee, do not Thou forget me."

He then rose to his feet and crying out ,"March on Boys," led the Royalist Foot into battle. The Foot advanced, as James II tells us, "with a slow steady pace, and a very daring resolution."

A Parliamentarian soldier later recalled the brave advance:

"...their Foot, came up all in front, and after some playing with the cannon on both sides, that part of it which was on their left, and towards our right wing, came on very gallantly to the charge."

To the advancing Royalist infantry things must have seemed promising. They had seen the success of their own cavalry, and morale must have been high as they sensed the rewards of victory.

Their confidence would have been reinforced by the fact that the Parliamentarian brigade of Charles Essex 'wholly disbanded and ran away, without ever striking stroke a blow'.

By this time Astley's Brigades were at push of pike with the Parliamentarian Foot. Now began the terrible struggle, later so well described by the Royalist Clarendon.

"The foot of both sides stood their ground with great courage; they kept their ranks; and the execution was great on both sides, but much greater on the Earl of Essex's party."

To make matters worse, the seven remaining Parliamentarian regiments six thousand strong, were now engaged in mortal combat with something like ten thousand Royalist Foot.

But by a minor miracle of courage and tenacity which has never been satisfactorily explained, after a bitter struggle, both sides simply stopped fighting, as one eyewitness recalled:

"Each side, as if by mutual consent, suddenly unlocked ranks and retired a few paces, there they struck down their colours, and continued to fire at one another until nightfall; a thing so very extra-

S.R. GARDINER ON THE ENGLISH CIVIL WAR

Prince Rupert was a handsome and dashing figure, as can be seen from this surviving portrait.

"If Rupert had been as fit to meet all the exigencies of war as he was to lead a charge of cavalry, it would have gone hard with the King's enemies. As it was, he knew how to inspire his followers with his own dashing energy and untiring courage; but though he was as capable of planning a campaign as he was of conducting a charge, he was apt to lose his head in the heat of battle; and to despise his enemies too much to take into account the full strength of their resistance. Charles at once appointed him General of the Horse. From one point of view no better selection could be made. There was no fear now that the Royal Cavalry would turn their backs upon the enemy as, three years before, they had turned their backs, under Holland's command, upon the Scots at Kelso. From another point of view the appointment was disastrous. Rupert demanded and obtained the privilege of taking orders from the King alone."

ordinary, that nothing less than so many witnesses as were there present could make it credible."

It was now that the initiative passed to the few Parliamentarian cavalry who had not routed from the field. Beyond question the credit for this goes to their Lieutenant-General, Sir William Balfour.

He gathered up the few available horsemen and launched a furious assault upon the Royalist Foot.

He struck the brigade of Colonel Richard Fielding, broke through a regiment that had green colours, "beat them to their cannon, where they threw down their arms, and ran away."

The King could now see his centre give way and come streaming back towards the hill with the Parliamentarian Foot in hot pursuit.

The King's Lifeguard meanwhile, was locked in combat with Constable's Regiment and Sir Edmund Verney, the Knight Marshal, who bore the King's Banner Royal, was killed in the swirling melee. He was struck down by Ensign Arthur Young and the King's standard was snatched from his lifeless hand.

But Young's triumph was short-lived. He was seen by the Royalist Captain Smith, who galloped up, crying, "Traitor, deliver the Standard!" and though wounded himself he killed one Roundhead, hurt another and routed the rest, who fled leaving the Standard in his possession. It is said that the King's Standard only remained in Parliamentarian hands for some six minutes.

Bulstrode again recalled this episode in the struggle.

"In this pursuit I was wounded in the head by a person who turned upon me and struck me with his pole-axe, and was seconding his blow, when Sir Thomas Byron being near, he shot him dead with his pistol, by which means I came back. In fine, by meeting these three regiments, we were obliged to return back to our army and then found our great error, in leaving our Foot naked who were rudely handled by the enemy's Horse and Foot together in our absence, who fell principally upon the King's royal regiment of Foot guards, who lost eleven of thirteen colours, the King's Standard–Bearer, Sir Edmund Verney, killed, and the Royal Standard taken, which was presently retaken by Captain John Smith, who was knighted for it that night by the King, under the Standard Royal and made a banneret with the usual ceremonies; and had after-

wards a large medal of gold given him, with the King's picture on the one side, and the banner on the other, which he always wore to his dying day, in a large green watered ribband, cross his shoulders."

As an obscure back-bencher, Oliver Cromwell had formed a troop of horse but he arrived too late and saw only the aftermath of the conflict which saw the flight of much of Parliament's untrained cavalry. Already his acute military mind was beginning to work as he observed to his commander after Edgehill.

"At my first going into this engagement, I saw our men were beaten at every hand... and I told him I would be serviceable to him in bringing such men in as I thought had a spirit that would do something in the work... 'Your Troopers', said I, 'are most of them old decayed servingmen and tapsters and such kind of fellows; and', said I, 'their troopers are gentlemen's sons, younger sons and persons of quality; do you think that the spirits of such base and mean fellows will be ever able to encounter gentlemen that have honour and courage and resolution in them... You must get men... of a spirit that is likely to go on as far as gentlemen will go, or else I am sure you will be beaten still."

(Continued on page 68)

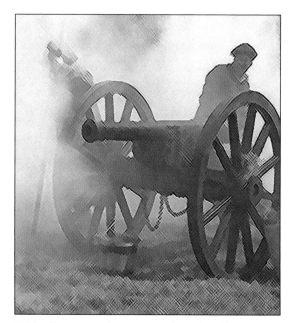

Field artillery was cumbersome to make and could be a logistical nightmare.

THE BATTLE OF EDGEHILL · 23RD OCTOBER 1642

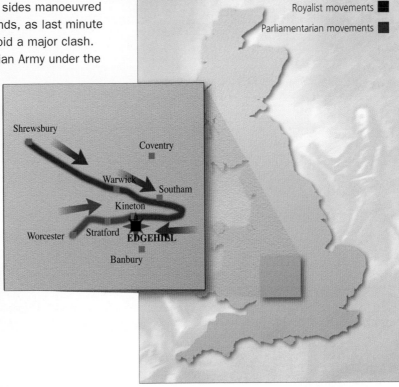

Edgehill was the first major battle of the English Civil War. In those early stages, a peaceful settlement was still a real possibility, and, in consequence, both sides manoeuvred uneasily through the Midlands, as last minute attempts were made to avoid a major clash.

Finally, the Parliamentarian Army under the Earl of Essex marched from Worcester, through Stratford-upon-Avon to the village of Kineton. The King and his army marched through Warwick and Southam to meet with the Parliamentarian forces on Edgehill, just south of Kineton.

The Battle of Edgehill featured some intense hand to hand fighting as the armies of the King and Parliament came to grips for the first time.

Royalist movements ■
Parliamentarian movements ■

Shrewsbury

Coventry

Warwick

Southam

Kineton

Worcester Stratford **EDGEHILL**

Banbury

Royalist movements
Parliamentarian movements

1. Prince Rupert and the Royalist Horse charge into Ramsay's Parliamentarian cavalry. The Parliamentarians break and rout from the field.

2. The Royalist left wing under Lord Wilmot charge and drive the Parliamentarian cavalry under Fielding from the field.

3. The foot regiments of both armies engage in fierce fighting.

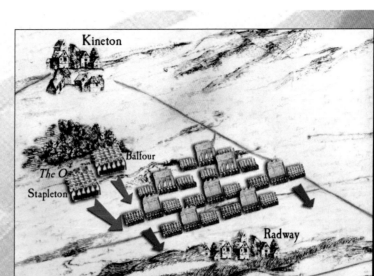

4. The Parliamentarian reserve cavalry under Balfour add their weight to the fight and the Royalists begin to give ground.

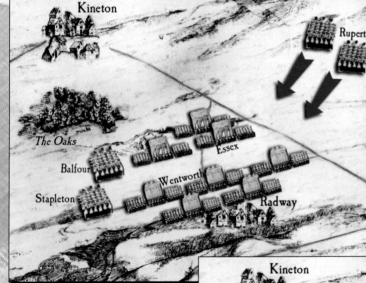

5. Scattered elements of Rupert's cavalry are back from the pursuit but are too late to influence the outcome.

6. Both sides are now fought to a standstill and the Parliamentarians begin to withdraw. Essex and his army march off the field in relatively good order towards Warwick.

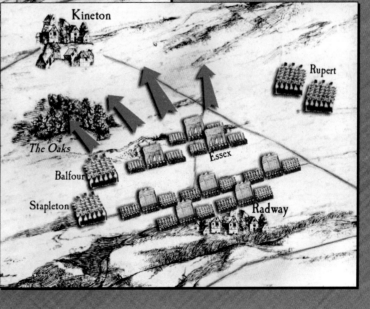

(Continued from page 64)

Cromwell soon saw the calibre of men which were required to defeat the Royalists and later reported his views to the Suffolk commissioners in 1643:

"I beseech you be careful what captains of horse you choose, what men be mounted; a few honest men are better than numbers. Some time they must have for exercise. If you choose godly honest men to be captains of horse, honest men will follow them... I had rather have a plain russet-coated captain that knows what he fights for and loves what he knows, than that which you call a gentleman and is nothing else."

Cromwell was to heed his own wise advice and he formed his own regiment of highly disciplined cavalry who were to become known as the famous 'Ironsides' of legend. He trained them well and their discipline, religious zeal and piety were to win them much fame as the war progressed. As the reputation of his regiment grew in fame so did the fortunes of their commander. He may have missed the battle at Edgehill but Oliver Cromwell was to rise rapidly from an obscure Captain of Horse in 1642, to become second in command of the Parliamentary forces behind Lord Fairfax in 1645.

When darkness put an end to the fighting on 23rd October, neither side had won the day.

One of the principal reasons was Rupert's cavalry, who cut down the fugitive Parliamentarians, many of whom they pursued for seven miles, and then began plundering Essex's baggage train in the village of Kineton.

Had the victorious cavaliers kept their discipline and returned to the field, they could have influenced the turning point of the battle.

Eventually, the armies simply became exhausted and gradually lost the will to fight. And so the two starved and bleeding armies, still within cannon-shot of one another, settled down to endure a night 'as cold as a very great frost and a sharp northerly wind could make it...'

The presence of the Royalist cavalry would almost certainly have won the day, but their lack of discipline in pursuing the fleeing Parliamentarian cavalry too far allowed the infantry of Parliament to rally. By their dogged persistence, they were able to hold the Royalists to a draw, but at a very high cost.

The Royalist, Bulstrode, writing at the time of the battle, confirmed this from his own experience.

Prince Rupert's attack on Essex's baggage train at Edgehill, as painted by Richard Beavis, 1824-1896.

Lord Lindsey, Royalist commander

"Now, when we returned from following the enemy, the night came soon upon us, whereas, in all probability, we had gained the victory, and made an end of the war, if we had only kept our ground after we had beaten the enemy, and not left our foot naked to their horse and foot. And, to add to our misfortune, a careless soldier, in fetching powder (where a magazine was) clapt his hand carelessly into a barrel of powder, with his match lighted betwixt his fingers, whereby much powder was blown up and many kill'd."

After a bitterly cold night Essex abandoned the battlefield to the King and retired northwards to the safety of Warwick Castle, leaving the way clear for the King to march on London.

The field of battle after the carnage, bore sad witness to the ferocity of the fighting:

"On Monday morning, being next after the battle, several parties were sent down to view the dead, the greatest part of the enemy having retired in the night to the town of Kineton, which was near them, and Mr Adrian Scroop having seen his father fall (being much wounded) desired the Duke of Lennox to speak to the King, that one of his coaches might go with him, to bring up his father's body; which

S.R. GARDINER ON THE ENGLISH CIVIL WAR

"The claim of victory advanced by either party is little to be heeded. The promise of future success was undoubtedly on the side of Essex. Only amongst the Parliamentary troops had there been that co-operation between infantry and cavalry which distinguishes an army from a fighting crowd. The immediate fruits of victory were reaped by Charles. He appointed Forth permanently to that nominal command of his forces which had hitherto meant so little, and he pushed on unmolested towards London. On the 27th Banbury surrendered to him, though its defence was entrusted to a whole Parliamentary regiment. On the 29th he entered Oxford in triumph at the head of his army, amidst the plaudits of citizens and scholars."

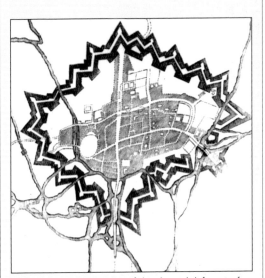

A contemporary engraving of the planned defences of Oxford. This elaborate scheme proved to be beyond the ability of the Royalists and the defences were never completed to this level.

being granted, he found his father stripped, with several very dangerous wounds, and that he was alive. Whereupon he lap'd him up in his cloak, and brought him in the coach, where he was presently dressed by the King's chirurgeon and by their care and skill was cured, and lived many years after, tho' he had seventeen wounds, and had died upon the place, but that the coldness of the weather stopp'd the bleeding of his wounds, which saved also several other men's lives that were wounded."

A few days after the battle, Sir Edward Sydenham, another who had fought in the Royalist ranks, wrote a letter to Ralph, the son of the brave Sir Edmund Verney:

"For all our great victory I have had the greatest loss by the death of your noble father that ever any friend did. He himself killed two with his own hands, and broke the point of his standard at push of pike before he fell, which was the last account I could receive of any of our own side of him. The battle was bloody on your side, for your horse ran away at the first charge and our men had the execution of them for three miles. It began at three o'clock and ended at six. The King is a man of the least fear and the greatest resolution and mercy that I ever saw and had he not been in the field we might have suffered.

God in mercy send us peace, and although your loss is as great as a son can lose in a father, yet God's children must bear with patience what affliction soever he shall please to lay upon them. You have a great trial. God in mercy give you grace to make a sanctified use of this great burden with patience. My humble service to your sad wife. God in his infinite mercy comfort you both shall be the prayers of your friend and servant."

With Essex out of the way, the impetuous Prince Rupert was all for making a dash with his cavalry to occupy London before Essex could reach the city with the battered remains of his army. The King, however, was disconcerted by the fact that matters had reached full scale war. He prevaricated in the hope of a peaceful settlement and the greatest Royalist opportunity of the war to capture the Parliamentary stronghold was lost.

Eventually, the whole Royalist army did march on London, but the initiative had been lost. The Parliamentarians who now mustered at Turnham Green to defend London were too numerous for his exhausted army and the King reluctantly withdrew to Oxford for the winter, there to establish his court. For the next four years the university city was to be the Royalist capital. The King was never to reach London, except as a prisoner of his enemies, to await his execution.

By November, Essex managed to slip past the Royalist 'full armies' and regain London. The forces of the King and Parliament were now joined in some indecisive fighting around Brentford and Hounslow to the West of London. One of those who joined the King's forces at this time was a young Welshman named John Gwynn, who witnessed the action which led to the destruction of Holles' Roundhead regiment:

"Myself and five comrades repaired from the Court at Richmond to the King's Royal Army, which we met accidentally that morning upon Hounslow Heath. We had no sooner joined with our worthy old acquaintance Sir George Bunckley, but we marched up to the enemy, engaged them and made them retreat into Brentford, and from thence to the open field, after firing we advanced up to push of pike and butt end of muskets, which proved so fatal to Holles and his butchers and dyers that day, that a great abundance of them were killed and taken prisoners, besides those drowned in their attempt to escape by leaping into the river."

Despite the advances they had made, Gwynn was forced to admit that the Royalist tide had reached its high water mark.

"No soldier or an impartial man could say that we could have advanced any further towards London than we did, because of the thick enclosures, with strong hedges and ditches, which were lined with men standing shoulder to shoulder by one another; on the common road were planted their artillery, with defensible works about them, so that we could not approach any nearer. As we were at so great a disadvantage, the King withdrew and marched for Hampton Court, where, for my further encouragement I had the care of the regiments colours conferred upon me in the hope that I would go on with as much resolution as I had begun."

THE CAVALIERS

JAMES BUTLER, DUKE OF ORMONDE

One of the most steadfast and loyal supporters of Charles I, was James Butler, Duke of Ormonde. Throughout the confused and changeable political and military events in Ireland, Ormonde stuck true to his duty to the sovereign.

During the latter times of the build up to the Civil War, the young Ormonde served Strafford, the Lord deputy in Ireland, as his right hand man.

Unfortunately, when Strafford was recalled to England, Charles rejected Strafford's advice that Ormonde be appointed Lord Deputy in his place and chose to appoint the older Sir John Borlase and Sir William Parsons in his stead.

Had Charles taken Strafford's advice, the rebellion in Ireland and with it, the whole of the Civil War might have been avoided.

As it was, the heavy handed rule of the English lords precipitated the Irish Rebellion, which was to have such a disastrous effect on the King's fortunes.

James Butler from a portrait painted shortly before the period of the Civil Wars.

Although he understood the Irish, Ormonde was a staunch Protestant and had no sympathy for the Catholic rising. At the head of the King's Army, Ormonde crushed the rebellion and was created Marquis of Ormonde and given a diamond by a grateful Parliament in 1642.

Throughout 1642, Ormonde was active in further suppression of the rebellion. Against his better judgment he arranged the cessation of 1643 which sent two thousand five hundred troops to aid the King in England.

However, the peace was to prove short lived and there was soon another Catholic army in arms against him. Eventually Ormonde was forced back and besieged in Dublin. Rather than allow the city to fall into the hands of the rebels, he surrendered it to the English Parliament and left for England.

During 1647, he acted as Charles' agent in bringing about the engagement of 1648.

With his part discovered, he fled into exile but came back to Ireland to lead the Irish rebels against the Parliamentary forces.

On the death of Charles in January 1649, Ormonde achieved the difficult task of uniting both Protestant and Catholic Irish forces against Parliament. Initially, his army enjoyed some success, but with the arrival of the all-conquering Oliver Cromwell, Ormonde's forces were swiftly crushed. Names like Rathmines and Drogheda have passed into legend.

With the restoration of Charles II, Ormonde was restored to his position and fortunes. He lived the rest of his years peacefully and died in 1688 at the age of seventy-eight.

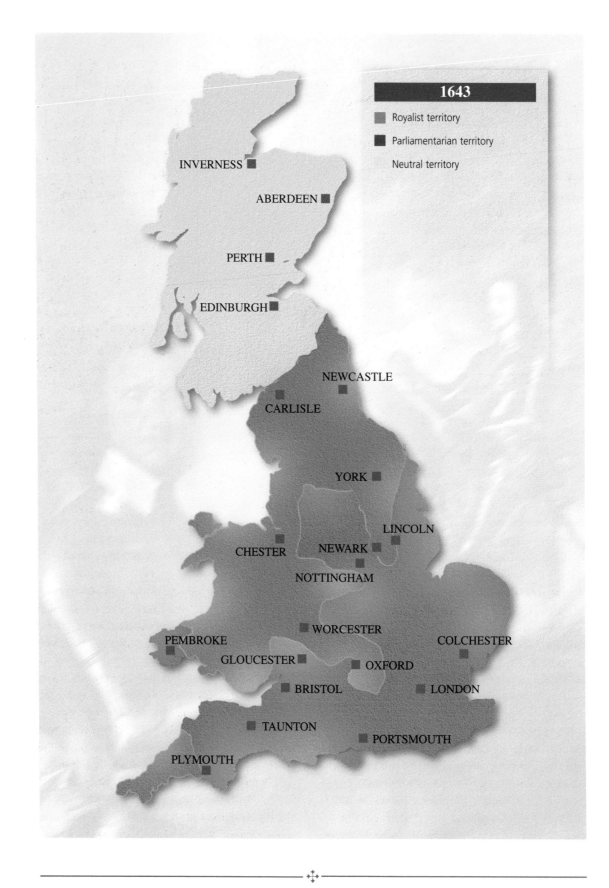

1643

◼ Royalist territory

◼ Parliamentarian territory

Neutral territory

INVERNESS ◼

ABERDEEN ◼

PERTH ◼

EDINBURGH ◼

NEWCASTLE ◼

CARLISLE ◼

YORK ◼

LINCOLN ◼

CHESTER ◼ NEWARK ◼

NOTTINGHAM ◼

WORCESTER ◼

PEMBROKE ◼ COLCHESTER ◼

GLOUCESTER ◼

OXFORD ◼

BRISTOL ◼ LONDON ◼

TAUNTON ◼

PORTSMOUTH ◼

PLYMOUTH ◼

THE WAR CONTINUES

A contemporary engraving from the Thirty Years War shows harquebusiers in battle against cuirassiers. It gives a very good idea of how cavalry were trained to use pistols in close combat. Their effectiveness may be overstated.

"All the counties of England no longer idle spectators, but several stages whereon the tragedy of the civil war was acted; except the Eastern Association, where Mr Oliver Cromwell by his diligence prevented the designs of the royal party."

Lucy Hutchinson 1643

As luck would have it, the winters of the early 1640's were particularly severe with unnaturally heavy and prolonged falls of snow. With a sudden thaw the primitive roads of seventeenth century England quickly turned into muddy quagmires which made movement impossible. Winter was therefore a time for small engagements between detachments and garrisons, while the main field armies waited for the spring and dry roads. All around the country, garrisons were attached, convoys were ambushed and there was a constant see-saw of raid and counter-raid.

During the summer of 1643 the two sides sought to improve their positions for the coming campaign season. Northumberland and Durham were already held for the King, and the Royalists were pushing southward into the Vale of York. On the other side of the Pennines, Cumberland and Westmorland were for the King, but in Lancashire the issue was still in some doubt.

Wales was dominated by the Royalists and most of East Anglia was Parliamentarian. In the south Sir William Waller captured Winchester from its Cavalier garrison shortly before Christmas, and was extending its influence into Devon. But in the far West Country his old friend and future opponent Sir Ralph Hopton had secured Cornwall and the south west for King Charles.

In the all-important Thames Valley and in the Midlands there was some jockeying for position as

The baggage train was vital for the survival of armies in the field. They also provided a tempting target for plunder, frequently at the expense of a battle-winning opportunity.

both sides prepared for the real war in the spring.

There is still some contention among historians of the Civil Wars as to whether there was a Royalist strategy for the year 1643. Some champion the prospect of the famous triple advance upon London, a three pronged assault including Newcastle's army from the north, Hopton's from the south west and, of course, the King's from the Midlands. These three prongs were to descend simultaneously upon the centre of Parliamentary control. Had London been captured in this manner, and Parliament with it, there is no doubt that the war would have come to an end in 1643. On the other hand, some scholars remain highly sceptical of Charles' decision making powers. After the Battle of Edgehill, the King, who combined indecisiveness in his character with a great deal of stubbornness, would not release Prince Rupert and his cavalry for a dash on London although, at that point, there was very little between them and the capital.

As the campaign season of 1643 opened, the King at first appeared to have the initiative but his army was crippled by a serious shortage of arms and ammunition. In some regiments there were many more pikemen than musketeers, which meant that

the Royalists would have to rely on brute strength rather than firepower in battle.

At the end of February, the Queen, who had gone to Holland to pawn the Crown Jewels and buy arms with the proceeds, landed at Bridlington in Yorkshire, and Newcastle prepared a great convoy to convey the arms to Oxford.

To cover this vital arms shipment, Prince Rupert moved into the Midlands and stormed the defences of Birmingham on the 3rd of April and took Lichfield after a short siege on the 21st. Emboldened by the Prince's absence however, Essex struck west and laid siege to Reading. Rupert returned in great haste, but both he and the King were powerless to prevent the garrison's surrender on the 27th of April 1643. Gwynn was, by now, a member of the hapless Reading garrison.

"Sir Arthur Aston, governor, received a letter upon the Castle-hill guard, looking about him, said 'Here are none but I may safely communicate the contents of my letter unto;' then arose from his chair, opened his letter, and went out of the door to peruse it, when there was no necessity to do so, but as his hasty fate would have it, he had scarce a minute to look it over, when a cannon-shot came through the guard-house and knocked of the tiles

from the roof. One fell upon his head and sunk him almost to the ground, before Colonel Lunsford and another officer caught him by both arms, held him up, brought him into the guard-house, put him into his chair, then presently he laid his hand on his head, under his cap, and faintly said, 'My head's whole, I thank God;' and spoke no more there at that time, but immediately was carried away to his house in the town, where, during the rest of the siege, he was speechless. A short time after the garrison was surrendered; then they broke their conditions with us, and plundered us."

Now that the issue of Reading had been decided, the two main field armies withdrew to their old positions, watching each other warily. The Round-head Army was crippled by a typhus epidemic, the first of many to sweep the three kingdoms in the armies' wake.

A highly romanticised Victorian view of the fate of Hampden at the Battle of Chalgrove. In this portrait the dying Earl is helped from the field by a party of cavalry whose dress is heavily influenced by the styles of the 1850's. The spiked helmets were probably more peculiar to the Victorian era than the English Civil Wars. The premature death of John Hampden in 1643 was a great blow to the possibility of a negotiated peace.

THE CAVALIERS

Sir Ralph Hopton fought a
chivalrous war with his old friend
and now adversary, Sir William Waller.

SIR RALPH HOPTON

Sir Ralph Hopton was one of the most
successful Field Commanders on the
Royalist side during the years of the Civil War.

He raised his own regiment and fought a
gentleman's war against his old friend and now
rival, Sir William Waller. This conflict between
them was characterised by the fact that they did
not allow personal animosity to cause them to
become enemies.

Hopton eventually defeated Waller at the
Battle of Lansdown and finally defeated his
army at Roundway Down. Thereafter, Hopton
served with the King on the campaign of
Cropredy.

After the defeat at Naseby, Hopton became
the commander of the King's artillery. He
finished the war as he had started, serving with
the last active Royalist in the south west.

To break the deadlock, a major victory was required which could alter the delicate balance in favour of one side or the other, but this was not likely to emerge from the pattern of minor battles and skirmishes which characterised the opening months of 1643.

Although many of the fights and skirmishes which took place all over England in the early months of 1643 were fairly small scale affairs, they were no less vicious and many of these seemingly inconsequential actions were contested as hotly as any of the main pitched battles of the war. We are fortunate that a number of good accounts of these small-scale actions survive.

The Royalist Captain Richard Atkyns described the tough fighting in one minor battle at Little Dean.

"No sooner had I received the word of command but my charging horse fell as trembling and quaking that he could not be kept upon his legs; so that I must lose my honour by an excuse, or borrow another horse; which with much ado I did of the Lord Chandos' gentleman of the horse, leaving twice as much as he was worth with him. The charge was seemingly as desperate as any I was

ever in, it being to beat the enemy from a wall which was a strong breastwork with a gate in the middle, possessed by about 200 musketeers besides horse. We were to charge down a steep plain hill, of above twelve score yards in length, as good a mark as they could wish. Our party consisting of between two and three hundred horse. Not a man of them would follow us, so the officers, about ten or twelve of us, agreed to gallop down in as good order as we would and make a desperate charge upon them.

The enemy seeing our resolution never fired at us at all, but ran away and we (like young soldiers) after them doing execution upon them. But one Captain Hammer, being better horsed than myself, in pursuit fell upon their ambuscade and was killed horse and man. I had only time enough to turn my horse and run for my life. This party of ours, that would not be drawn on at first, by this time seeing our success came into the town after us and stopped our retreat. And, finding that we were pursued by the enemy, the horse in the front fell back upon the rear and they were so wedged together that they routed themselves, so as there was no passage for a long time. All this while the

Leading Royalists gather together in a contemporary pamphlet which describes 'England's monumental mercies in her miraculous preservation from manifold plots, conspiracies and papists'.

THE ROUNDHEADS

JOHN HAMPDEN

Born in London 1594, John Hampden was at the forefront of the years of political and religious unrest which led to the English Civil War.

He first took his seat in Parliament in 1621 and was to remain a thorn in the side of King Charles and the Royalists until his premature death at Chalgrove Field in 1643.

Hampden was a leading opponent of the ship money tax levied by Charles and fought a test case against the extension of this maritime tax to inland counties.

Although King Charles won the case, the ship money issue was to provide a rallying point for his enemies.

Hampden was one of the leading figures in the impeachment of Strafford and Laud. He believed that the public welfare required that Strafford should be convicted and executed. He got his way. Strafford was executed in 1641, Laud in 1644.

In matters of religion Hampden was an independent, and although God-fearing, did not share the extreme views of others in the party.

With his death in 1643, Parliament would greatly miss his abilities as a negotiator and a force for conciliation in their dealings with the Royalist party, which may just have brought about a peaceful solution.

A continental engraving by Jacques Callot described as 'Man in Military Dress'. It gives a very good impression of the dress of the 1630's. Some of these fashions would have survived into the Civil Wars period although the ruff collar would not have done.

enemy were upon me, cutting my coat upon my armour in several places and discharging pistols as they got up to me, being the outermost man, which Major Sheldon declared to me very great advantage. But, when they pursued us to the town. Major Leighton had made good a stone house and so prepared for them with musketeers that one volley of shot made them retreat. They were so near me that a musket bullet from one of our own men took off one of the bars of my cap I charged with and went through my hair and did me to hurt. But this was only a forlorn party of their army to face us, whilst the rest of their army marched to Gloucester."

The main chance to strike a real strategic blow fell to the Royalists. Sir Ralph Hopton, the Royalist leader in the West, drew up his army to face the Parliamentarians, led by Sir William

Waller, who in former days had been a close friend. They met at Lansdown Hill outside Bath on the 5th of July.

The tragedy of a civil war can be clearly seen in the surviving letters between Hopton and Waller, two old friends who found themselves on different sides of a bitter conflict.

"To my noble friend Sir Ralph Hopton at Wells
Sir,
The experience I have had of your worth and the happiness I have enjoyed in your friendship are wounding considerations when I look upon this present distance between us. Certainly my affections to you are so unchangeable that hostility itself cannot violate my friendship to your person, but I must be true to the cause wherein I serve. The old limitation usque ad aras holds still, and where my conscience is interested all other obligations are swallowed up. I should most gladly wait on you according to your desire, but that I look upon you as you are engaged in that party beyond a possibility of retreat and consequently incapable of being wrought upon by any persuasion. And I know the conference could never be so close between us, but that it would take wind and receive a construction to my dishonour. That great God which is the searcher of my heart, knows with what a sad sense I go upon this service and with what a perfect hatred I detest this war without an enemy, but I look upon it as opus domini, which is enough to silence all passion in me. The God of peace in his good time send us peace and in the meantime fit us to receive it. We are both upon the stage and must act those parts that are assigned us in this tragedy. Let us do it in a way of honour and without personal animosities. Whatsoever the issue be, I shall never willingly relinquish the dear title of your most affectionate friend and faithful servant, William Waller."

Despite the friendship between their leaders, the war between the two armies in the west was as vigorously pursued as in any other theatre. The battle of Lansdown was to provide a much needed victory for the Royalists. They may have been relatively small affairs, but the fighting was vicious and as dangerous as any, as Richard Atkyns was later to testify.

A Victorian engraving depicting the capture of the Royal Standard at Edgehill from Sir Edmund Verney. In reality the Standard was not to remain long in Parliamentarian hands and it was recaptured fairly swiftly by the Royalist Captain Smith.

"As I went up the hill, which was very steep and hollow, I met several dead and wounded officers brought off, besides several running away, that I had much ado to get up by them. When I came to the top of the hill I saw Sir Bevil Grenville's stand of pikes, which certainly preserved our army from a total rout with the loss of his most precious life. They stood as upon the eaves of an house for steepness, but as unmoveable as a rock. On which side of this stand of pikes our horse were, I could not discover, for the air was so darkened by the smoke of the powder that for a quarter of an hour together (I dare say) there was no light seen, but when the fire of the volleys of shot gave; and 'twas the greatest storm that ever I saw, in which though I knew not whither to go, nor what to do, my horse had two or three musket bullets in him immediately, which made him tremble under me at a rate, and I could hardly with spurs keep him from lying down, but he did me the service to carry me off to a led horse and then died.

By the time I came up to the hill again, the heat of the battle was over and the sun set but still pelting at one another half musket shot off. The enemy had a huge advantage of ground upon our men, for their foot were in a large sheep-cot, which had a stone wall about it as good a defence against any thing but cannon as could be, and ours upon the edge of the hill, so steep that they could hardly draw up. 'Tis true there were shelves near the place like Romish works where we quartered that night, but so shallow that my horse had a bullet in his neck. We pelted at one another till half an hour before day, and then we heard not any noise, but saw light matches upon the wall, which our commanders observing sent one to discover whether they had quit the field or not, who brought news that they were gone."

Another Royalist eyewitness at Lansdown was Lieutenant-Colonel Walter Slingsby, who also

Armoured cavalry; from a continental engraving of around 1650.

described the closing stages of the battle from the point of view of the King's party. He was with the Royalist Foot and described the manoeuvres by which Waller was able to withdraw with his army relatively intact.

"The rebels' Foot took example by their horse and quit their breastworks retiring behind a long stone wall that runs across the down. Our Foot leaps into their breastworks, our horse draws up upon their ground. Our two wings that were sent to fall into the two woods had done their business and were upon the hill as soon as the rest.

The enemy, observing our front to enlarge itself upon the hill and our cannon appearing there likewise, began to suspect himself and drew his whole strength behind that wall, which he lined well with musketeers and in several places broke down breaches very broad that his horse might charge if there were occasion, which breaches were guarded by his cannon and bodies of pikes.

Thus stood the two armies taking breath looking upon each other, our cannon on both sides playing without ceasing till it was dark, at which time our right wing of shot got much nearer their army, lodging themselves amongst the many little pits betwixt the wall and the wood from whence we galled them cruelly.

About 11 of the clock we receiv'd a very great volley of small shot but not mix't with cannon by which some of us judg'd that he was retreating and gave this at his expiring. But the general apprehension through our army was that the enemy had intention to try a push in the night for their ground, which they had so dishonourably lost. For we were then seated like a heavy stone upon the very brow of the hill, which with one lusty charge might well have been roll'd to the bottom.

It was not long before we knew certainly that they were gone. At their departure they left all their light matches upon the wall and whole bodies of pikes standing upright in order within the wall as if men had held them. We were glad they were gone for if they had not I know not we had, within an hour. But indeed had our horse been as good as the enemy's the rebels had never gone off the field unruin'd."

Despite this escape from Lansdown the writing was on the wall for Waller and his army.

Hopton's victorious western cavaliers moved finally to destroy Waller's army at the battle of Roundway Down on the 13th of July 1643. There Lord Wilmot, Sir John Byron and a strong body of cavaliers inflicted a shattering defeat on Waller. Atkyns took part in the battle and left us an exact account of the fighting. His graphic description includes the almost comic account of the pursuit and temporary capture of Sir Arthur Haselrigg, who was able to resist numerous attempts to impede his progress by taking off the extra thick cuirassier armour he was wearing and throwing it away.

"The next morning I had orders that the rendezvous was about Marlborough, whither I went with several horse quartered at Farringdon, and came timely thither. The Lord Wilmot was sent with a recruit of horse from Oxford, and I suppose all the horse at that rendezvous were about eighteen hundred and two small pieces of cannon.

We lost no time but marched towards the enemy, who stood towards the top of the hill; the Foot in the middle between two wings of Horse, and the cannon before the Foot. Although the Royalist force was relatively small the cavalry still enjoyed something of an art of invincibility and without waiting for the Royalist Infantry to arrive, the order was given to charge the entire Parliamentary Army. The charge was so sudden that I had hardly time to put on my arms. We advanced at a full trot three deep and kept in order. The enemy kept their station and their right wing of horse, being cuirassiers, were I'm sure five if not six deep, in so close order that Punchinello himself, had he been there, could not have gotten into them.

All the horse on the left hand of Prince Maurice's regiment, had none to charge; we charged the very utmost man of their right wing. I cannot better compare the figure of both armies than to the map of the fight at sea, between the English and Spanish Armadas, only there was no half-moon, for though they were above twice our numbers – they being six deep in close order and we but three deep and open

THE ROUNDHEADS

SIR WILLIAM WALLER

William Waller was born in Sussex in 1604. He was to come to embody all of the virtues of dignity, honour and faithfulness which were all too often absent in the murky events of the Civil War.

As a young man he fought against the Catholic armies on the continent and formed a firm friendship with a young Ralph Hopton, who was to become his main opponent in the English Civil Wars. It is typical of Waller that although he was at war against Hopton, he would not allow personal animosity to intrude into the relationship. His famous letter written to Hopton on the night before the battle of Lansdown is a model of dignity in an otherwise undignified world.

"Certainly my affections to you are so unchangeable, that hostility itself cannot violate my friendship to your person, but I must be true to the cause wherein I serve... We are both upon the stage and must act those parts assigned us in this tragedy: let us do it in a way of honour, and without personal animosities; whatsoever the issue be, I shall never willingly relinquish the dear title of your most affectionate friend and faithful servant, Wm Waller."

Like all the other politicians except Cromwell, Waller lost his position of command in the army under the Self-Denying Ordinance of 1645.

He also lost the religious debate by siding with the Presbyterians against the Independents in the political arguments of 1647.

Although the Presbyterians controlled Parliament, Parliament could not defeat the army and Waller found himself cast in the role of Parliament's

William Waller was one of the few figures to survive and enjoy relative peace and prosperity during the years of political turmoil which followed the first Civil War.

agent, acting against the unruly army elements.

In the middle of June 1647, Waller and ten other Presbyterian MP's were impeached for allegedly creating hostility between Parliament and the army in order to instigate a new Civil War.

In return for Waller agreeing to withdraw from Parliament, the army withdrew from its threatened march on London.

The London Apprentices demonstrated for the return of the Presbyterian MP's to the house and the eleven MP's including Waller, returned to the House in triumph. In response, the army marched on London and Waller fled into exile.

With his return to England, Waller was imprisoned for a long stretch by the army, on whose behalf he had fought so long and hard.

By 1648, Waller, in common with the other Presbyterian leaders, had effectively become a cavalier in sympathy.

He was bitterly opposed to the execution of the King in 1649. Although he took no part in subsequent cavalier insurrections, he was frequently arrested on suspicion of cavalier sympathies. At one time he was even interrogated by Cromwell himself. Waller noted with disappointment that Cromwell pretended not to know him.

He lived to see the restoration of King Charles II and was granted a pardon for his Roundhead past. He spent his last years quietly at Osterley and died in September 1668. In recognition of his upright conduct throughout the years of the Civil War, he was buried with full military honours by those who had formerly been his enemies.

by reason of our sudden charge – we were without them at both ends. The cannoneers seeing our resolution did not fire their cannon. No men ever charged better than ours did that day, especially the Oxford horse, for ours were tired and scattered, yet those that were there did their best.

T'was my fortune in a direct line to charge their General of Horse which I supposed to be so by his place. He discharged his carbine first but at a distance not to hurt us, and afterwards one of his pistols, before I came up to him and missed with both. I then immediately struck into him, and touched him before I discharged mine; and I'm sure I hit him, for he staggered and presently wheeled off from his party and ran on.

I pursued him, and had not gone twenty yards from him, but I heard a voice saying "'Tis Sir Arthur Haselrigg - Follow him!" But from which party the voice came I knew not, they being joined, nor never did know till about seven years since. But follow him I did and in six score yards I came up to him, and discharged the other pistol at him, and I'm sure I hit his head for I touched it before I have fire and it amazed him at that present, but he was too well armed all over for a pistol bullet to do him any hurt, having a coat of mail over his arms and a headpiece (I am confident) musket proof his sword had two edges and a ridge in the middle, and mine was a strong tuck. After I had slackened my pace a little, he was gone twenty yards from me, riding three quarters speed and down the side of a hill, his posture was waving his sword on the right and left hand of his horse, not looking back to see whether he were pursued or not (as I conceive) to daunt any horse that should come up to him.

In about six score more yards I came up to him again (having a very swift horse that Cornet Washnage gave me) and stuck by him a good while, and tried him from head to the saddle and could not penetrate him nor do him any hurt. But in this

(Continued on page 88)

The leading figures in the Roundhead movement from a contemporary publication 'Broadside' which offers 'a perfect list of all the victories obtained by Parliament's forces'.

THE BATTLE OF LANSDOWN HILL - 5TH JULY 1643

The Battle of Lansdown was contested by the pikemen of both sides who became locked in a fierce hand to hand combat.

B y July 1643, after a prolonged series of engagements with the Royalists, the situation still hung in the balance.

Finally, Waller brought his army to Lansdown Hill, just north of Bath, seeking a decisive engagement with the Royalists, under Lord Hopton. Hopton brought his army from the south to confront Waller on 5th July 1643. Once again, the engagement would prove indecisive.

Royalist movements ■

Parliamentarian movements ■

Chippenham

Marshfield

LANSDOWN HILL

Roundway Down

Bath

Melksham

Bradford on Avon

Trowbridge

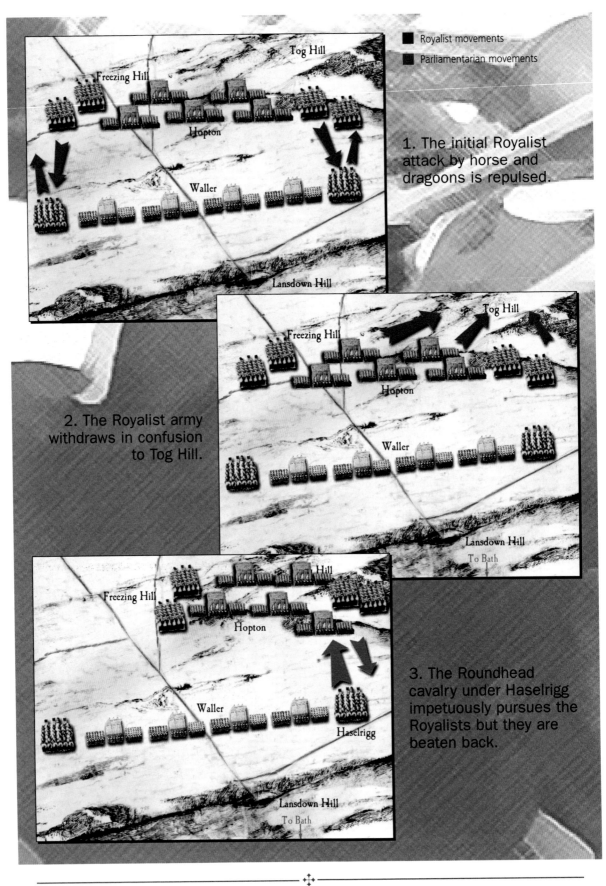

Royalist movements
Parliamentarian movements

1. The initial Royalist attack by horse and dragoons is repulsed.

2. The Royalist army withdraws in confusion to Tog Hill.

3. The Roundhead cavalry under Haselrigg impetuously pursues the Royalists but they are beaten back.

4. The retreat of the Parliamentarian cavalry is the signal for the Royalist Foot to begin a fierce assault on the Parliamentarian position on Lansdown Hill.

5. There is a bitter hand to hand fight on the steep slopes in which Grenville's regiment gradually gain the ascendancy.

6. At nightfall Waller draws off the Parliament-arian Army in good order, leaving the Royalists in control of the field at Lansdown.

Sir Bevil Grenville, leader of the Cornish Royalists.

(Continued from page 84)

attempt he cut my horse's nose, that you might put your finger in the wound, and gave me such a blow on the inside of my arm amongst the veins that I could hardly hold my sword. He went on as before and I slackened my pace again and found my horse got up to him again, thinking to have pulled him off his horse. But he having now found the way, struck my horse upon the cheek, and cut off half the headstall of my bridle; but falling off from him, I ran his horse into the body and resolved to attempt nothing further than to kill his horse; all this time we were together hand to fist.

In this nick of time came up Cornet Holmes to my assistance, (whoever failed me in time of danger), and went up to him with great resolution, and felt him before he discharged his pistol, and though I saw him hit him, 'twas but a flea-biting to him. Whilst he charged him, I employed myself in killing his horse, and ran him into several places, and upon the faltering of his horse his headpiece opened behind and I gave him a prick in the neck, and I had run him through the head if my horse had not stumbled at the same place. There came in

Captain Buck, a gentlemen of my troop, and discharged his pistol upon him also, but with the same success as before, and being a very strong man, and charging with a mighty sword, stormed him and amazed him but he fell on again. By this time his horse began to be faint with bleeding, and fell off from his rate, at which said Sir Arthur, "What good will it do you to kill a poor man?" Said I "Take quarter then", with that he stopped his horse and I came up to him, and bid him deliver his sword, which he was loathe to do. And being tied twice about his wrist, he was fumbling a great while before he would part with it. But before he delivered it, there was a runaway troop of theirs that had espied him in hold. Says one of them, 'My Lord General is taken prisoner!'; says another, 'Sir Arthur Haselrigg is taken prisoner! Face about and charge!' With that they rallied and charged us, and rescued him; wherein I received a shot with a pistol, which took off but the skin upon the blade bone of my shoulder."

This story being related to the King at a second or third hand, his answer was, 'Had he been victualled as well as fortified, he might have endured a siege of seven years.'

Despite the fact that they had seen this cavalry chased from the field the Parliamentarian infantry stood its ground. By moving the men into a hedgehog of pikes they formed a solid wall which the Royalists could not breach. Atkyns again takes up the story.

"When we came back to the army, (which in so confused a field was difficult to do), we found the enemy's foot still in close body, their muskets lined with pikes and fronting every way, expecting their horse to rally and come to their relief. In the meantime our horse charged them, but to no purpose; they could not get into them. At last, when they saw our foot march from Devizes and come within a mile of them, they asked quarter, and threw down their arms in a moment."

The perils of the battlefield were plain to see but Atkyns had not allowed for the presence of the other primary factor in a war zone, the opportunist chiefs who seek a quick profit for the misfortunes of others. In this case the villain appears in the form of his own groom.

"*When I alighted I found my horse had done bleeding, his cuts being upon the gristly part of his nose, and the cheek near the bone. I bade my groom have a great care of him, and go into quarters immediately, but instead this rogue went directly to Oxford, left my hurt horse at Marlborough with a farrier, and sold another horse of mine at Oxford and carried my portmanteau with him into the North which had all my clothes and linen in it, and other things worth above £100 and I never saw him more. For want of a shift (my wound having bloodied my linen) I became so lousy in three or four days that I could not tell what to do with myself. And when I have got a shift, which was not till we took Bath, my blood and the sweat of my body had so worn it, that it fell off into lint.*"

The curious code of honour which still prevailed over many of the combatants is illustrated by Atkyns in his concern over whether or not a Lieutenant Sandys, captured by the Parliamentarians and honour bound to surrender himself at Bristol, was still governed by this compulsion, even after his recapture by his own side.

In the swirling crush of the cavalry melee, both swords and pistols could be employed.

S.R. GARDINER ON THE ENGLISH CIVIL WAR

A contemporary engraving of Sir Ralph Hopton when he was still Governor of Bristol, completed prior to 1645.

"So far everything had gone well with Hopton. If his mind was weighed down with anxiety, it was not from fear of the enemy. The horsemen who followed Hertford and Maurice were full of energy and courage, but they were desperate plunderers. As a commander of those Cornish soldiers who were as stainless in this matter as even Cromwell's troopers, Hopton was gravely dissatisfied with the evil which he was powerless to stay, and he was all the more vexed because he was himself a native of Somerset, and they were his own friends and neighbours who complained in vain of the ravages to which they were subjected."

THE FIELD ARMIES - ROYALIST

WESTERN ROYALIST ARMIES

The prime mover in the Royalist military activities in the west was Sir Ralph Hopton. An able and gifted commander, he led the Western Royalists to victory at Braddock Down and Stratton.

Always hampered by the refusal of Hopton's Cornish troops to fight outside the country, Hopton was also to endure failure at Plymouth and Southern Down.

The Western Royalists really became a force to be reckoned with only when the forces of the Marquis of Hertford and Prince Maurice were united under the effective command of Hopton in 1643.

Together they were victorious at Lansdown, and Roundway Down. Once again, however, they could not accomplish a successful capture of Plymouth.

After the disastrous defeat at Cheriton, the forces under Hopton were incorporated into the King's Oxford Army for the campaigns of 1644.

Lord Goring assumed command of the Royalist forces for the campaign of 1645 but with the destruction of Charles' Oxford Army at Naseby, only an unremitting run of failure lay ahead. Even the appointment of Hopton in January 1646 could not save the day and the last Royalist forces in the west surrendered in March 1646.

Listed below is a selection of regiments that served at various times in the Western Royalist Armies:

Foot
- Lord Hopton
- John Tevanion
- Thomas Bassett
- Bevil Grenville
- William Godolphin
- Sir Nicholas Slanning
- Prince Maurice

Horse
- Lord Mohun
- Earl of Caernavon
- Sir George Vaughan

THE FIELD ARMIES - PARLIAMENTARIAN

THE WESTERN ASSOCIATION

Under the leadership of Sir William Waller, the Parliamentarian Armies in the West of England fought an unequal struggle against the Royalists before they were finally annihilated in the Battle of Roundway Down.

Nonetheless, Waller still managed to wield considerable influence and took part in the great debate of 1644 which led directly to the formation of the New Model Army.

The famous letter from Sir Ralph Hopton to Waller is an enduring example of the trials of triumph and adversity.

Listed below is a selection of regiments who served at various times under Sir William Waller:

Foot
- Sir William Waller
- Hardress Waller
- Edward Cooke
- Col. Sam Jones

Horse
- Sir Arthur Haselrigg
- Richard Norton
- George Thompson
- Jonas Van Druske
- Edward Popham

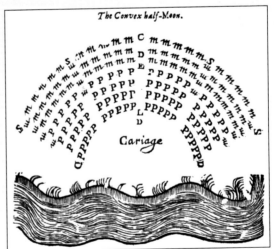

An unusual formation of pikes and muskets from Barriffe's 'Military Discipline'.

A Victorian view of hand-to-hand combat in the Civil Wars. Although the dress feels accurate, cavalry standards were much smaller than the huge flag which the soldier in the centre is trying to snatch from the man on horseback

THE BATTLE OF ROUNDWAY DOWN - 13TH JULY 1643

The Battle of Roundway Down was finally decided by the arrival of the Royalist Foot, who attacked the Roundheads who had been deserted by their own cavalry which had routed from the field pursued by the Royalists.

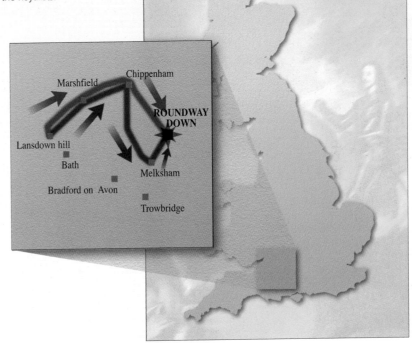

Royalist movements ■
Parliamentarian movements ■

Marshfield
Chippenham
Lansdown hill
ROUNDWAY DOWN
Bath
Melksham
Bradford on Avon
Trowbridge

After the Battle of Lansdown, Waller marched first to Chippenham then on to Roundway Down near Devizes, where Waller drew up his cavalry. They were pursued by Hopton and his cavalry, who then came face to face with the Parliamentarians on Roundway Down in July 1643.

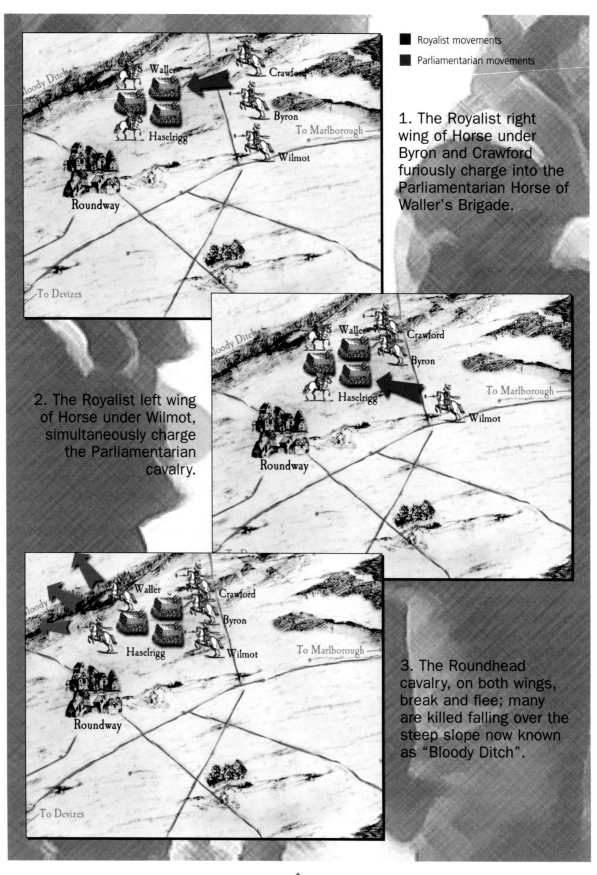

Royalist movements
Parliamentarian movements

1. The Royalist right wing of Horse under Byron and Crawford furiously charge into the Parliamentarian Horse of Waller's Brigade.

2. The Royalist left wing of Horse under Wilmot, simultaneously charge the Parliamentarian cavalry.

3. The Roundhead cavalry, on both wings, break and flee; many are killed falling over the steep slope now known as "Bloody Ditch".

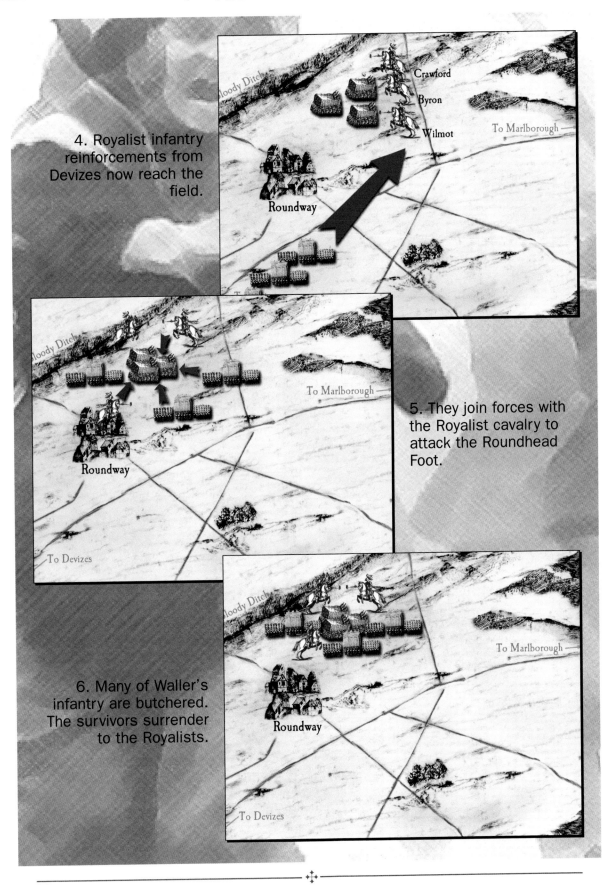

4. Royalist infantry reinforcements from Devizes now reach the field.

5. They join forces with the Royalist cavalry to attack the Roundhead Foot.

6. Many of Waller's infantry are butchered. The survivors surrender to the Royalists.

THE FIELD ARMIES - PARLIAMENTARIAN

THE EASTERN ASSOCIATION

Nominally commanded by the Earl of Manchester, the army of the Eastern Association was the training ground for the man who was to become synonymous with the whole of the Civil War - Oliver Cromwell.

Cromwell's double regiment of horsemen formed the backbone of the cavalry in the army. They were present at most of the fights with the Earl of Newcastle's army and, in addition, fought at 2nd Newbury and Marston Moor.

In the fallout between the Presbyterians and the Independents, Manchester lost his influence in the army and it was Cromwell who went on to command the regiment of the Eastern Association in the New Model Army.

Listed below is a selection of regiments who served at various times with the Earl of Manchester:

Foot
- Earl of Manchester
- Sir Miles Hobart
- Francis Russell
- Edward Montague
- John Pickering

Horse
- Algernon Sydney
- Oliver Cromwell
- Charles Fleetwood

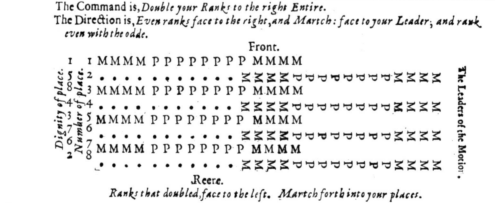

A contemporary formation from Barriffe's drill book: how to double ranks.

(Continued from page 89)

"*After we were refreshed in our quarters, we marched to Bath, which town the enemy had newly quitted, and marched or rather retreated to Bristol. There I found my Lieutenant, Thomas Sandys, formerly taken prisoner, recovering of his wounds but not well able to go abroad. We were very glad to see each other, and I desired him to tell me the manner of his being taken. He told me he pursued the enemy too near their body, and they sent out fresh horse upon him and took him and gave him quarter without asking. But after he was their prisoner, a Scot shot him into the body with two pistol bullets, which were still in him so that he was very near death.*

When he was brought to the town, Sir William Waller enquiring what prisoners were taken, heard of his name, and came to see him. He seemed exceedingly angry at the inhumane action that befell him, and sent for his own chirurgeon presently and saw whatever he called for, and he would see him paid, that whatsoever woman he sent for to attend him, should be admitted, and lent him ten broad pieces for his own private expenses, and before he marched to Bristol, he came to see him again, and finding him not able to march, took his parole to tender himself a true prisoner to him at Bristol which I answered that he was now made free by as good authority as took him prisoner, and that I expected he should return to his command, upon which we struck a hear and at last referred the business to the Lord Caernarvon to determine.

The case was agreed to be 'whether a prisoner upon his parole to render himself to the enemy, being afterward redeemed by his own party, ought to keep his parole or not.' His Lordship heard arguments on both sides, at last said thus, that there had been lately a precedent in the Council of War in a case of like nature, wherein it was resolved that if the prisoner, (being redeemed by a martial power without any consent of his own), shall afterwards refuse the command he was in before and attempt to render himself prisoner to the enemy, he shall be taken as an enemy, and be kept prisoner by his own party; the reason seems very strong because he may be prevailed upon by the enemy to betray his own party; and the freeing

Cuirassier armour from a Victorian engraving. This elaborately finished suit would have been designed for a wealthy individual.

General Sir Phillip Skippon, known as 'Old Robin', was a much-loved commander of Parliamentarian infantry. It was Skippon who led the London apprentices, who knew him affectionately as 'Old Robin'.

of his person, gives him as it were a new election; and if he choose rather to be a prisoner than a free man, it demonstrates his affection to be there. But this did not satisfy my lieutenant, for he would not take his place as before but marched along with the troop as my prisoner, till the taking of Bristol (the place where he promised to render himself) and there he thought he was fully absolved from his parole, and betook himself to his employment again."

Roundway Down was a disaster for Parliament, and particularly for the cavalry, so it is fortunate that a survivor has been able to give a glimpse of what it meant to be on the receiving end of such a calamitous defeat.

On 15th July 1643, Captain Edward Harley wrote an account of the battles in the west country, from the Parliamentarian viewpoint. He commanded a troop in Waller's own regiment of horse at Roundway Down.

"As soon as ever we came there were a very great body of the enemy, which we found afterward to be between forty and fifty colours besides dragoons. But at the very first charge all our horse ran away and left our foot, who behaved themselves very bravely as long as they were able to defend themselves, and then shifted for themselves. We have not lost many men, considering what a miserable rout we were in. All our cannon, baggage and ammunition are lost and very many arms. We must look upon this as the hand of our God, mightily against us for 'twas he only that made us fly. We had very much self-confidence, and I trust the Lord has only brought this upon us to make us look more to him, whom I am confident, when we are weakest, will show himself a glorious God over the enemies of his Truth. So this time nothing has been gained by us with multitudes, and I beseech the Lord give us faith to live by that, and then I doubt not but our broken bones shall prevail over the enemy's mighty strength.

Postscript - Sir, I lost ten horse, and two men in the fight last week and this last time I have lost five or six more, so that my troop is now very weak.

Sir Arthur Haselrigg is hurt in three places, but not mortal. My brother Robert humbly begs your blessing. I thank God we are both well having the mercies of our God very great to us in preserving us safe. I beseech you pardon this scribbling for I have not been in a bed these twelve nights before."

THE STORMING OF BRISTOL

Buoyed up by Hopton's success, the Royalists moved swiftly. A second arms convoy arrived in Oxford two days later and leaving a scattering of garrisons to mask the main Roundhead Army, the Royalists marched on Bristol.

The city's hastily constructed earth defences were rather too extensive for the small Parliamentarian garrison and they proved incapable of repelling a furious Royalist assault on the 26th of July. The storming of the defences of the city of Bristol was to prove one of the most savage day's fighting of the whole war.

Royalist casualties were high, the dead lay piled high on the ramparts.

"As gallant gentlemen as ever drew sword lay upon that ground - like so many rotten sheep."

Although losses were high, the gain to the Royalist cause was incalculable. Bristol was the second city in the Kingdom, a major port with sufficient ships still in it, to form the nucleus of a Royalist fleet. Less spectacularly, but no less importantly, the city also had gun manufacturers, capable of turning out hundreds of muskets a week. These were greatly welcomed by the under supplied Royalists. By the end of the war, most Royalist infantry regiments were wholly armed with Bristol made muskets, and had abandoned pikes entirely.

With Bristol secure, some of the King's advisers advocated turning immediately to attack London. If the city fell it would mean the end of the war, but Charles again hesitated and instead it was decided to first capture Gloucester, the last remaining major Parliamentary stronghold in the west. It was unlikely to be able to hold out for very long. So confident was Charles of victory that he allocated a portion of his precious forces to undertake a simultaneous siege of Exeter. After the fall of these two Roundhead strongholds it was planned that the combined Royalist armies would then advance on London with their rear secure.

Once again, Charles had chosen the way. Sickened by the losses at Bristol, Charles would not permit Gloucester to be stormed, preferring instead to starve the defenders into submission.

The governor, Colonel Massey, confounded the King's army by holding out, and by doing so thwarted Charles' great design for 1643. It was to prove a near run thing, however, but the Royalist will to continue with the siege was finally broken by an unseasonable downpour of rain.

The Puritan Chaplain, John Cobat, recalled the events of the siege:

"Certainly the care of a higher Providence preserved and brought of those many several parties, when the vanquishing of any one of them must needs run the city upon extreme hazard; for our whole strength remained upon the works day and night except the reserve of a hundred and twenty men at the main guard. One rate and slender rank were to receive the storm without seconds, yet the safety of the whole did require those frequent sallies, a desperate remedy to a despairing city, not only to cast back the enemy's preparations but to

S.R. GARDINER ON THE ENGLISH CIVIL WAR

William Waller from a contemporary engraving.

"Although the news from Roundway Down, following close upon the news from Adwalton Moor, was a terrible blow to the Parliamentary leaders, it brought with it no thought of surrender. It rather gave life to that scheme for calling in the Scots which they had long entertained, but which even the House of Commons had hitherto shrunk from putting into execution.

There can be little doubt that between Pym and Argyle a good understanding had for some time existed. It was under Argyle's influence that the various bodies which together acted as the government of Scotland resolved on May 10th to summon a Convention of Estates - a kind of informal Parliament - to meet on June 22nd without the royal consent."

Detail from a continental engraving of siege operations at the time of the Civil Wars. The guns are protected by wicker baskets filled with earth, known as gabions.

amaze them, that the soldiers should be held up in such height of resolution and cause them to expect more hot service from within the works. Our men likewise were to be kept in the heat of action to prevent the feigning of the spirits, their hands also imbrued in blood did the more enrage them. Not by safer means could they over come, the terror which by the reputation of the King's army might possess their minds. The enemy were kept waking by continual alarms to waste and whensoever their cannon had been silent for a while, one or two of our guns gave fire to disturb the calm and signify to the country that we were yet alive. For the besiegers ever and anon scattered reports of the taking of the town with a purpose to prevent our relief. All things within did presage a deliverance.

The sadness of the times did not cloud the countenance of the people. They beheld their fortunes with a clear brow, and were deliberate and cheerful in the endeavours of safety. No great complainings were heard in our streets, no discontent seized on the soldiers, at other times prone to mutiny; men of suspected fidelity did not fail in action; every valuable person was active in his own place. The usual outcries of women were not then heard, the weakness of whose sex was not overcome by the terrible engines of war. And our becalmed spirits did implore divine assistance without confusion. The Governor personally performed, ready at every turning of affairs, and gracing the business with speech and gesture. Upon the least intimation of diffidence he pretended rational hopes of success, adding withal that our late yielding could not mollify the King's army, and if in the close we must needs be lost, no surer means of safety than by the utmost gallantry to constrain honourable conditions.

The enemy still prepared for a general storm, meanwhile seeking to waste our magazine, which they knew must needs suddenly fail, expended their own store, and daily acted to the terror of the inhabitants; shooting grenades, fire-balls, and great stones out of their mortar-pieces, and had now planted a battery on the southside westward, unto which the lower part of the town was open. Thence in one night they shot above twenty fiery melting hot iron bullets, some eighteen pound weight, others two-and-twenty pound weight, which were seen to fly through the air like the shooting of a star. They passed through stables, and ricks of hay, where the fire by the swiftness of the motion did not catch, and falling on the tops of houses, presently melted the leads, and sunk through, but all the skill and industry of the enemy could not set one house on fire.

They still played their great shot against the walls, and wrought hard in filling up the moat with faggots and earth at the place, where they battered, where also they built a gallery over the head of the trench, the breadth of four abreast in the shelter whereof they had almost worked themselves over the moat. Then we found that they had sunk a mine under the east gate; whereupon the governor commanded a counter-mine in two places, but finding the springs, left off, conceiving for the same reason the endeavour of the enemy to no purpose. To discover or interrupt this work, a sergeant with five daring men were put forth at a port hole in the dungeon at the east gate, came close to the mouth of their mine, took off the board that covered it, and for a while viewed the miners. One of these cast in the hand-grenade amongst them, whilst the four musketeers played upon them as they ran forth, and with the noise of our men from the walls gave the whole league a strong alarm, and crept in at the port-hole without harm. Wherefore discovering that the enemy notwithstanding the springs, went on with their mine, we renewed our countermine for they had sunk a great depth under the moat, and extremely toiled in drawing up the spring water, till at length they had gotten under the gate that our miners could hear them work under them and did expect to spoil them by pouring in water or stealing out their powder.

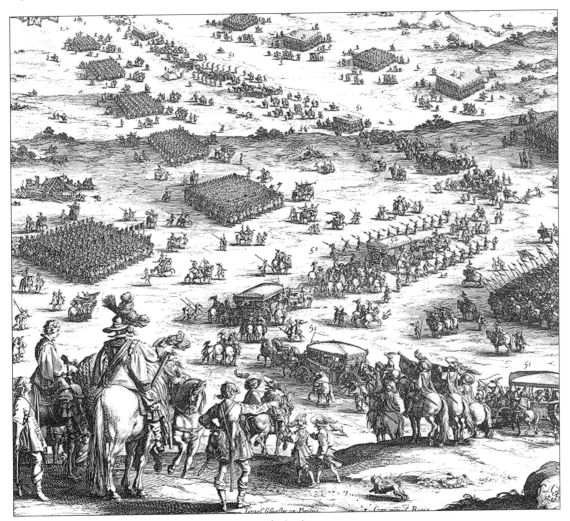

Detail of a French army of the period drawn up in readiness for battle.

John Hotham, Governor of Hull. His steadfastness deprived the King of vital munitions at the outbreak of war.

As the soldiers within were heated with their own performance, so the enemy without being wasted in a lingering design before the hour of service came, grew feeble in their own thoughts and to us contemptible. Our common soldiers took to themselves a liberty to revile, presented and confounded for the enemy with the self-same language in which they were wont to abuse and scorn our party, which contumely, though it begets a more deadly hatred and desire of revenge in generous minds, at the time did deject exceedingly and debase the spirits of their private soldiers, who had never performed one gallant achievement and to whom the sturdiness of our men was well known. The slowness of their design in that form of a leaguer, proceeded from the desire of saving their foot, with this presumption, that there was no power to raise the siege; which confidence deceived them, till too late, for their foot after those many knocks, and the first fury spent, were not so capable of the service, without the help of many tedious preparations. Wherefore, besides their mine and battery, they framed great store of those imperfect and troublesome engines to assault the lower parts of the city. Those engines ran upon wheels with planks, musket proof, placed on the axle-tree with holes for

musket shot and a bridge before it, the end whereof, (the wheels falling into the ditch), was to rest upon our breast works."

With the breathing space gained from the protracted siege of Gloucester, the Earl of Essex was able to assemble a relief force from London by filling out his typhus-ravaged ranks with several regiments of militia from the London trained bands.

Not all of those in the ranks were cheered on their way to war. Letters from London, captured by the Royalists, were published in their propaganda magazine, Mercurius Rusticus, among them this embarrassing plea from his wife to a Parliamentarian soldier, John Owen under Lieutenant-Colonel West in the Blue regiment.

"Most tender and dear heart, my kind affection remembered unto you. I am like never to see you more I fear, and if you ask the reason why, the reason is this, either I am afraid the Cavaliers will kill you or death will deprive you of me, being full of grief for you, which I fear will cost me my life. I do much grieve that you be so hard-hearted to me. Why could not you come home with Master Murphy on Saturday? Could not you venture as well as he? But you did it on purpose, to show your hatred to me. Here is none of our neighbours with you that has a wife but Master Fletcher and Master Norwood and yourself. Everybody can come but you. I have sent one to Oxford to get a pass for you to come home, but when you come you must use your wits. I am afraid if you do not come home, I shall much dishonour God more than you can honour him. Therefore if I do miscarry you shall answer for it. Pity me for God's sake and come home. Will nothing prevail with you? My cousin Jane is now with me and prays for your speedy return. For God's sake come home So with my prayer for you I rest your loving wife."
London September 5

Susan Owen

Despite the dubious quality of some of his regiments and with the garrison down to a single barrel of powder, Essex raised the siege of Gloucester on the 4th of September. Essex was to throw away his success by, once again, allowing the Royalist Army to get between him and his base at London. The King was able to force Essex to fight him on ground of his choosing. The two forces met at Newbury. John Gwynn was present at both the siege and the battle.

"I was at the siege of Gloucester, we would probably have captured the town, but a great glut of rain fell, flooding our works, and we were forced to remove the next day.

At Newbury we beat the enemy from the town's end to the top of the hill by the heath, a wing of Essex his horse moving gently towards us, made us leave our execution upon the enemy, and retreat into the next field, there were several gaps to get to it, but not near my way; yet with the colours in my hand, I jumped over the hedge and ditch, otherwise I would have died by a multitude of hands. We kept this field until midnight and until some intelligence came that Essex was marching away with a great part of his army, and that had buried a great many of his great guns. Near unto this field, upon the heath, lay a whole file of men, six deep, with their heads all struck off with one cannon shot of ours."

As the action at Newbury has been so well documented by participants, on both sides, we can use their memoirs to piece together an unusually comprehensive portrait of the battle as seen from both sides.

On the Parliamentarian side, the gruesome events were recalled with equal clarity:

"The next morning, September 20, early before day, we had drawn up all our army in their several regiments and marched away by break and then advancing towards the enemy with most cheerful and courageous spirits. The Lord Robartes' soldiers had begun to skirmish with them before we came up to the enemy, which we hearing, put us to a running march till we sweat again, hastening to their relief and succour.

When we were come up into the field, our two regiments of the trained bands were placed in open company upon the right wing of the whole army. The enemy had there planted eight pieces of ordnance, and stood in a great body of horse and foot, we being placed right opposite, against them and far less than twice musket shot distance from them. They began their battery against us with their great guns above half an hour before we

(Continued on page 108)

S.R. GARDINER ON THE ENGLISH CIVIL WAR

A contemporary study of Robert Devereux, Earl of Essex, who was the driving force behind the early stages of the Parliamentarian war efforts.

"London now made itself ready for a supreme effort. Every shop was closed, that no man might plead the calls of business as a bar to the fulfilment of duty. The pulpits rang with exhortations to go forth to the help of the Lord against the mighty. Patriotic and religious emotions beat in unison.

On August 22nd Essex reviewed eight thousand men on Hounslow Heath, ready to start on the perilous enterprise."

King Charles is depicted as he desperately tries to rally his life-guard to make a final charge at the Battle of Naseby. In reality Charles was prevented from leading the charge by the aged Scots Earl of Carnwath who grabbed the bridle of his horse and led the King away from the field.

THE 1ST BATTLE OF NEWBURY - SEPTEMBER 1643

The first Battle of Newbury demonstrated that Charles was an able strategist but it also highlighted the fact that his resources were unlikely to carry the war to a successful conclusion.

After the relief of Gloucester, Essex took his Parliamentarian army first north to Pershore, then directly south to Cirencester. Thinking he had evaded the King he began marching direct to London via Newbury. On hearing this, the King moved due south in an effort to cut off his opponent. The two armies met at Newbury with the King once again blocking Essex's path to London.

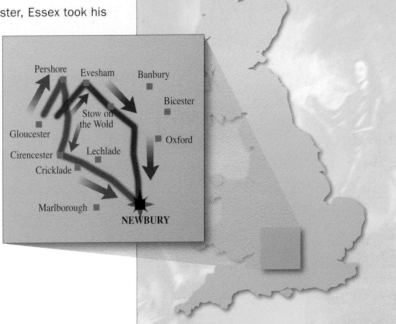

Royalist movements ■

Parliamentarian movements ■

Pershore Evesham Banbury

Bicester

Stow on
the Wold

Gloucester

Cirencester Lechlade Oxford

Cricklade

Marlborough

NEWBURY

Royalist movements
Parliamentarian movements

1. Royalist Horse under John Byron and Foot under Nicholas Byron begin their attack on the Roundhead centre.

2. The Parliamentarian Horse advance over Wash Common to attack the Royalist cavalry

3. The bloody fight for Roundhill continues with neither side giving ground.

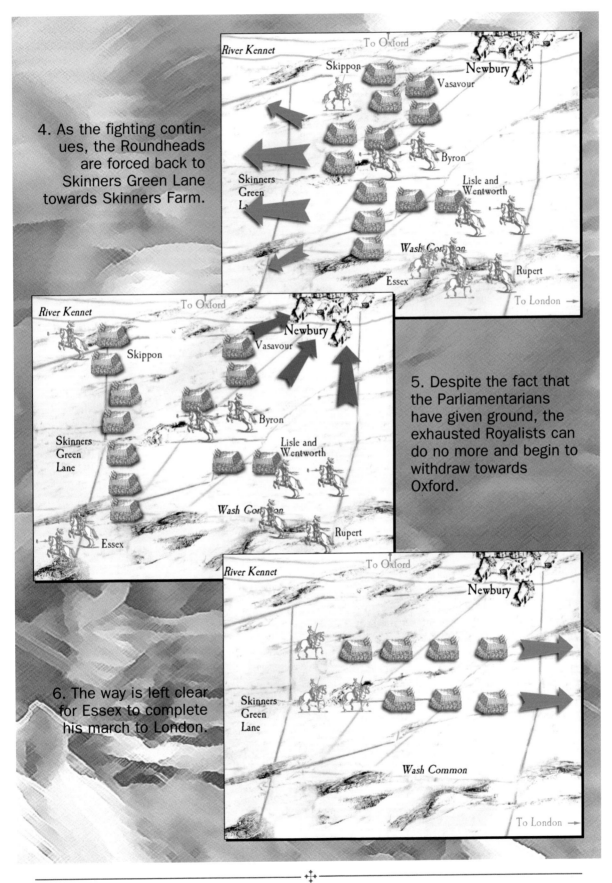

4. As the fighting continues, the Roundheads are forced back to Skinners Green Lane towards Skinners Farm.

5. Despite the fact that the Parliamentarians have given ground, the exhausted Royalists can do no more and begin to withdraw towards Oxford.

6. The way is left clear for Essex to complete his march to London.

(Continued from page 103)

could get any of our guns up to us. Our gunners dealt very ill with us, delaying to come up to us. Our noble Colonel Tucket fired piece of ordnance against the enemy, and aiming to give fire the second time was shot in the head with a cannon bullet from the enemy. The Blue Regiment of the trained bands stood upon our right wing, and behaved themselves most gallantly. Two regiments of the King's Horse, which stood upon their right flank afar off, came fiercely upon them and charged them two or three times, but were beat back with their musketeers, who gave them a most desperate charge and made them fly.

This day, our whole army wore green boughs in their hats to distinguish us from our enemies; which they perceiving one regiment of their horse had got green boughs and rid up to our regiments crying 'Friends! Friends!' but we let fly at them and made many of them and their horses tumble, making them fly with a vengeance. The enemy's cannon did play most against the Red Regiment of trained bands, they did some execution amongst us

at the first, and were somewhat dreadful when men's bowels and brains flew in our faces. But blessed be God that gave us courage, so that we kept our ground and after a while feared them not. Our ordnance did very good execution upon them, for we stood at so near a distance upon a plain field that we could not lightly miss one another. We were not much above half our regiments in this place; for we had sixty files of musketeers drawn off for the forlorn hope, who were engaged against the enemy in the field upon our left flank.

Where most of the regiments of the army were in fight they had some small shelter of the hedges and banks, yet had a very hot fight with the enemy and did good execution and stood to it as bravely as ever men did. When our two regiments of the trained bands had thus played against the enemy for the space of three horse, or thereabouts, our Red Regiment joined to the Blue which stood a little distance from us upon our left flank, where we gained the advantage of a little hill, which we maintained against the enemy half an hour. Two regiments of the enemy's Foot fought against us all this

The death of Lucius Carey, Viscount Falkland, from a Victorian engraving of the Battle of Newbury.

The triumphant entry of Essex back into London at the head of his army, which included the trained bands who had marched out from the city on their way to the relief of Gloucester.

while to gain the hill, but could not. Then two regiments of the enemy's Horse which stood upon our right flank, came fiercely upon us and so surrounded us that we were forced to charge upon them in the front and rear, and both flanks, which was performed by us with a great deal of courage and undauntedness of spirit, insomuch that we made a great slaughter among them and forced them to retreat. But presently the two regiments of the enemy's Foot in this time gained the hill, and came upon us before we could well recover ourselves, that we were glad to retreat a little way into the field, till we had rallied up our men and put them into their former posture, and then came on again.

If I should speak any thing in the praise and high commendations of these two regiments of the trained bands, I should rather obscure and darken the glory of that courage and valour God gave unto them this day. They stood like so many stakes against the shot of the cannon, quitting themselves like men of undaunted spirits, even our enemies themselves being judges. It might be expected that something should be spoken of the noble and valiant service performed by the rest of the regiments of the army, both Horse and Foot; but their courage and valour itself speaks, which was performed by them on that day, our men fighting like lions in every place, the great slaughter made amongst the enemies testifies.

My noble and valiant Captain George Massie, who was with the forlorn hope, received a shot in the back from the enemy of which wound he is since dead. This 20 September we lost about sixty or seventy men in our Red Regiment of the trained bands, besides wounded men, we having the hottest charge from the enemy's cannon of any regiment in the army. Also that worthy and valiant gentleman Captain Hunt was slain in this battle, whose death is much lamented. These two poor regiments were the very objects of the enemy's battery that day and they have since made their boast of it. It is conjectured by most, that the enemy lost four for one. Seventy chief commanders were slain on their side. This is most certain, that they did acknowledge *themselves to be beaten. It is credibly informed by those that were this day in the King's Army, that the King himself brought up a regiment of Foot and another of Horse into the field and gave fire to two pieces of ordnance, riding up and down all that day in a soldier's grey coat.*

The next day I viewed the dead bodies. There lay about one hundred stripped naked in that field where our two regiments stood in battalia. This night the enemy conveyed away about thirty cart loads of maimed and dead men, as the town-people credibly reported to us, and I think they might have carried away twenty cart loads more of their dead men the next morning. They buried thirty in one pit. Fourteen lay dead in one ditch. This battle continued long. It begun about six o'clock in the morning and continued till past twelve o'clock at night. In the night the enemy retreated to the town of Newbury and drew away all their ordnance. We were in great distress for water or any accommodation to refresh our poor soldiers, yet the Lord himself sustained us that we did not faint under it. We were right glad to drink the same water where our horses did drink, wandering up and down to seek for it. Our word this day was 'Religion', theirs was 'Queen Mary' in this field."

Detail from a portrait of Lucius Carey, Viscount Falkland, painted just prior to the outbreak of the Civil Wars.

WINTER CLOSES IN

With Reading recaptured and an indecisive outcome from the Newbury battle, the winter of 1643 closed in on another stale-mate. Once again, small scale actions, sieges and skirmishes marked the course of the war.

We are unusually well supplied with accounts of the actions like this, which were fought out in a variety of the bitterly contested small affairs in the area just to the west of London in the dying months of the year. The bulk of the Royalist forces came from Lord Hopton's army, while Parliament relied on the forces of the London trained bands (who were increasingly mutinous over their prolonged absence from home) to provide the bulk of the forces fighting under the command of Sir William Waller. With numbers and resources reasonably in the balance, both sides could have secured victory over the other in the close fighting

during the harsh winter of 1643. Much of that fighting took place around Basing House in Hampshire, home of the Marquis of Winchester. These particular actions took on an especially vicious dimension, as the catholic Marquis represented the personification of everything to which the zealous puritans of the London trained bands were opposed.

Lieutenant Elias Archer of the Yellow Auxiliaries described the type of action which was fought between the Parliamentarian forces around Farnham and those of the Royalists, under Ralph Hopton:

"While we were thus close under the walls, the women which were upon the leads of the house threw down stones and bricks, which hurt some of our men; in the meantime, the rest of our forces continued firing against other parts of the house, and performing such other service as it was possible, for men to do in such a desperate attempt till it was dark night that we could not see their loop-holes (although we were within pistol shot of the walls) then we were drawn off into several grounds and fields near adjoining, where we quartered that night.

I know something is expected should be spoken of the loss we there sustained. I conceive our loss of men in all the three days service against the house,

One of this sequence of Callot's etchings shows the pillage of a town in France. Although this is an engraving from the continent, such scenes would have been common place in England at the time of the Civil Wars.

and march homewards on the morrow. And about an hour and a half before night Sir William came into the park to us and at the head of every regiment of our London Brigade, he gave us many thanks for our service past, and told us that according to his promise and our expectation, we were to be discharged and march homewards on the morrow, and said he would not detain us, (if we were so sent homewards that we would stay no longer). But withal he told us that yet we could not return with much honour in respect of the bad success we had in our chiefest service, certifying us with all, that at the present there was an opportunity which might much avail the States and bring honour both to God and ourselves, if we would but lend him our assistance till the Monday following, engaging himself upon his honour and credit, that we should be no longer detained. Which we considering gave our full consent to stay, for which he gave us many thanks, in a very joyful expression advising us presently to prepare for the service because delays are dangerous.

Whereupon most of our men went presently into the town to refresh and prepare themselves for the service, where although they before gave their general consent many of them stayed behind and went not with their colours. Nevertheless we advanced without them and marched all that night pretending at the first setting forth to go towards Basing. But having marched that way about two miles, we returned to the left, and, (in a remote way between the wood and hills), marched beyond Alton, and about 9 o'clock on Wednesday morning December 13 came upon the west side of the town, where we had both the wind and hill to friend.

Then Sir William's own regiment of foot, Sir Arthur Haselrigg's five companies and five companies of Kentishmen went on upon the north and north-west side and gave the first onset by lining of hedges and the like, but could not (as yet) come to any perfect execution, in respect that our London regiments were not come in sight of the enemy, and therefore, they bent all their force against those three regiments and lined divers houses with musketeers. Especially one great brick house near the church was full, out of which windows they fired very fast, and might have done great prejudice to those men, but that when our train of artillery, came towards the foot of the hill, they made certain shot which took place upon that house and so forced them to forsake it."

THE FIGHT AT ALTON CHURCH

Although it hardly merits a mention in the text books, Archer's account of the fighting for the church at Alton provides a graphic insight into just how bitter these small actions could be. This was still very much a transitional phase in warfare where individual conspicuous acts of gallantry or courage were required to rally the flagging spirits of men who had lost their appetite for the fight.

Baron Byron painted at the time of the Civil Wars.

Despite the fact that they had been under arms for a least a year, the forces of Parliament still displayed the attributes of civilians at war. It took the courage of men such as Guy and Shambrooke to provide the example which would inspire the men of the Parliamentarian forces to do their duty as soldiers and ultimately to obtain the victory over the Royalists. Visitors to the church today can still see the signs of the struggle which took place on that bitter Tuesday afternoon in 1643.

"In the meantime our London regiments and four companies which belong to Farnham Castle came down the hill. Then the Red Regiment and the Greencoats, which Greencoats are the four companies of Farnham Castle, set upon a half-moon and a breast-work, which the enemy had managed, and from whence they fired very hot and desperately till the Green Auxiliaries marched on the other side of a little river into the town with their colours flying and, (being in the wind of the enemy), fired a little thatched house and so blinded them, that this regiment marched forwards and coming in part behind the works, fired upon them, so that they were forced to forsake the said half-moon and breast-works, which they had no sooner left but presently the Greencoats, and part of the musketeers of the

Red, and our Yellow regiment entered, while the rest of our regiment marched into the town and their colours flying.

Now was the enemy constrained to betake himself and all his forces to the church, churchyard, and one great work on the north side of the church, all which they kept near upon two hours very stoutly and (having made scaffolds in the church to fire out at the windows) fired very thick from every place till divers soldiers of our regiment and the Red regiment, who were gotten into the town, fired very thick upon the south-east of the churchyard, and so forced them to forsake that part of the wall, leaving their muskets standing upright, the muzzles whereof appeared above the wall as if some of the men had still lain there in ambush and our men seeing nobody appear to use those muskets, concluded that the men were gone, and consulted among themselves to enter two or three files of musketeers promising Richard Guy, one of the Captain's sergeants (who was the first man that entered the church-yard) to follow him if he would lead them. Whereupon he advanced, and coming within the church-yard door, and seeing most of the Cavaliers firing at our men, from the south and west part of the church-yard, looked behind him for the men which promised to follow him and there was only one musketeer with him. Nevertheless he flourishing his sword, told them if they would come, the church-yard was our own.

Then Simon Hutchinson, one of Lieutenant-Colonel Willoughby's sergeants, forced the musketeers and brought them up himself. Immediately upon this, one of the sergeants of the Red regiment (whose name I know not and therefore cannot nominate him as his worth deserves) brought in another division of musketeers who together with those which were there before, caused the enemy's forces to betake themselves towards the church for safeguard. But our men followed them so close with their halberts, swords, and musket-stocks that they drove them beyond the church door, and slew about ten or twelve of them, and forced the rest to a very distracted retreat, which when the others saw who were in the great work on the north side of the church-yard they left the work and came thinking to help their fellows, and coming in a disorderly manner to the south-west corner of the church, with their pikes in the rear (who furiously charged on, in as disorderly a manner as the rest led them) their front was forced back upon their own pikes, which hurt and wounded many of the men, and broke the pikes in pieces.

By this time the church-yard was full of our men, laying about them stoutly, with halberts, swords and musket-stocks while some threw hand-grenades in the church windows, others attempting to enter the church being led on by Major Shambrooke, (a man whose worth and valour envy cannot stain) who in the entrance received a shot in the thigh (whereof he is very ill). Nevertheless our men vigorously entered and slew Colonel Bowles, their chief commander at the present, who not long before swore, "God damn his soul if he did not run his sword through the heart of him which first called for quarter". He being slain, they generally yielded and desired quarter, except some desperate villains which refused quarter, who were slain in the church and some others of them wounded, who afterwards were granted quarter upon their request.

They being all subdued, all the prisoners which were taken about the church were all put into a great barn which joined to the church-yard, and after the church was cleared of our men, they were all put into the church, and the rest which were taken in several houses in the town were put to them, and there they were coupled together and brought to Farnham, the number of them being eight hundred and seventy-five among whom were about fifty commanders, besides horsemen which were taken in pursuit of the Lord Crawford, who ran away from the town as soon as we gave the first assault upon their works. What service our horse did I cannot punctually relate because I saw it not, but it seems they were not idle, for (I heard) they made our numbers of prisoners near eleven hundred, many of those prisoners being men of considerable respect in the King's Army.

One thing I had almost forgotten (which I know is expected) that is to speak of the loss of men either side sustained in this service, our loss was not above eight or nine men at the most, besides what were wounded, and I conceive their loss of men to

S.R. GARDINER ON THE ENGLISH CIVIL WAR

A Victorian engraving of an officer of foot at the time of the Civil Wars.

"Experience was, in fact, teaching the Parliamentary chief that the trained-band system, admirably adapted as it was for the suppression of passing tumults, was entirely unsuited for a prolonged war. The very Londoners, whose conduct - at Newbury - had roused the admiration of their opponents, shrank from the continuous abandonment of their duties as civilians. The Commons were not slow to perceive that the remedy lay in the encouragement of the system of standing armies, raised for permanent military service, and attached to the standards by the regularity of their pay. That system already existed, and it had only been the stress of danger which had led to its being supplemented by the temporary expedient of an appeal to local forces."

be about fifty or sixty, most of which were slain in the church and church-yard after we had entered.

Neither side, it seemed, was strong enough to win the war without outside help. So both parties earnestly set about the business of securing outside intervention.

THE BATTLE OF NANTWICH

Frustrated in his attempt to bring in a French army, a cease-fire with the Irish rebels brokered by his loyal servant Ormonde allowed the King to ship home thousands of troops and to form a new army in Cheshire and North Wales. But it was to prove a short-lived hope. This new army was defeated and dispersed at Nantwich in January 1644.

Living near to Nantwich was Richard Gough, who later wrote a history of the village of Myddle. Like many small settlements, Myddle was not left untouched by the events of the war and Gough's account is an interesting picture of the events of the war upon a small town. He begins his Civil War account with a list of these from the Parish who became embroiled in the Civil War.

"First, Thomas Formeston of Marton, a very hopeful young man, but at what place he was kill'd I cannot say.

Secondly, Nathaniel, the son of John Owen of Myddle, the father was hang'd before the wars, and the son deserved it in the wars, for he was a Cataline to his own country. His common practice was to come by night with a party of horse to some neighbour's house and break open the doors, take what they pleased, and if the man of the house was found, they carried him to prison, from whence he could not be released without a ransom in money, that no man here about was safe from him in his bed; and many did forsake their own houses. This Nat Owen was mortally wounded by some of his own party in an alehouse quarrel near Bridgenorth, and was carried in a cart to Bridgenorth to be healed, but in the meantime the Parliament party laid siege to Bridgenorth and the garrison soldiers within the town set the town on fire and fled into the Castle. In which fire, this Owen, being unable to help himself, was burnt to death.

Thirdly, Richard Chaloner of Myddle, bastard son of Richard Chaloner, brother of Allen Chaloner, blacksmith. This bastard was partly maintained by the parish, and being a big lad, went to Shrewsbury, and was there listed, and went to Edgehill fight, (which was October 23rd, 1642) and was never heard of afterwards in this country.

Fourthly, Reece Vaughan, he was brother to William Vaughan a weaver in Myddle, and brother to Margaret the wife of Francis Cleaton. He was killed at Hopton Castle in this country, where the garrison soldiers refusing fair quarter, when they might have had it, were afterward cut in pieces when the Castle was taken by storm.

Fifthly, John Arthurs, a servant of my father's, who was kill'd at the same Castle.

Sixthly, Thomas Hayward, brother to Joseph Hayward the innkeeper then in Myddle was killed in the wars, but I cannot say where.

Seventhly, Thomas Taylor, son of Henry Taylor of Myddle, was killed, I think at Oswaldstry.

Eighthly and ninethly, William Preece of the cave, (who was commonly called Scogan of the Goblin hole) went for a soldier in the King's service and three of his sons (i.e.) Francis, Edward, and William, two of them Francis and William were killed at High Ercall. The old man died in his bed, and Edward was hanged for stealing horses.

Tenthly and Eleventhly, Richard Jukes and Thomas Jukes, sons of Roger Jukes, sometime innkeeper in Myddle.

Twelfthly, John Benion, a tailor, who lived in Newton in the house where Andrew Paine lives.

Thirteenthly, an idle fellow who was a tailor and went from place to place to work in this parish, but had no habitation. These four last named went for soldiers, when the King was at Shrewsbury, and were heard of no more, so that it was supposed that they all died in the wars. And if so many died out of these three towns, we may reasonably guess that many thousands died in England in that war.

There were but few that went out of this parish to serve the Parliament, and of them, there was none killed (as I know of) nor wounded except John Mould, son of Thomas Mould of Myddle Wood. He was a pretty little fellow, and a stout adventurous soldier. He was shot through the leg with a musket *bullet, which broke the musket bone of his leg and slew his horse under him. His leg was healed but was very crooked as long as he lived."*

SKIRMISHES AND SMALL ACTIONS

Mercifully for the inhabitants of Myddle, their village did not become a battlefield; however, there were very few towns or settlements of any size in England which did not witness at least some violence during the years of the Civil Wars. Although they were spared from the horrors of a greater conflict, even this tiny village did witness a skirmish between the opposing forces to which Richard Gough was a witness.

"There happened no considerable act of hostility in this parish during the time of the wars, save only one small skirmish, in Myddle, part of which I saw, while I was a schoolboy at Myddle, under Mr Richard Rodericke, who commanded us boys to come into the church, so that we could not see the whole action, but it was thus. There was one Cornet Collins, an Irishman, who was a garrison soldier for the King, at Shrawardine Castle. This Collins made his excursions very often into this

parish, and took away cattle provision, and bedding, and what he pleased. On the day before this conflict, he had been at Myddle taking away bedding, and when Margaret, the wife of Allen Chaloner, the smith, had brought out and shewed him her best bed, he thinking it too coarse, cast it into the lake before the door, and trod it under his horse feet. This Cornet, on the day that this contest happened, came to Myddle and seven soldiers with him, and his horse having cast a shoe, he alighted at Allen Chaloner's shop to have a new one put on.

There was one Richard Maning, a garrison soldier at Morton Corbett, for the Parliament. This Maning was brought up as a servant under Thomas Jukes, of Newton, with whom he lived many years, and finding that Nat Owen (of whom I spoke before) did trouble this neighbourhood, he had a grudge against him, and came with seven more soldiers with him, hoping to find Owen at Myddle with his wife. This Maning and his companions came to Webscott, and so over Myddle Park, and came into Myddle at the gate by Mr Gittin's house at what time the Cornet's horse was a shoeing. The Cornet hearing the gate clap, looked by the end of the shop and saw the soldiers coming, and thereupon he and his men mounted

Artists of the Victorian period tended to favour the Royalist cause, principally because of its romantic associations. In this famous painting, entitled 'When did you last see your father', the Royalists' women and children are portrayed as the victims of the heartless Parliamentarian inquisition.

their horses, and as the Cornet came at the end of the shop, a brisk young fellow shot him through the body with a carbine shot, and he fell down in the lake at Allen Chaloner's door. His men fled, two were taken and as Maning was pursuing them in Myddle Wood field, which was then unenclosed, Maning having the best horse overtook them, while his partners were far behind, but one of the Cornet's men shot Maning's horse which fell down dead under him, and Maning had been taken prisoner had not some of his men came to rescue him. He took the saddle under his arm, and the bridle in his hand, and went away to Wem, which was then a garrison for the Parliament. The horse was killed on a bank near the further side of Myddle field, where the widow Mansell has now a piece enclosed. The Cornet was carried into Allen Chaloner's house, and laid on the floor, he desired to have a bed laid under him, but Margaret told him she had none but that which he saw yesterday, he prayed her to forgive him, and lay that under him which she did.

Mr Rodericke was sent for to pray with him. I went with him, and saw the Cornet lying on the bed, and much blood running along the floor. In the night following a troop of horse came from Shrawardine, and pressed a team in Myddle, and so took the Cornet to Shrawardine, when he died the next day.

Those two soldiers that were taken at Myddle were Irishmen, and when they came to Wem were both hang'd. For the Parliament had made an ordinance, that all native Irish, that were found in actual arms in England should be hang'd upon which thirteen suffered. Which thing, when Prince Rupert heard, he vowed, that the next thirteen that he took should be so served; which happened not long after. For Prince Rupert in the summer after, viz 1644, came with a great army this way, and made his rendezvous on Holloway Hills (as he had done once before, and his brother Prince Maurice at another time) and took his quarters all night at Cockhutt, and the next day he made his rendezvous at Ellesmeare. At which time, Mr Mitton of Halston, was General of the Parliament forces in this county, and was a valiant and polite commander and hearing the Prince made only his

rendezvous at Ellesmeare and intended to go forward, the General hoping to find some stragglers in Ellesmeare, that stayed behind the army, came with a troop of horse through byways, but when he came to the gate that goes out of Oateley Park, he found that he was come too soon, for there was three or four troops of horse at Oateley Hall, which got between him and home, and therefore, when he and all his men were come through the gate they shot a horse dead up to the gate, to keep it from opening. But the others soon broke down two or three ranks of pales, and followed so close, that all the General's men before they came to Ellesmeare were taken, except the General, and one George Higley (a little fellow). At last, one that had a good horse overtook the General, and laid his hand on his shoulder and said "You are my prisoner". But Higley struck the other in the face with his sword, which caused him to fall, and so the General and Higley turned down the dark lane that goes towards Birch Hall and others went straight into the town. But the General and Higley

The Earl of Manchester played a significant part in the events up until 1645 but thereafter he quickly faded from the scene; one of the leading supporters of the Presbyterian cause in England was lost.

A detail of hand-to-hand cavalry combat from Callot's etchings which were executed in the 1630's and therefore give a real flavour of what cavalry combat at the time of the Civil Wars may have looked like.

escaped, and when they came to Welsh Frankton there they made a stay and one other of his men came to them. The General had lost his hat, and being furnished again, he went to Oswaldstry, a garrison for the Parliament."

AN ACTION AT NOTTINGHAM

In the larger towns, the effects of the war were more marked. Lucy Hutchinson, wife of the Governor, described the events in the Parliamentarian strong-hold of Nottingham after messengers brought word of a Royalist advance in January 1644.

Lucy Hutchinson's memoirs are particularly interesting as they provide an eyewitness account of the fighting from a female perspective. We do however need to treat her material with some caution, as the reader does get the strong impression that some of the books in which they appear may been slanted to present the memory of her husband in the best possible light.

Nonetheless, her lucid account of the attempt by the Royalists under Sir Charles Lucas to capture the Puritan town is an exciting and wonderfully detailed description of the kind of action which was being fought throughout England in late 1643 and early 1644. If Lucy Hutchinson's experience was typical of other towns of this size it is not too difficult to understand why the rate of mortality was so great. It has been estimated that the Civil War took a proportionately higher toll on the men of Great Britain than the Great War and the constant repetition of events like these no doubt played their part.

"The Horse, perceiving the enemy's body to be a great one, retreated to the Castle, and the Foot seeing them gone, and none of the townsmen come forth to their assistance, made also an orderly retreat back to the Castle, in which there was not a man lost nor wounded. The works being unperfect and quitted were easily enter'd though the cannon that play'd upon them from the Castle took off

Lord John and Lord Bernard Stuart by Anthony van Dyck, 1638

THE IMPACT OF WAR

By 1643 the whole of England was paying a terrible price for the continuation of the war. The prospect for a negotiated peace at that time would still appear to have been very real, but the stubbornness of Charles and the superior political skills of the hawks in the parliamentary camp, combined to ensure that the war continued, despite the appalling consequences for the country.

Robert Baillie, one of the Scottish commissioners sent to London in 1643, sent a letter home describing the state of England as he found it in the second year of Civil War.

"That country is in a most pitiful condition, no corner of it free from the evils of a cruel war. Every shire, every city, many families, divided in this quarrel; much blood and universal spoil made by both where they prevail."

The appearance of a Scots Army in support of Parliament had been feared by the Royalist Party for some time. They had long been in discussion on friendly terms with the Parliamentary Commissioners, but it was not until September 1643 that Parliamentarians and Scots Commissioners signed the Solemn League and Covenant which bound the Scots to bring in an army on the side of Parliament.

wholly the second file of musketeers that enter'd the gates, and kill'd them. The first was led up by Lieutenant-Colonel Cartwright, who two days before had sent to the Governor for a protection to come in and lay down arms. The enemy being enter'd possessed themselves of St Peter's Church and certain houses near the Castle, from whence they shot into the Castle yard and wounded one man and killed another, which was all the hurt that was done our men that day.

The Parliamentarians were to be more successful than the Royalists in their search for outside help. A few days before the King's Irish Regiments were routed at the battle at Nantwich, the Scots had finally come to Parliament's aid and crossed the border near Berwick with a mighty army, some twenty thousand strong. Suddenly, the whole complexion of the war was altered.

It also committed both countries to establishing a common form of worship. The Scots Commissioners assumed from the discussion that this would be Presbyterianism – according to the "example of the best reformed churches". The English, however, added the phrase "according to the word of God", thus making the whole agreement a good deal more ambiguous. The Scots carelessly assumed that this meant that the English would adopt a Presbyterian system of organisation of the Church like that of Scotland. Ultimately this misunderstanding would lead to the break up of their alliance, but by then the Parliamentary forces would have had what they needed from their new allies.

Although Parliament still held the upper hand numerically, both sides were simply too exhausted to overcome the other unaided. Outside help had to be sought and the most obvious place to look for it was in Scotland.

A Victorian view of Oliver Cromwell in the House of Commons. As well as being an able leader on the battlefield, Cromwell also proved himself a great politician whose forceful energy resulted in the passage of the Self-Denying Ordinance.

An extract from the Royalist newspaper Mercurius Rusticus which sought to demonstrate the numerous grievances the Roundheads had inflicted on England. Newspapers like this were used by both sides for propaganda purposes.

Large numbers of Scots mercenaries were already fighting for both King and Parliament, but the Scottish government itself had so far remained neutral.

Charles recognised that his religious differences with the Scots were such that they were unlikely to ally themselves to him; it would be asking too much to expect their active support for his cause. He therefore directed his diplomatic efforts to ensuring that they stayed neutral.

Parliament, however, was far closer to the Scots in the complex matter of religious worship.

To court favour of Scotland, it seemed that the Parliamentarian commissioners negotiating with the Scots were even prepared to accept the adop-

tion of Presbyterianism as the official religion in England. In practice, the majority of Parliament had no real intention of imposing the Scots form of Church government on England, but they gave an excellent impression of appearing to do so. It was Parliament, therefore, who succeeded in persuading the Scots that they should both unite in a common cause.

When the English Parliament tried to gain Scots allies, they thought that they could obtain the services of the veteran Scots army, which had been sent to protect Scots settlers in Ulster from the Irish rebels. It had been sent there in 1641 and 1642 after the outbreak of the Catholic uprising. Initial negotiations centred around bringing this army back from Ireland to fight in England, because it was obviously a very experienced, battle-hardened army, but the English suddenly discovered that this was not going to be possible because the army in Ireland had not actually been paid for years. They had got three months pay when they first went across there, and had not been paid since. They were now on the verge of mutiny. The army was, in fact, in secret negotiation with loyalist agents to come over to the King's side, not through any deeply held conviction, but simply because the King promised to pay them. It was therefore decided that the best thing to do was to leave the Scots Army in Ireland where it was safe enough fighting the Irish rebels. In Ireland, the Scots Army had a reason to fight the Irish rebels, because they were Catholics. It was decided instead to raise a new army to fight in England, on the same basis, by universal conscription throughout Scotland, and then use that army of twenty thousand men to invade.

There can be little doubt that if the twenty thousand men which the Scots brought over into England had been put straight into effective action, they could have altered the war. It would certainly have been difficult for the King's cause to survive in the north of England. As it was, however, the seven thousand strong army of the Earl of Newcastle was reinforced by five thousand more, a little later on, from Ireland under Lord Byron. This influx added a new context to the war. The first massacres of prisoners now took place. Many of the reinforcements from Ireland were Catholics. There was now a straightforward division between Catholicism on the one hand and the presbyterians and puritan parties on the other and it was not going to have an ameliorating effect on the war.

In the 17th century, Scotland armies were raised not by beating up for volunteers, as was the case in England, but by a form of conscription.

The Scots regiments were territorially based and local communities often took a great pride in raising their own regiments and following their progress with keen interest.

From time immemorial, when an army was required to be raised, a muster, or Wapinschaw, would be held in each Scottish district. At this muster, equipment was inspected and the names were taken of each unmarried man between the ages of sixteen and sixty who was fit for military service.

Once the orders were given for mobilisation, one man in four from the list was to be called up. The Sheriffdom in which he was raised was responsible for kitting him out and paying him for the first forty days of his service, and only after that time did his upkeep become the government's responsibility.

In the years before the Great Civil War, thousands of Scots had served overseas in the various armies engaged in the German wars. Now, in order to make the best possible use of their experience, it was directed that while each Colonel of each regiment should naturally be a local nobleman, his second in command was to be a professional soldier. This sound principle applied throughout the army.

The musketeers accounted for about two-thirds of the average regiment's strength and were armed with matchlock muskets, simple muzzle-loading weapons fired by means of a piece of match or slow-burning fuse.

The pikemen were less numerous, armed with sixteen-foot long pikes, and although they were expected to fight against other pikemen when the fight came to close quarters, their real task was to protect the musketeers against enemy cavalry.

Like their English counterparts, most Scots cavalrymen wore little armour. Often a thick leather buff-coat and a helmet was considered enough, but some of them were armed quite differently.

In battle, Scots cavalry regiments were normally formed up into two squadrons. One of them was composed of men armed with swords, pistols and carbines in the usual manner. The other was often armed with lances, a weapon which had gradually fallen into disuse in much of Europe and which was now quite unknown in England.

The General commanding this mighty host was himself one of the most highly regarded professional soldiers in Christendom: Alexander Leslie, the recently created Earl of Leven.

On the 19th of January 1644, Alexander Leslie, the Earl of Leven, led his blue-bonneted army across the River Tweed into the north of England.

Alexander Leslie was a very experienced general. He really was one of the first rank, and although there were some who were ready enough to criticise him as being too old by the time of the Civil War, he did actually demonstrate that in practice he had a very firm grip on strategy. He may not have been quite so good on battlefield tactics, but he was the one who actually got the Scots Army mobilised into England. Many Civil War generals would have sat down outside the City of Newcastle, in order to try and clear supply lines before moving further south. But Leslie saw very clearly that his first priority was to destroy the Royalist field army.

Endymion Porter, Royalist soldier, by van Dyck.

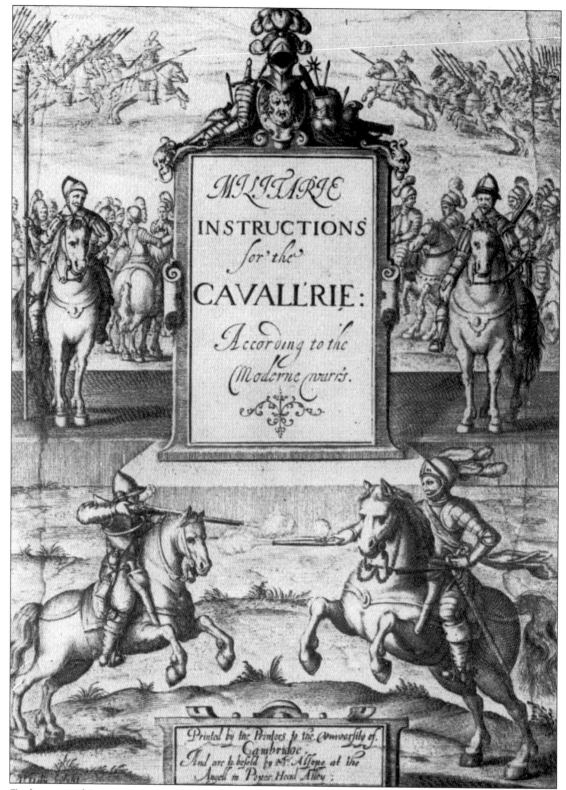

The front page of Carouso's instructions for the cavalry provides one of the few glimpses of cavalrymen of the period from the English perspective.

THE WAR IN THE NORTH

As the war progressed the proportion of musketeers in each regiment began to increase as pikemen grew fewer in numbers.

"The enemy is mighty and master of the field, plentifully supplied
from His Majesty and the Papists and malignant parties,
with money and all necessities."

Lord Fairfax to Parliament, 1643

The north had been won for the King by the Marquis of Newcastle's victory over the Northern Parliamentarians at Adwalton Moor in 1643. Since then it had been a secure rear area for the Royalists.

William Cavendish, the Earl of Newcastle, was a fabulously wealthy landowner who had spent an enormous portion of his own personal wealth on the King's war. He was, however, to prove a less than effective commander when the occasion really demanded.

Freed from Parliamentarian interference, the north not only provided recruits for the Royalist armies, but coal, the chief product of the region,

was shipped out from the Tyne to pay for the arms and ammunition.

These munitions were landed by blockade runners who slipped past the stronger Parliamentarian navy. Twice, so far, Newcastle had supplied convoys of imported ammunition to the King at critical moments, and without these crucial supplies the war in the south might already have been lost.

Now the Scots invasion threatened to choke off this vital supply route and simultaneously to destroy one of the King's most important sources

(Continued on page 130)

THE CAVALIERS

WILLIAM CAVANDISH, EARL OF NEWCASTLE

The principal supporter of the Royalist cause in the north of England was William Cavendish, created Earl of Newcastle by Charles I in 1628.

Newcastle was a fabulously wealthy landowner and probably the richest man in England at the outbreak of the Civil War.

He was appointed General of the King's Forces north of the Trent in 1642, and successfully held the north for the King for the first two years of the war, defeating Fairfax at Adwalton Moor, but failing to capture Hull or the Eastern Association counties.

In 1644 the arrival of the Scots Covenantor Army made life very difficult for the Northern Royalists, and Newcastle's army was destroyed utterly in their defeat at Marston Moor.

Newcastle could not face what he described as "the laughter of the court", and fled into exile after the debacle at Marston Moor.

He returned to England on the restoration of Charles II and set to work to rebuild his fortune.

He lived to the ripe old age of eighty-four.

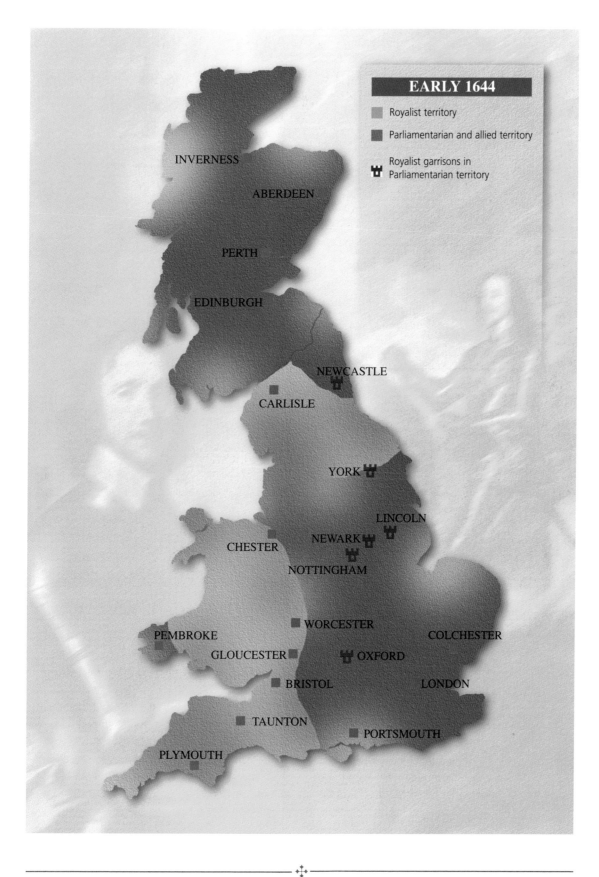

EARLY 1644

Royalist territory

Parliamentarian and allied territory

Royalist garrisons in Parliamentarian territory

INVERNESS

ABERDEEN

PERTH

EDINBURGH

NEWCASTLE

CARLISLE

YORK

LINCOLN

CHESTER

NEWARK

NOTTINGHAM

WORCESTER

PEMBROKE

COLCHESTER

GLOUCESTER

OXFORD

BRISTOL

LONDON

TAUNTON

PORTSMOUTH

PLYMOUTH

THE FIELD ARMIES - PARLIAMENTARIAN

FAIRFAX'S ARMY

The armies of the Ferdinando, 2nd Lord Fairfax and his son, Thomas Fairfax, fought an uneven struggle against the superior Royalist forces in Yorkshire and the north of England, which were led by the Earl of Newcastle.

The forces under Fairfax suffered a disastrous defeat at Adwalton Moor in June 1643 but the young Lord Fairfax in particular was not one to give up a struggle lightly. The Northern Army was reformed and fought at Nantwich and Marston Moor in 1645. Thomas, or 'Black Tom', went on to be Lord General of all Parliamentarian forces in 1645 and took up command of the New Model Army on its creation.

Listed below is a selection of regiments who served at various times in Fairfax's army:

Foot
- Lord Fairfax
- John Bright
- Sir William Constable
- Robert Overton
- John Lambert
- Col. Boynton

Horse
- Lord Fairfax
- Sir Thomas Fairfax
- Sir Hugh Bethyell
- John Lambert
- Lionel Copley

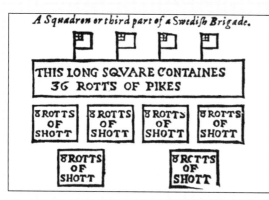

Pike formation from Barriffe's 'Military Discipline' shows a regiment drawn up as part of the Swedish brigade formation.

THE FIELD ARMIES - ROYALIST

THE NORTHERN ROYALIST ARMY

The story of the Royalist Army in the north is inextricably bound up with that of its commander, the fabulously wealthy William Cavendish, Earl of Newcastle.

Newcastle was the King's champion in the north and successfully prosecuted the war against the northern Parliamentarians with his victories at Seacroft Moor and Adwalton, although

they had proved less than capable with defeats at Hull, Grantham, Gainsborough and Winceby at the hands of the Eastern Association. Newcastle's army did a good job of keeping the invading Scots at bay in 1644 but was eventually besieged at York by the combined armies of Leven, Fairfax and Manchester.

Despite the great wealth of their leader, many of the regiments in his armies were clad in plain, undyed white woollen coats which led to them being nicknamed Newcastle's Lambs.

The Lambs went to the slaughter at Marston Moor in 1644 when Newcastle's Army was all but destroyed in the battle which followed the lifting of the siege. A broken man, Newcastle himself left for exile on the continent because he felt he "could not bear the laughter of the court".

Listed below is a selection of regiments who served at various times in the Northern Royalist Army:

Foot
- Sir Thomas Glemham
- Sir John Belayse
- Sir Henry Slingsby
- John Lamplugh
- Sir Richard Hutton
- Sir William Lambton
- Col. John Tempest

Horse
- Col. Samuel Tuke
- Sir Francis Carnaby
- Sir Richard Dacre
- Sir Marmaduke Langdale
- Lord Henry Cavandish

(Continued from page 125)

of recruits. All that stood in Alexander Leslie's path was the bad weather and a bare handful of untrained and poorly equipped military units.

Responding at once to the danger, the Earl of Newcastle raced northwards in a desperate attempt to at least hold the line of the River Tyne against the invading army.

Now a fresh disaster struck. Emboldened by Newcastle's absence in the north, the Yorkshire Parliamentarians, led by Lord Fairfax and his son, Sir Thomas Fairfax, fell upon Newcastle's rear. Storming the market town of Selby on the 11th of April, they destroyed the field army left by the Earl to cover the city of York.

THE SIEGE OF YORK

York was the Royalist northern capital and was now in grave danger. All hope of halting the Scots advance was abandoned and Newcastle turned round and hurried southwards to save York.

It was now that Leven revealed his true worth as a strategist. In crossing the River Tyne he had been forced to abandon his line of communication with Scotland. This was now firmly blocked by the Royalist garrisons on Tyneside and a small Royalist field army led by Sir Robert Clavering which was also operating in the area. As a result, all of the Scots' supplies had to be brought south by sea and landed at Sunderland.

It would therefore have been both prudent and sensible for Leven to stay in the north. There he could reduce those garrisons and secure his supply routes. Nevertheless, the sixty-four year old general acted boldly. Recognising that his primary objective was to destroy the Earl of Newcastle's field army and to capture the city of York, Leven took a calculated risk. He headed southwards in hot pursuit.

By the 22nd of April he was united with the English Parliamentarian forces led by Fairfax. They met outside York and Newcastle's army was promptly besieged within the ancient walls.

Unless relief could come soon, the Royalists would be starved into submission, the north lost and ultimately perhaps the fortunes of the King himself would be ended.

The baggage train was often the target for plunderers who would have been better employed on the battle fields.

Royalist reserves by this stage of the war were practically non-existent. The only quarter from which aid could realistically be expected to come to the relief of York was from the King's own Oxford Army.

Unfortunately, the Kings Oxford Army had its own problems and was in no condition to assist anyone. At the end of March 1643, the Royalist thrust towards London had been heavily defeated at the battle of Cheriton, and ever since then the King had been forced on to the defensive, with the increasingly feeble Royalist forces entrapped around Oxford held by far superior Parliamentary forces.

Nevertheless, for the King to lose York and his grip on the north was quite unthinkable, so Charles ordered his nephew, Prince Rupert, to break out from Oxford and head northwards to relieve the city of York.

As the situation in the south was so critical, only Prince Rupert's own regiments of infantry and cavalry could be spared from the main field army. Rupert was therefore to assemble his relief army as best he could, from the scattered Royalist forces he met en route to York.

In January, a small Royalist army made up of fresh regiments from Ireland had been defeated by Fairfax at Nantwich in Cheshire. The remnants of that army were now at Shrewsbury and Rupert marched to begin his preparations there. The army gained strength but, even with the aid of other locally raised units, there still were not nearly enough men available to attempt a march on York. Undaunted, Rupert then hatched an ambitious plan.

At the beginning of the war much of Lancashire declared for the King, but in the spring of 1643 Parliament gained the upper hand after the battle of Whalley Ridge. Rupert now reasoned that if he could retake Lancashire for the King he would then be able to recruit the additional men he needed for the relief of York.

As the worried Puritan inhabitants of the northern towns looked to their God for help in their hour of need, Rupert had his eyes more firmly on earthly matters. On the 16th of May 1644, Rupert moved north to begin his campaigning. He stormed Stockport on the 25th and three days later took

William Cavendish, Earl of Newcastle, the King's champion in the north.

Bolton. Next, the Prince turned his attention to Liverpool, which he captured on the 10th of June after a short siege. With his objective of capturing Lancashire now virtually complete, he set about filling up the ranks of his battered regiments, and even raised some new ones.

THE FATEFUL LETTER

Meanwhile, back in Oxford, in Rupert's absence, the war was going very badly for the King. With two Parliamentarian armies, led by the Earl of Essex and Sir William Waller, operating against him, he was very hard pressed indeed. In his desperation the King decided to concentrate the Royalist forces at the loyal town of Worcester. He wrote to Rupert in an attempt to recall his forces for that rendezvous, but the letter was couched in such ambiguous terms that it was actually to precipitate the fateful battle of Marston Moor.

"If York be lost I shall esteem my crown little less; unless supported by your sudden march to me; and a miraculous conquest in the South, before the effects of their Northern power can be found here.

THE ROUNDHEADS

THOMAS LORD FAIRFAX

Lord Thomas Fairfax was born in 1612 in the West Riding of Yorkshire, and was nicknamed "Black Tom" for his dark hair and his looks. He was one of the few figures to emerge from the turmoil of the Civil War to see out the years of the Restoration in peace.

Possibly the most astute politician of the entire period, Fairfax waged a solitary war with Newcastle's Northern Army during 1643. Although his forces were destroyed at Adwalton Moor, Fairfax was to make a comeback and ultimately played a major part in the victory at Marston Moor in 1644.

Fairfax was not disqualified by the Self-Denying Ordinance from service in the army, and was appointed the first commander of the New Model Army in 1645.

As an Independent in matters of religion, he used the army to support Cromwell and Ireton against the Presbyterians in the great struggle between Parliament and the army in 1647. In the following year he stood for the Grandees of the army against the levellers.

Throughout all the military machinations and political upheavals of the following year, Fairfax remained firmly in command of the army. He also commanded its respect.

It was Fairfax who crushed the Royalist ring in Kent while Cromwell dealt with the Scots Army at Preston.

Fairfax had the wisdom to avoid being one of the judges of Charles I and was able to retire into quiet obscurity during the years of the Commonwealth and the Protectorate. Even after the restoration, Fairfax was left alone by his former enemies. He lived on for eleven years under the rule of Charles II.

But if York be relieved, and you beat the rebels army of both kingdoms, which are before it; then (but otherwise not) I may possibly make a shift upon the defensive to spin out time until you come to assist me. But if that be either lost, or have freed themselves from besiegers, or that, for want of powder, you cannot undertake that work, that you immediately march with your whole strength, directly to Worcester, to assist me and my army; without which, or your having relieved York by beating the Scots, all the successes you can afterwards have must infallibly be useless unto me."

The fateful letter was certainly badly drafted, and on reading it Sir John Culpeper, one of the King's most trusted advisors is said to have commented:

"Before God you are undone, for upon this peremptory order he will fight, whatever comes on't."

Nevertheless, the actual message should have been clear enough. The King was in serious trouble and he urgently required the assistance of Prince Rupert and his army. If Rupert was ready to march, and was able to relieve York by beating the Scots, he had permission to do so. But come what may, win or lose, he must still march south again as soon as possible to meet the King at Worcester.

Rupert appears to have received this letter five days later, by which time Royalist prospects were beginning to look equally bleak in York. The city was still well stocked enough with food and ammunition, but the two original besieging armies, led by Leslie and the Fairfaxes, had since been joined by a third one under the Earl of Manchester, and surrender was now only a matter of time. Weighing up all the options, Rupert quickly came to a decision. If he marched at once to rejoin the King, York would certainly be lost. On the other hand the King's letter hinted that he still had a few days grace, so once again displaying the single minded determination which is so typical of him, Rupert decided to chance his luck and relieve York first.

The problem remained, however, that the three armies besieging York still outnumbered his own by at least two to one. He had taken on such odds before and emerged triumphant, but this time, with so much at stake, he knew he had considerably to reduce the odds before he could risk a battle.

His solution was once again bold and imaginative, and it very nearly worked. Setting off across the Pennines he reached the small market town of Knaresborough on the 30th of June. By that time the Allied commander-in-chief, General Leslie, knew that he was coming and next day he assembled the three Allied armies to fight the approaching Royalists on Marston Moor, a broad stretch of open ground about five miles west of York.

To their surprise, however, there was no sign of the Royalists that day. Instead of marching due eastwards from Knaresborough, Rupert had struck northwards. He crossed one tributary of the River Ouse at Boroughbridge and then another at Thornton Bridge, before turning south again, having completely outflanked the Allies.

That night, as his weary infantry flung themselves down to rest, Rupert's cavalry pushed on to York and relieved the city to the untrammelled joy of its exhausted defenders.

Together the two Royalist armies now mustered a total of six thousand cavalry and eleven thousand

A painting from the Civil War period of Colonel Richard Neville gives a better idea than many of the engravings of just how rich and flamboyant much of the dress of the period could be.

Herring's romantic view of Roundhead cavalry during the war.

infantry. Although he was still slightly outnumbered by the Allies, Rupert now had enough men to fight his battle on roughly equal terms - or so he thought.

The problem was that the troops in York did not share his martial enthusiasm. Having just weathered a long siege, the men of the Earl of Newcastle's army were in no mood for a fight and crucially, neither was his Scottish chief-of-staff, Lord Eythin.

Eythin's basic problem was that while he had been happy enough to fight against the English Parliamentarians, he was less than happy at the prospect of fighting against his fellow countrymen. Indeed many of Newcastle's men were Scots and they had already abandoned him to rejoin their country's army.

Realising that the city had been relieved, the Allies abandoned any plans for a further siege and instead moved southwards in the hope of trapping Rupert once he moved south himself.

Eythin, with the city relieved, argued that there was no need whatever to rush into a battle immediately. Both of the Royalist armies were exhausted and it would be much better to rest them for a few days before moving out to fight the Allies.

On the other hand, Rupert still had the King's letter summoning him urgently to that rendezvous at Worcester. He believed he could not afford to delay, even for a single day. Furthermore, if he marched south without beating the Scots, there would of course be nothing to prevent their coming back to resume the siege once he was gone. There was no alternative, he argued, but to fight and to fight now. Reluctantly, Newcastle and Eythin bowed to his wishes.

What Prince Rupert could not know, however, was that just three days earlier, the King had actually defeated the army of Sir William Waller at Cropredy Bridge. The pressure was relieved and he no longer needed Rupert's assistance in the south.

With the primitive communications of the day, Rupert could not know of this good news. Still thinking that he had to move fast, he set off in pursuit of the retreating Allies early next morning and he soon caught up with their rearguard on Marston Moor.

PRELUDE TO MARSTON MOOR

On the Parliamentarian side was the Scots Major, General Sir James Lumsden. He recalled the events of the day:

"When Prince Rupert advanced on York we lifted our siege to meet him, he having an order intercepted from the King, that nothing but impossibilities should stay him from beating the Scots. As we marched he put the River Ouse between us and came to York without hindrance, so that we lay four miles therefrom, and on the morrow we set off for Tadcaster to attend his retreat.

Our foot were in the van and the message came that Prince Rupert was advancing with his whole army. This made us march back at once to the position we had just left, where we found him drawing up on a field three miles in length and as many broad, the finest ground for such use I had ever seen in England.

Finding Prince Rupert so near, and with no possibility of our foot coming up for another two hours, we kept the advantage of the hill with our Horse until the Foot came up and were put in order of battle."

The cavalry regiments making up the Parliamentarian rearguard were positioned on a low ridge stretching from east to west, overlooking Marston Moor, but there was still no sign of the Roundhead infantry.

The fiery Prince Rupert would certainly have attacked before the Allied Foot returned, if he had been given a chance, but the operation was already beginning to go badly wrong for Rupert.

Although Rupert's cavalry had reached York the previous night and so had only a short distance to march on to the moor, his infantry were still camped some miles back up the road at Tollerton and had not even reached York as yet. As a result it was some hours before they reached the battlefield.

On the Royalist side, there was equal cause for concern, as there was still no sign at all of the white-coated infantrymen belonging to Newcastle's army.

When the Allies lifted the siege on the previous day, Newcastle's euphoric men had gone plundering in the abandoned Parliamentarian trenches. They had spent their time, understandably enough, getting drunk and celebrating their relief.

Now they were hung over and mutinous. They refused to march out of the city until they received their arrears of pay. Lord Eythin, who was just as reluctant to fight, made little effort to impose any discipline on them and it was very late in the day before they eventually arrived on the moor.

The delay had given the Roundheads the time they needed to re-group the three armies and now

(Continued on page 140)

'England's Wolf', a depiction of the evils brought upon the country by the voracious cavaliers.

CIVIL WAR SIEGES

At the time of the Civil War, England was dotted with strong places of safety, a hangover from the mediaeval era. They varied from individual houses and fortified manors to full scale castles.

At this period, artillery did not fire exploding shells with any great accuracy or reliability and generally stormings of towns were few and far between. The preferred method was to attempt to starve the defenders into submission.

THE FIRST SIEGE OF HULL

Defender: Sir John Hotham for Parliament.

Besieger: King Charles I for the Royalists.

Duration: July 1642.

The Result: The siege was raised due to the lack of materials and men.

THE SIEGE OF SKIPTON CASTLE

Defender: Colonel Sir John Mallory for the Royalists.

Besieger: Colonel John Lambert for Parliament.

Duration: From 23rd December 1642 to 21st December 1645.

The Result: The Castle was surrendered by the Royalists on honourable terms.

THE FIRST SIEGE OF NEWARK

Defender: Sir John Henderson for the Royalists.

Besieger: Major General Thomas Ballard for Parliament.

Duration: From 27th January to 9th February 1643.

The Result: The Parliamentary attackers are repulsed.

Micklebar Gate in York.

THE SIEGE OF READING

Defender: Sir Arthur Aston for the Royalists.

Besieger: The Earl of Essex for Parliament.

Duration: From 15th to 28th April 1643.

The Result: The siege was surrendered on terms by Aston's Deputy, Col. Richard Fielding, 27th April.

THE SIEGE OF YORK

Defender: William Cavendish, Earl of Newcastle, for the Royalists.

Besieger: Alexander Leslie, Earl of Leven, Ferdinando, Baron Fairfax and Edward Montagu, Earl of Manchester for Parliament.

Duration: From 21st April to 16th July 1643.

The Result: The siege was surrendered on terms.

A contemporary illustration showing Civil War siege machines.

THE SIEGE OF CHESTER

Defender: Sir Nicholas Byron for the Royalists.

Besieger: Sir William Brereton for Parliament.

Duration: Intermittently between 18th July 1643 and 3rd February 1646.

The Result: The Royalists surrendered on terms.

THE SIEGE OF GLOUCESTER

Defender: Colonel Edward Massey for Parliament.

Besieger: King Charles of the Royalists.

Duration: From 10th August to 5th September 1643.

The Result: Gloucester was relieved by the Earl of Essex with the Garrison down to almost the last of its gunpowder.

THE FIRST SIEGE OF BRISTOL

Defender: Colonel Nathaniel Fiennes for Parliament.

Besieger: Prince Rupert for the Royalists.

Duration: From 23rd to 26th July 1643.

The Result: The siege was surrendered on terms after being stormed by the Royalists.

THE SECOND SIEGE OF HULL

Defender: Ferdinando Lord Fairfax for Parliament.

Besieger: The Earl of Newcastle for the Royalists.

Duration: From 2nd September to 12th October 1643.

The Result: The Royalists raised the siege after a series of inspired actions by Fairfax.

THE SIEGE OF PLYMOUTH

Defender: Colonel James Wardlaw for Parliament.

Besieger: Prince Maurice for the Royalists.

Duration: From 30th September to 22nd December 1643.

The Result: The Royalists abandoned the siege.

THE SECOND SIEGE OF NEWARK

Defender: Sir Richard Byron for the Royalists.

Besieger: Sir John Meldrum for Parliament.

Duration: From 29th February to 21st March 1644.

The Result: The besieged were relieved by Prince Rupert.

THE FIRST SIEGE OF LATHOM HOUSE

Defender: Charlotte, Countess of Derby for the Royalists.

Besieger: Sir Thomas Fairfax for Parliament.

Duration: From 28th February to 27th May 1644.

The Result: The siege was relieved by Prince Rupert.

THE SIEGE OF LYME

Defender: Garrison Commander Colonel John Were and Governor Colonel Ceeley for Parliament.

Besieger: Prince Maurice for the Royalists.

Duration: From 20th April to 15th June 1644.

The Result: The siege was abandoned upon the approach of a relief force.

THE SECOND SIEGE OF LATHOM HOUSE

Defender: Colonel Edward Rosthern for the Royalists.

Besieger: Major General Egerton for Parliament.

Duration: From July 1644 to 2nd December 1645.

The Result: The house was surrendered on terms.

THE SIEGE OF DONNINGTON CASTLE

Defender: Colonel John Boys for the Royalists.

Besieger: For Parliament: Lieutenant General John Middleton – 31st July 1644, Colonel Jeremy Horton – 29th September 1644, Earl of Manchester and Sir William Waller – October 1644, Colonel John Dalbier – November 1645 – April 1646.

Duration: Collectively for one year and nine months.

The Result: The Royalists surrendered on terms on 1st April 1646.

A contemporary plan of Newark, which remained loyal to Charles into 1646.

THE SIEGE OF BASING HOUSE

Defender: John Paulet Marquis of Winchester for the Royalists.

Besieger: Colonel Richard Norton and Oliver Cromwell for Parliament.

Duration: From 15th August to 4th October 1645.

The Result: The House was stormed and burnt to the ground on 4th October 1645 by Parliament.

THE SIEGE OF WINCHESTER CASTLE

Defender: Lord Ogle for the Royalists.

Besieger: Lieutenant General Oliver Cromwell for Parliament.

Duration: From 28th September to 6th October 1645.

The Result: The Castle was surrendered on terms to Oliver Cromwell.

THE SECOND SIEGE OF BRISTOL

Defender: Prince Rupert for the Royalists.

Besieger: Sir Thomas Fairfax for Parliament.

Duration: From 23rd August to 10th September 1645.

The Result: Bristol was surrendered on terms after being stormed by Parliament.

King Charles blames Rupert for the failure and accuses him of dereliction of duty.

THE THIRD SIEGE OF NEWARK

Defender: Lord John Belayse for the Royalists.

Besieger: Alexander Leslie, Earl of Leven for the Scots.

Duration: From 26th November 1645 to 8th May 1646.

The Result: On the order of the King, Belayse and his troops surrendered to the Parliament forces.

A Victorian view of Basing House as it may have looked in the aftermath of the siege.

(Continued from page 135)

they could count on a single force of seven thousand cavalry and twenty thousand infantry. On the left were the Eastern Association cavalry led by one Oliver Cromwell, still a lesser known MP, but also a gifted commander who, like Rupert, had grasped the essence of cavalry fighting was to charge home at the gallop and drive the enemy from the field.

Although he was not the figure he would later become, Cromwell's reputation was growing both on and off the field. His cavalry were already renowned for their fierce courage and excellent discipline.

Behind Cromwell's men was a brigade of cavalry under a professional Scots soldier named David Leslie. These soldiers were destined to play a crucial role in the battle. In the centre stood the combined allied infantry of the two armies, commanded by two more Scots professionals, Laurence Crawford and Sir James Lumsden. On the right wing was Fairfax's cavalry and another Scots brigade. The Royalist dispositions left much to be desired; Rupert had intended that Newcastle's and his own should be drawn up side by side.

The late appearance of the Northern Infantry, however, meant that his own men had to be spread thinly across the front, while the latecomers eventually grouped together at the rear. Rupert assumed that it was too late in the day to fight, and the battle would be fought the next day, but the Earl of Leven had other ideas. After all, he reasoned, a summer's evening is as long as a winter's day. No sooner had the Royalists begun to relax than the Allied army rolled down off the ridge and crossed the moor at a running march to attack them.

Earlier that day the Royalists had lined the ditch with musketeers, but this thin skirmish line was quickly overrun as the Allied Infantry came forward.

On the left Cromwell's men crashed into Lord Byron's cavaliers. Almost at once Byron gave way, but then Cromwell was counter-charged by the Royalist second line, led by Prince Rupert himself.

In the swirling melee, Cromwell received a slight wound and hastily retired from the field in order to have it dressed.

King Charles and the Earl of Denbigh hold a council of war.

Musketeer with matchlock.

which identified him as one of the Allies, and rode alone to join Cromwell on the victorious right flank.

Encouraged by the success of Langdale, Sir Charles Lucas then charged forward at the head of the Royalist reserves. The undefended flank of the Allied infantry had been exposed by the flight of Fairfax's men, and Lucas with his fresh cavalry carved deep into it.

Regiment after regiment of Scots infantrymen took to its heels and ran; one witness described how a great shoal of Scots ran past him crying out, "Woe's us, we're undone!" Alexander Leslie and his staff fled too, believing the battle to be lost.

Leslie's abrupt departure from Marston Moor has naturally been criticised but in the circumstances it is, to an extent, understandable. He was standing in the centre of the allied line at the time when it was hit by a very strong Royalist counter-attack which rolled up the flank and sent thousands of troops scurrying away to the rear. The army had every appearance of breaking up and it was quite understandable that he should have assumed it was all over. However, as a General, he should have participated in the stout resistance which was put up by some of the Scots infantry brigades and by his counterpart in the cavalry, David Leslie.

Sir Marmaduke Langdale.

Undaunted, David Leslie brought up his brigade of lancers and with the enthusiastic support of some Parliamentarian infantry commanded by another Scots mercenary named Laurence Crawford, he sent Rupert's Cavaliers fleeing backwards towards York.

As if to compensate for this reverse, however, on the other flank disaster had struck the Roundheads.

As Sir Thomas Fairfax led his cavalry forward across the ditch he ran into a storm of musketry and was then charged by two Royalist cavalry brigades under Lord Goring and the grim Sir Marmaduke Langdale.

At first Fairfax did well and routed the two regiments which Rupert had posted on that wing.

Unfortunately, as he looked around for support to exploit his success, his cavalry was swept aside by Goring's triumphant Cavaliers.

As the Parliamentarians fled, Sir Thomas saved himself by plucking the white paper from his hat

Others, however, were made of sterner stuff than Leslie, among them Lumsden, who stayed on the field despite the flight of his men.

"The service went very hot on all sides. They that fought stood it extremely well to it, whereof my Lord Lindsay and his brigade were one. Those brigades which fled were soon replaced by Kilhead's and Dunfermline's Regiments.

I was at the head commanding the foot of Loudon's and Buccleugh's Regiments, but they misbehaved and I could not persuade them to stand, for they would not come up to the charge, but before they were attacked. The enemy of course charged at once and our greatest losses were among these regiments."

Despite the flight of many of the Scots regiments, two Scots units, standing on the extreme right of the allied front line, formed a hedgehog of pikes against the cavalry and stood like a rock, giving a trio of Scots officers the chance to turn the tide.

First, Lieutenant General William Baillie rallied the four regiments in the crumbling centre, and as the Cavalier assault broke upon the resolute skil-trons of pikemen, the crisis was averted almost as quickly as it had arisen.

At much the same time, Cromwell judged it safe to rejoin David Leslie in a renewed attack upon the Royalists' right flank.

Sir Thomas Tyldesley struggled vainly to hold them, as the combined Allied Cavalry and Infantry destroyed his Royalist regiment. Prince Rupert himself had been ignominiously chased into a beanfield by the victorious Allied Cavalry and in his absence, with ammunition running low, a general retreat began.

So far, Newcastle's white-coated infantry had played no real part in the battle, but now when they tried to withdraw eastward in good order, they found their line of retreat blocked by the Atterwith Enclosures. As the Allies closed in, they turned at bay behind the ditches and hedges, and a fierce fight of renewed intensity began. The outcome of the battle once more hung in the balance.

That balance looked like being finally tipped in favour of the Royalists. Near Long Marston, Lord Goring had gathered up his victorious Cavaliers and was forming them up for another charge. A heavy Royalist counter-attack now could have devastating consequences.

Realising the danger, David Leslie had now taken command of all the horse on the left wing and he sent Oliver Cromwell to deal with Goring, while he and his Scots took on the stubborn whitecoats.

At first Leslie was unable to make any impression on this defiant band, but then he brought up Colonel Fraser's Dragoons. Dismounting, they poured a volley into the whitecoats at point-blank range and as the pikes came tumbling down, Leslie sent his men into the gap.

Unable to retreat but yet still stubbornly refusing to surrender, the whitecoats at last went down in a bitter struggle to the last man.

The long day was drawing on, but Cromwell had still time enough to see off Goring's remaining cavaliers.

The one thing that Cromwell is best known for is the discipline of his mounted troops which was quite at variance with the corresponding indis-cipline of Prince Rupert's cavalry. On the Royalist

The difficulties of moving field artillery can be clearly seen from this contemporary drawing.

Alexander Leslie, General of the Scots army which invaded England in 1644.

left wing at Marston Moor, the Royalist cavalry actually broke through the parliamentary right wing, but they then went on to plunder the baggage train which was, by now, fairly standard practice in the Royalist armies. Cromwell's victorious troops, the Ironsides, did not follow suit. Cromwell was able to halt his men after the charge and dispatch troops to pursue the broken enemy. He was then able to rejoin the infantry battle with his cavalry intact and defeat the Royalist attack. And so Cromwell saved the day at Marston Moor as he was later to do at Naseby.

"Truly England and the Church of God hath had a great favour from the Lord, in this great victory given unto us, such as the like never was since this war began. It was obtained by the Lord's blessing upon the godly party principally. We never charged but we routed the enemy. The left wing, which I commanded, being our own horse, saving a few Scots in our rear, beat all the Prince's horse. God made them as stubble to our swords, we charged their regiments of foot with our horse, routed all we charged.

Sir, God hath taken away your eldest son by a cannon shot. It brake his leg. We were necessitated to have it cut off, whereof he died.

Sir, you know my trials this way; but the Lord supported me with this; that the Lord took him into the happiness we all pant after and live for. There is your precious child full of glory, not to know sin nor sorrow any more. He was a gallant young man, exceeding gracious. God give you His comfort.

(Continued on page 147)

THE FIELD ARMIES - PARLIAMENTARIAN

THE COVENANTERS

The army which Scotland sent to intervene in the war in England was unusual for the Civil War period in that it was a nation army raised from the whole of Scotland and with ranks filled by soldiers who had a common vision of what they fought for.

This was also the case with the Covenanter Army of 1639, 1640 and 1648. The Scots enjoyed a good supply system and they were generally well equipped and clothed in hoden-grey, which marked them for Scotsmen.

They also wore the blue bonnets which became synonymous with the Covenanters.

Their biggest contribution to the war on the battlefield was in their victory at Marston Moor in 1644.

Listed below is a selection of regiments who served at various times with the Scots Covenanter armies:

Foot
- Marquis of Yester
- Sir Mungo Campbell of Lawer
- Lord Coupar
- Master of Cranstoun
- Earl Marischel

Horse
- Earl of Ballcarre
- Sir John Browne Of Fordell
- Earl of Dalhousie
- Lord Gordon

THE FIELD ARMIES - ROYALIST

IRISH REINFORCEMENTS

Throughout the early years of the Civil War, King Charles placed a great deal of faith in his ability to draw upon the support of pro-Royalist forces in Ireland. Although he was never to receive the extensive support that he hoped for, the cessation of 1643 did allow the first few thousand men to be landed in England.

They were deployed in the north-west of England under Lord Byron, where they were defeated by the forces of Fairfax and Brereton at Nantwich in January 1644.

They were joined by a new influx in February 1644 which added Regiments under Broughton and Tillier to the King's forces.

All fought at Marston Moor where they were roughly handled. Although the survivors served in the Naseby campaign, their effectiveness was questionable and their numbers never really added significantly to the Royalist war effort.

Listed below is a selection of regiments who came from Ireland.

- Col. Henry Warren.
- Col. Robert Broughton
- Col. Sir Michael Erney
- Col. Richard Gibson
- Col. Henry Tillier
- Sir Robt. Byron
- Sir Fulke Honcke

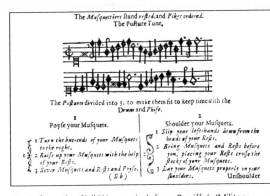

Music from the Civil Wars period, from Barriffe's 'Military Discipline', used to indicate the postures for 'poise your muskets' and 'shoulder your muskets'.

A DOGS ELEGY,
OR
RVPERT'S TEARS,

For the late Defeat given him at *Marston-moore*, neer *York*, by the Three Renowned Generalls; *Alexander Earl of* Leven, *Generall of the Scottiſh Forces*, Fardinando *Lord* Fairefax, *and the Earle of* Manchefter *Generalls of the* Engliſh *Forces in the North.*

Where his beloved Dog, named *B O Y*, was killed by a Valliant Souldier, who had skill in *Necromancy.*

Likewiſe the ſtrange breed of this Shagg'd Cavalier, whelp'd of a Malignant Water-witch; With all his Tricks, and Feats.

york

Sad Cavaliers, *Rupert* invites you all   ⎰ Cloſe-mourners are the Witch, Pope, & devill,
That doe ſurvive, to his Dogs Funerall. ⎱ That much lament yo'r late befallen evill.

An illustration from a Roundhead broadsheet depicting the death in battle of Prince Rupert's beloved dog, Boye.

A continental image from roughly the Civil Wars period depicting the grim aftermath of battle. The practice of stripping and looting the dead produced some revenue for men who were almost always months in arrears of pay.

(Continued from page 143)

Before his death he was so full of comfort that... he could not express it, it was so great above his pain. This he said unto us. Indeed it was admirable."

In many ways the struggles for command in the army were helped by Cromwell's political skills. Besides his undoubted genius as a military commander which saw his forces' victory at Marston Moor, he also knew how to achieve results by political machination.

One should not forget, however, the contribution of the Scots. Cromwell had been criticised for dismissing the Scots as 'a few Scots behind him', in a letter after the battle, but it is fairly clear that Leslie's troopers played a significant part in the battle and without their help the parliamentary infantry would have been in trouble.

By now, the Royalists must already have known that the battle was lost and in the ensuing melee they were routed just as swiftly and decisively as Fairfax

had been. James Lumsden witnessed the action:

"The horse on our right wing were beat, although my Lord Eglinton and his men distinguished themselves. Our left flank of Horse under the command of General Cromwell and General Leslie carried themselves bravely and under God were responsible for our victory, though Manchester's Foot also did good service under the command of Major General Crawford. We lost Lord Dudhope and Lieutenant Colonel Bryson, two captains and some soldiers, but we took Sir Charles Lucas and Major General Porter and some colonels and some of their officers, while sundry of their chief officers were killed. We slew more than two thousand of them, took fifteen-hundred prisoners, twenty cannon, which was all they had, all their ammunition, all their baggage, ten thousand arms, all their foot colours, and many horse cornets."

The behaviour of Scots soldiers at Marston Moor was, at best, patchy. Some of them ran, some of

Victorian artist Ernest Crofts' atmospheric representation of Cromwell after his victory at Marston Moor, a battle which was to be crucial to the outcome of the entire war.

them fought very stoutly indeed. But to consider the circumstances under which this happened, the regiments which ran were on the right flank of the allied army and ran because the allied cavalry, on their immediate right, was routed by the Royalists. The second wave of Royalist cavalry came at them, not from the front, as they were expected, but from the flank. Not surprisingly, they panicked and started running. Further in towards the centre of the Scots line, regiments which had time to see that something was going badly wrong were able to turn around, face the cavalry threat, and put themselves in a suitable posture of defence.

Eventually, they were able to beat off the Royalist counter-attack and pave the way for the massive Allied victory which followed.

The Royalists are now known to have lost nearly twice the two thousand reported by Lumsden, and the losses fell particularly hard upon the officers. No fewer than ten Colonels were killed, including Posthumous Kirton, the commander of Newcastle's own regiment of whitecoats and at least twenty-three captains - a quarter of them belonging to just one regiment, Sir Thomas Tyldesley's.

Marston Moor was an utter disaster for the King. Weary and dispirited, Rupert led the survivors of his broken army north to Richmond and then back across the Pennines to rejoin the King. Newcastle and Eythin both fled into exile on the continent. Newcastle, it is said, because he did not want to suffer the laughter of the King's court at his defeat.

Abandoned to its fate, York surrendered two weeks later. The north was lost.

The Civil War dragged on for two more years, but for the King, the end was now inevitable. The only possible outcome was ignominious defeat.

The bloody battle of Marston Moor had been the first major step on that bitter road to surrender.

Marston Moor was the largest battle ever fought on British soil, but the allies gained very little from their famous victory. York surrendered two weeks later, but Newcastle-Upon-Tyne held out until October and Carlisle until the following June. Only the Earl of Manchester's Eastern Association Army was free to turn south, and without it Parliament might still have lost the war.

THE BATTLE OF MARSTON MOOR - 2ND JULY 1644

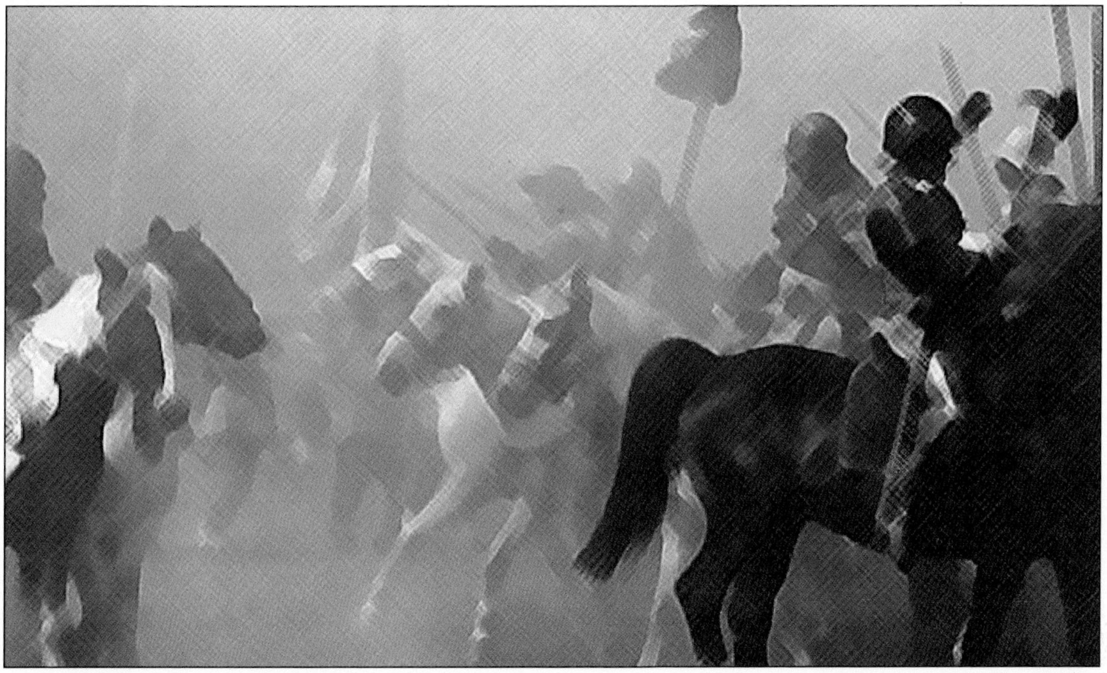

The cavalry played a major role in the battle of Marston Moor.

The Battle of Marston Moor was fought as a consequence of the relief of the Siege of York by Prince Rupert. Rupert and his relief force had marched from Oxford through the Midlands, during which a number of Puritan towns were attacked and burnt. The flying army came to the relief of Liverpool and then marched through Preston before swinging south to York. He was opposed by three Parliamentarian armies, the Scots Covenanters, the armies of Fairfax operating in York and the army of Manchester, which had marched from the Eastern Association counties. With five armies present, Marston Moor was to be the largest single battle ever fought on English soil.

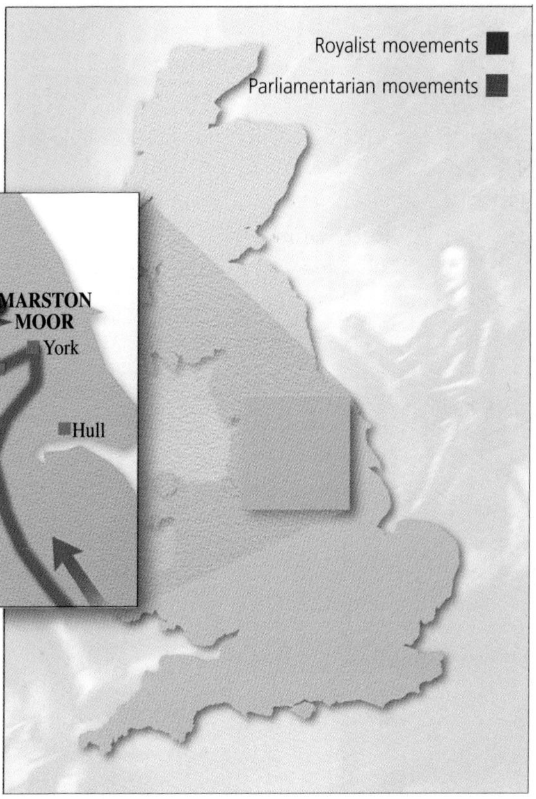

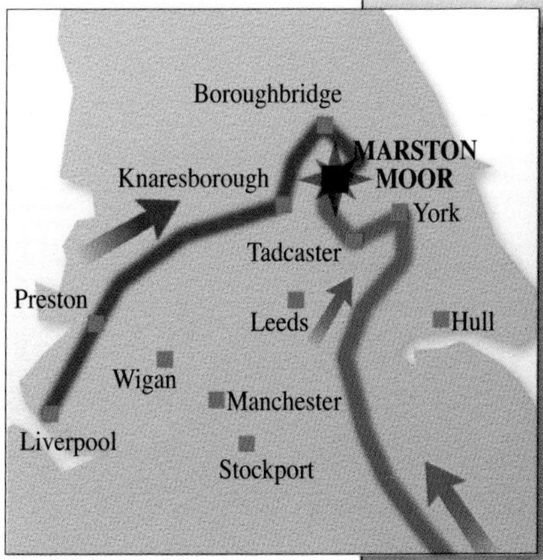

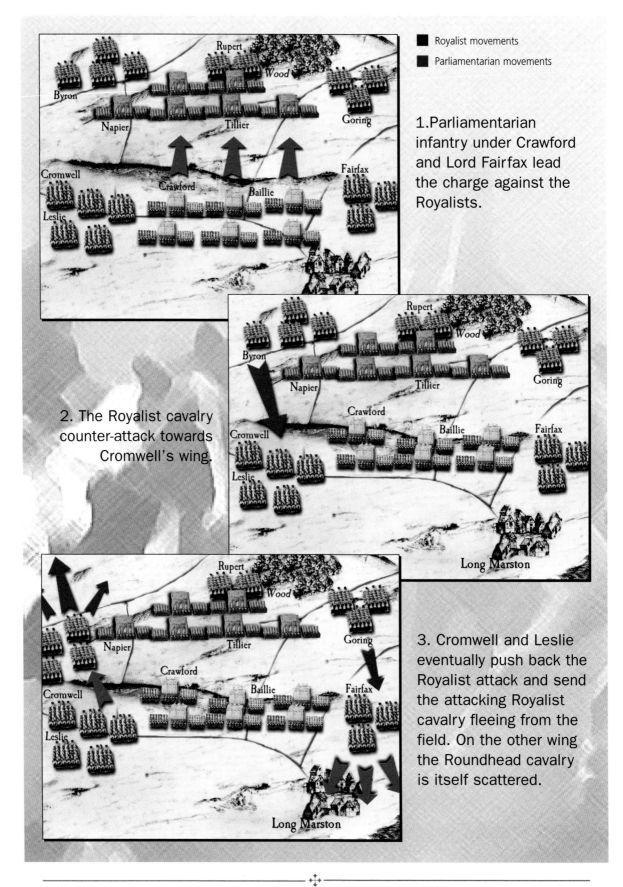

■ Royalist movements
■ Parliamentarian movements

1. Parliamentarian infantry under Crawford and Lord Fairfax lead the charge against the Royalists.

2. The Royalist cavalry counter-attack towards Cromwell's wing.

3. Cromwell and Leslie eventually push back the Royalist attack and send the attacking Royalist cavalry fleeing from the field. On the other wing the Roundhead cavalry is itself scattered.

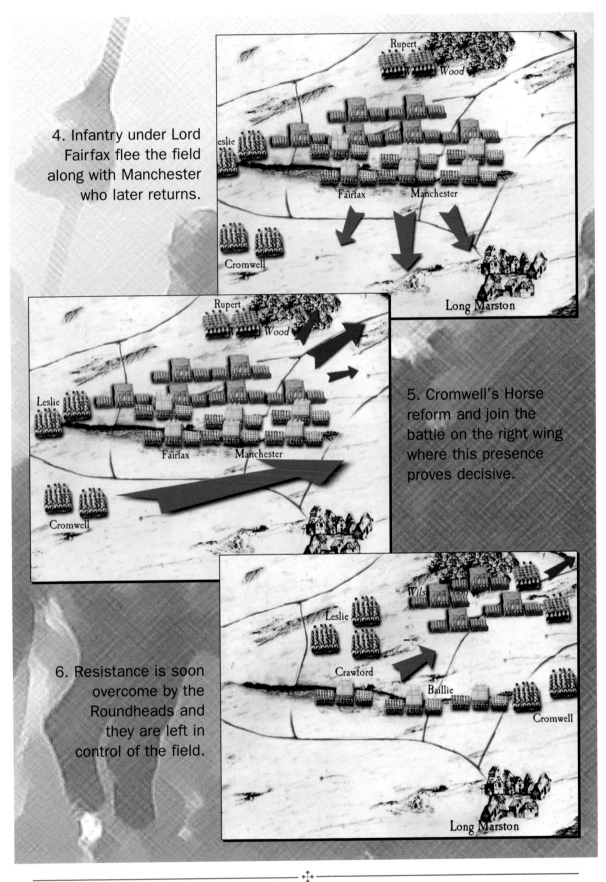

4. Infantry under Lord Fairfax flee the field along with Manchester who later returns.

5. Cromwell's Horse reform and join the battle on the right wing where this presence proves decisive.

6. Resistance is soon overcome by the Roundheads and they are left in control of the field.

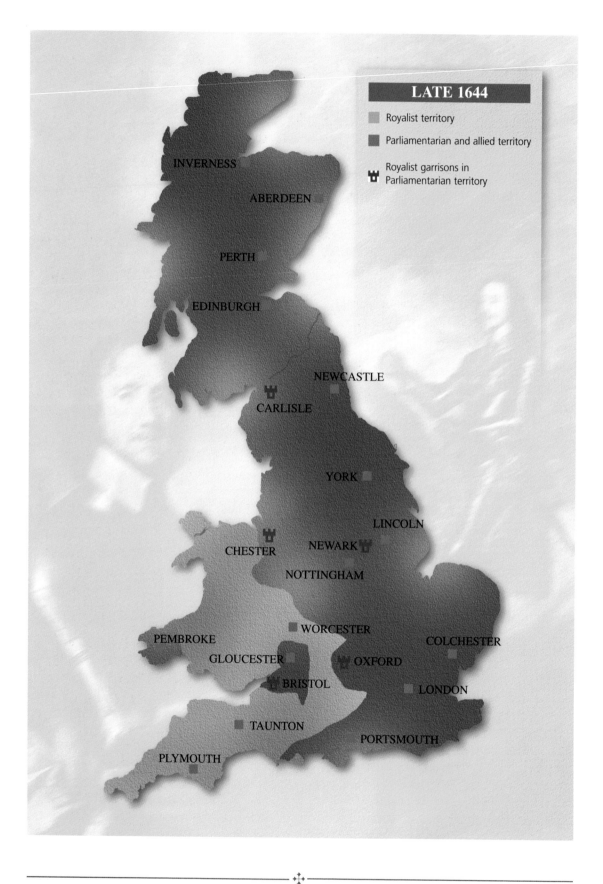

LATE 1644

Royalist territory

Parliamentarian and allied territory

Royalist garrisons in
Parliamentarian territory

INVERNESS

ABERDEEN

PERTH

EDINBURGH

NEWCASTLE

CARLISLE

YORK

LINCOLN

CHESTER   NEWARK

NOTTINGHAM

WORCESTER   COLCHESTER

PEMBROKE

GLOUCESTER   OXFORD

BRISTOL   LONDON

TAUNTON

PORTSMOUTH

PLYMOUTH

THE KING HEADS WEST

Armies of the Civil Wars period were followed by the inevitable human tail in the form of camp followers, merchants and assorted hangers-on. After Naseby, many of the Irish women were cruelly mutilated by the victorious Parliamentarians.

"For General they chose Sir Thomas Fairfax, who had been in the wars beyond sea and had fought valiantly in Yorkshire for the Parliament...he was acceptable to sober men because he was religious, faithful, valiant and of a grave, sober, resolved disposition, very fit for execution and neither too great nor too cunning to be commanded by the Parliament."

Richard Baxter

While Rupert was in the north the King had been very hard pressed at Oxford by the combined armies of Essex and Waller.

Defeat for the King looked imminent but then the two generals, who harboured a personal hatred for each other, suddenly parted company.

The King at once seized his opportunity to attack each in turn and defeated Waller's army at Cropredy Bridge in Oxfordshire.

After his victory at Cropredy he then pursued the inept Earl of Essex into the Royalist West Country, once again interposing his own army between Essex and London. This time there would be no mistakes. In a week-long running-battle the Parliamentarians were harried to destruction at Lostwithiel in Cornwall. Most of Essex's cavalry eventually broke out under cover of rain and darkness, and he himself fled in a tiny fishing boat, but his infantry were forced to surrender on the 2nd of September. Marston Moor had been avenged and no end to the war was in sight.

Richard Symonds was present at the battle and described the condition of the Parliamentary soldiers who surrendered, as they marched past him on the long road back to London, through hostile lines of Royalist soldiers, gathered to mock their former foes.

"The King himself rode about the field and gave strict command to his chief officers to see that none of the enemy were plundered, and that all his soldiers should repair to their colours which were in the adjoining closes. Yet notwithstanding our officers with their swords drawn did perpetually beat off our foot, many of them lost their hats etc.

Yet most of them escaped this danger till they came to Lostwithiel, and there the people inhabitants and the country people plundered some of their officers and all, notwithstanding a sufficient party of Horse was appointed by his Majesty to be their convoy.

They all, except here and there an officer (and seriously I saw not above three or four that looked like a gentleman) were stricken with such a dismal fear, that as soon as their colour of the regiment was passed (for every ensign had a horse and rode on him and was so suffered) the rout of soldiers of that regiment pressed all of a heap like sheep, though not so innocent. So dirty and so dejected as was rare to see. None of them, except some few of their officers, that did look any of us in the face. Our foot would flout at them and bid them remember Reading, Greenland House (where others that did no condition with them took them away all prisoners) and many other places, and then would pull their swords, etc, away for all our officers still slashed at them.

The rebels told us as they passed that our officers and gentlemen carried themselves honourably but they were hard dealt with by the common soldiers.

This was a happy day for his Majesty and his whole army, that without loss of much blood this great army of rascals that so triumphed and vaunted over the poor inhabitants of Cornwall, as if they had been invincible, and as if the King had not been able to follow them, that 'tis conceived very few will get safe to London, for the country people whom they have in all the march so much plundered and robbed that they will have their pennyworths out of them."

On his return to Oxford from the victory at Lostwithiel, fresh Parliamentarian forces sought to trap the King at Newbury, but the Royalists fought their way clear in the second battle of Newbury. Angry recriminations followed and the Parliamentarians split into two factions.

On the one hand were the Presbyterians and their Scots allies, led by the old generals, Essex, Manchester and Waller. They were sickened by the fighting and ready for peace. The Presbyterians favoured the reorganisation of the Church of England along the same lines as that of the Church of Scotland. They were also more inclined to make peace with the King. Manchester was the chief spokesman.

"I beseech you, Let us consider what we do. The King need not care how often he fights. If we fight a hundred times and beat him ninety-nine he will be King still, but if he beats us but once or the last time, we shall be hanged and all our posterity undone."

On the other side were the Independents and their champion Oliver Cromwell. To Manchester Cromwell had the stern reply, *"If this be so, my Lord, why did we take up arms in the first? This is against fighting ever hereafter."*

On one point both the Independents and the Presbyterians were agreed. The organisation of the Parliamentarian forces had to be reviewed, for their performance in the field was poor. There were

(Continued on page 161)

Disembarking troops from a contemporary engraving by Callot.

THE BATTLE OF CROPREDY BRIDGE - 28TH JUNE 1644

Pikemen go into battle. Their densely packed ranks could provide an excellent target for musketeers.

A s the King began his manoeuvres in the west for the campaign of 1644, Waller and his Parliamentarian forces marched north from Worcester through Banbury to meet the King's Army at Cropredy.

They were soon in visual contact with the King's forces as both armies marched in sight of the other. There appeared to be little in the way of strategic planning, or manoeuvres. The armies met, north of Banbury on 28th June 1644, in the Battle of Cropredy Bridge.

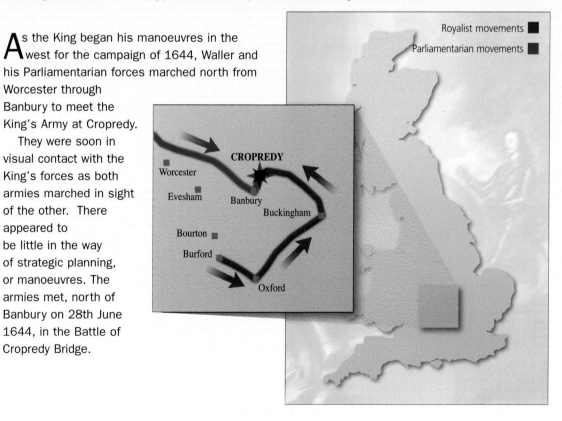

Royalist movements

Parliamentarian movements

CROPREDY

Worcester

Evesham

Banbury

Buckingham

Bourton

Burford

Oxford

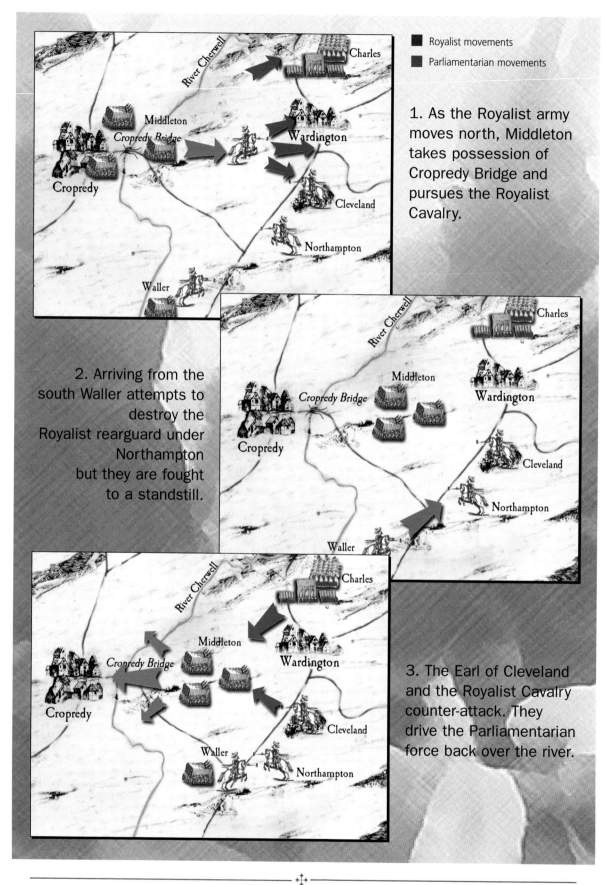

Royalist movements
Parliamentarian movements

1. As the Royalist army moves north, Middleton takes possession of Cropredy Bridge and pursues the Royalist Cavalry.

2. Arriving from the south Waller attempts to destroy the Royalist rearguard under Northampton but they are fought to a standstill.

3. The Earl of Cleveland and the Royalist Cavalry counter-attack. They drive the Parliamentarian force back over the river.

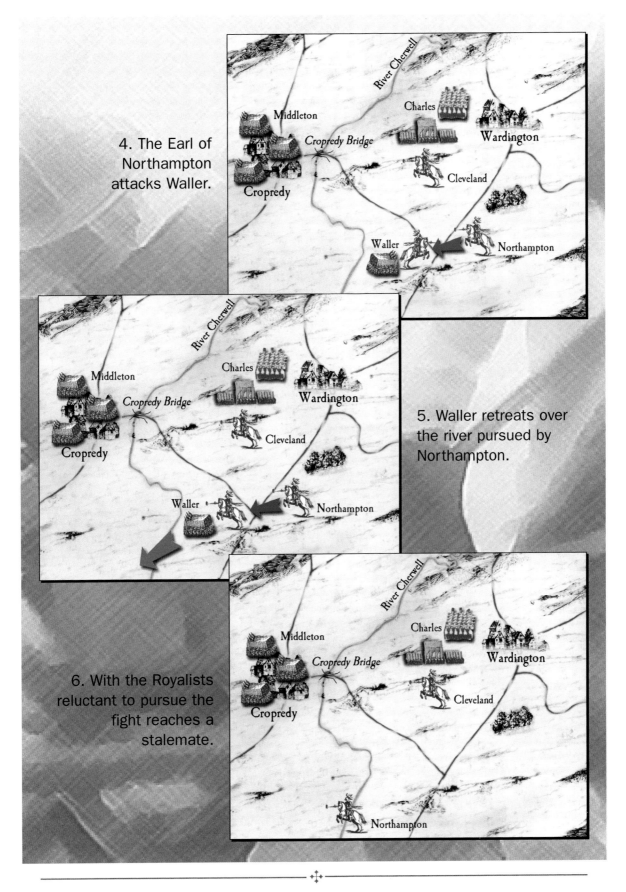

4. The Earl of Northampton attacks Waller.

5. Waller retreats over the river pursued by Northampton.

6. With the Royalists reluctant to pursue the fight reaches a stalemate.

A Victorian view by the famous military painter, Ernest Crofts, depicts the Royalists' surrender of the city of York in the wake of the disastrous Battle of Marston Moor.

THE ROUNDHEADS

EDWARD MONTAGU, SECOND EARL OF MANCHESTER

Despite being a leading figure in the road to war and the military events of the first civil war, Edward Montagu was a force for moderation and toleration at every opportunity. He was a leading opponent of the King in matters of politics and religion and was appointed to command the army of the Eastern Association. Although he was nominally head of these forces, the real power and military force was always Oliver Cromwell.

Despite the fact that Manchester outranked Cromwell, Cromwell was able to out-manoeuvre Manchester in his attempts to find a peaceful solution with the King. It was in an argument with Cromwell that Manchester made his famous plea against fighting the King in 1644.

"If we beat him ninety-nine times, he is still the King. If he beats us once we shall all be hanged and our posterity undone."

Cromwell angrily retorted that this was an argument against fighting ever again and if so, why had they taken up arms in the first place.

It was arguments like these which led to Manchester, a Presbyterian, being out-manoeuvred by the Independents in 1644. With the passage of the Self-Denying Ordinance, Manchester gave up his commission and faded from the military scene.

Politically, the Presbyterians were to prove impotent against the power of the army and once again Manchester failed to influence the debates of 1647, from which the army emerged victorious.

Leading Parliamentarian commanders as depicted in 1644. It is interesting to note that as Cromwell has not yet taken centre stage, he is still depicted as a minor figure by comparison with the Earl of Essex.

Another of Callot's etchings gives a good flavour of camp life and the inevitable tail which followed the armies of the period.

(Continued from page 154)

too many regiments and too many officers but all too few soldiers. The solution was to break up the existing units and draft the men into fewer but larger regiments. Nomination of officers became a trial of strength between the two factions. The Independents won and Sir Thomas Fairfax was appointed General. But the overriding influence in the army was that of Oliver Cromwell.

In 1644, despite the fact that Parliament had won a number of victories over the Royalists, still no end to the war lay in sight. Cromwell was firmly of the opinion that many of the politicians in charge of the army were actually happy to prolong the war as it gave them untold power and influence which they would never wield in peacetime.

Cromwell picked his moment and in one of the most skilful pieces of timing in his career, he made what was probably one of his finest speeches. His impassioned oratory directly resulted in the passage of the Self-Denying Ordinance of 1644, which ultimately removed all politicians except Cromwell himself from positions of command in the army. It also led directly to the formation of Parliament's new, all-powerful weapon – the New Model Army which was to win the war for Parliament.

"It is now the time to speak, or forever hold the tongue. The important occasion now is no less than to save a nation out of a bleeding, nay almost dying, condition... casting off all lingering proceedings, like those of soldiers of fortune beyond the sea, to spin out a war...

The Members of both Houses have got great places and commands, and the sword into their hands; and, will perpetually continue themselves in grandeur, and not permit the War speedily to end, lest their own power should end with it... I know the worth of those commanders, Members of both Houses, who are still in power. But, if I may speak my conscience without reflection upon any, I do conceive if the Army be not put into another method, and the War more vigorously prosecuted, the people can bear the War no longer, and they will enforce you to a dishonourable peace.

But this I would recommend to your prudence, and I hope we have such true English hearts and zealous affection towards the general weal of our Mother Country as no Member of either House will scruple to deny themselves, and their own private interests, for the public good."

Cromwell got his way. The politicians were removed from command and the New Model Army took the field in time to defeat the King at Naseby in 1645.

THE ARMY WAS NEW MODELLED

The Battle of Naseby.

"The Army was New Modelled and a new General was proposed to command it. For which, by the votes of the two Houses of Parliament, myself was nominated though most unfit and so far from desiring it... I was induced to receive the command."

Fairfax

Despite the great reverse at Marston Moor, 1644 had ended with some very real causes for optimism for the Royalists and Charles had genuine reason to think he might yet win the war.

Things seemed to be going the King's way. He had just had news of Montrose's victory at Auldern, which effectively neutralised Leven up in the north. The Parliamentary ranks were riven with strife and dissension and as a result some very ill-judged decisions were made; in particular, that which pinned Fairfax around Oxford despite all the evidence from the earlier course of the

Civil War that sieges were very wasteful and that it was armies free in the field that won victories. That decision gave Charles a free hand. With Fairfax engaged in a protracted siege at Oxford, the King could not only move wherever he liked in the Midlands, he was also able to move north or south. While this was a massive advantage for Charles, it did lead to a certain amount of dissent in his own ranks. There was some tension between two contrary opinions in the Royalist camp. On the one hand was Rupert, who wanted to march north and recruit people from Yorkshire, because he believed that they could actually build up the army significantly that way. Then there was a second party led by Digby, who wanted to march south and take all the Royalist concentration in that direction.

As he met with Goring and Rupert to plan the coming campaign, the King had some grounds for measured optimism. In some respects he was even cheerful. In attempting to appease all of the competing factions, Charles Stuart was once again displaying the indecision which was to plague his cause. Arrayed against him was the New Model Army, ably led by its commander Sir Thomas Fairfax. It was not yet the force it would become. But Fairfax himself was a formidable opponent, and the New Model Army had been brought about chiefly by the energy of Oliver Cromwell.

It was he who had grown tired of the politicians who had used their military positions for their own ends rather than for the common good.

In a famous speech he moved the House of Commons towards the famous Self-Denying Ordinance which forced all existing members of Parliament to resign their places of command in the army.

Whereas Essex, and all of the other MP's who held positions resigned and never again took up senior positions, Cromwell survived. This was probably thanks to Fairfax, who felt the great man

indispensable to the Parliamentarian cause and petitioned Parliament to that effect.

Accordingly, Cromwell was allowed to take up his position as Commander of the Cavalry in the New Model Army. The faith and trust Fairfax placed in him was to prove entirely correct.

Common knowledge suggests that Cromwell somehow managed to avoid a personal obligation under the Self-Denying Ordinance. This is often used as evidence that Cromwell was both a hypocrite and somewhat manipulative. In many respects that would appear to be unfair. The Self-Denying Ordinance that was finally passed by both Houses of Parliament did not actually prohibit members of parliament from holding commissions in the army. It did require officers holding current commissions from Parliament to lay down those commissions within forty days after the act had been passed. There was nothing, however, in the Self-Denying Ordinance which precluded the reappointment of officers. Cromwell did so.

In the field, the New Model Army mustered some fifteen thousand men.

Against this formidable foe, the King chose to concentrate only eleven thousand men, leaving the rest of his forces to hold garrisons in towns and castles scattered throughout the land.

A coach being attacked by soldiers.

Some scholars have argued that ultimately it may have been his downfall, but it has often been suggested that, had he been more resolute in his ambition, a single field army of twenty thousand Royalists could theoretically have taken the field in May 1645.

In reality, Charles and the Royalists had very little territory left, and that territory which remained had to be defended against Parliamentary garrisons which ringed them.

In the north they virtually had nothing. In the Midlands they had one or two scattered garrisons. They were strong only in the south west, and even here the Parliamentarians had three very strong garrisons which effectively neutralised the troops that the Royalists mustered in that area.

The only real source of extra troops that Charles had would have been Goring's small but intact detachment. Had Goring obeyed orders and joined the King's Oxford Army, then that would have brought Charles' army up to near parity with the New Model Army.

Goring, however, was ambitious; he saw himself as a replacement for Hopton. He dallied around in the south-west and did not come to Charles' aid when he was so ordered.

Effectively, Charles could not really have afforded to field a larger army, because that would have meant conceding territory to the Parliamentarians, which was something he was desperate to avoid.

So it was that Charles Stuart gathered about him the last great army that he was to call into the field.

As the regiments left Oxford, the remaining garrison silently watched them march out. There was a great deal of tension in the still air. The King's capital was already being loosely blockaded. Oxford had already survived one siege and there were rumours of a new Roundhead army marching to besiege the city again.

The Siege of Oxford, from a contemporary painting. Oxford was besieged or at least heavily blockaded almost continually for most of the war.

Even with the reinforcements which joined him, the King's forces for the campaign of Naseby never amounted to more than twelve thousand men. He was about to face the New Model Army, fifteen thousand strong.

More than three hundred and fifty years on, opinion is very much divided as to what Charles hoped to achieve in this last campaign.

The strategic situation was, of course, very difficult for the Royalists.

The territory which could be said to be Royalist controlled had shrunk during 1644, from approximately half the area of England and Wales to a little more than a quarter. Royalist territory was now exclusively located in Wales and the south west. Worse still, these were among the least opulent areas of the country.

The prosperous areas around London remained firmly in Roundhead hands as they had done since the outbreak of the war. These areas also supplied far greater numbers of men and munitions.

Only in Scotland was there a glimmer of hope for Charles.

In the remote north of the country, the daring Marquis of Montrose had won a string of victories. His small royalist force had caused the powerful Scots Army operating in the north of England, on behalf of Parliament, to turn and keep a wary eye on its homeland.

The New Model Army was therefore deprived of what could have been a powerful second pincer in a grand encircling movement, designed to crush the King's capital from the north and south.

In the spring of 1645 Charles hoped to march north and join forces with Montrose, whose rising star was beginning to eclipse that of even his favourite, Prince Rupert.

In early May, news reached him of yet another famous victory by Montrose, this time at Auldern. A link-up with this great new General seemed to be the most obvious hope of salvation for the hard pressed Royalists.

Montrose was to become one of the great romantic figures of the Civil War. A very brave man and a fine soldier, his achievements in Scotland were all the more remarkable as his army was very small and had a habit of disappearing at regular intervals.

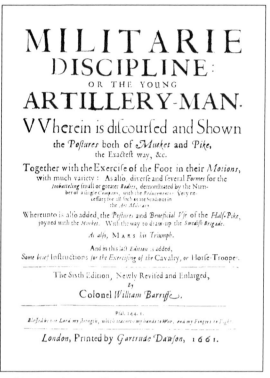

Drill books such as Barriffe's 'Military Discipline' were hugley popular with the large numbers of amateur soldiers who formed the trained bands..

He was badly supplied and it is fair to say that at first King Charles had not taken Montrose very seriously.

Certainly he was not provided with the men or equipment he had asked for, and he was more or less ordered to go away and do whatever he could in the north.

Nevertheless, the King was deeply impressed by Montrose's series of great successes. The triumph at Auldern was followed up later by another victory at Alford, another small, ill-equipped army where Montrose's was able to defeat the Scottish National Army, which was much better equipped and resourced.

Respected historians such as S R Gardiner have put forward the opinion that Montrose was a superb strategist, a very good tactician, but he was also a romantic and what he was chasing, was, in the end, quite unrealistic. Montrose was one of the first signatories of the National League and Covenant. He was a Presbyterian and obviously believed in the Presbyterian system of Church

Charles I at the battle of Naseby. This Victorian engraving represents the moment when Charles is supposed to have tried to lead his lifeguard in one final charge.

Government. It was his fond hope that Charles could be brought to support the Presbyterian system of Church Government throughout Britain. That is something that Charles would not do, as subsequent history demonstrated.

With the continued success in the north, Charles was still the object of two competing schools of advice from his council. The first group, led by the vocal Prince Rupert, urged that the King move north as soon as possible to join forces with the Marquis of Montrose.

The other school, led by Goring and Digby, recognised the danger posed by the New Model Army and urged that the King take the field against this dangerous new foe while it was still in its infancy.

The New Model Army was not yet the invincible machine recorded by history. It was badly supplied, disorganised and even the famous red coats were still to be issued to many units of the army.

Despite this fleeting opportunity, Charles, as usual, made a muddled compromise; he appears to have attempted to appease both parties.

As a result, there was little in the way of a coherent plan for the last campaign of Charles I. The various factions within the court still vied for power and no clear overall strategy was ever established.

As he joined his King for the last campaign of 1645, Goring was as intractable as ever. And the King, therefore, became the victim of the power struggle between Goring and Prince Rupert. Torn between two competing objectives, it would appear that Charles could not choose between either counsel. In the end he moved north as Rupert counselled.

But in reality, the defeat of the New Model Army was his only real chance left to win the war; in his heart Charles must have known this to be true.

As is often the case in military campaigns, error can seem to compound error and at this point Charles I was to make another of the grave mistakes which characterised his handling of the first Civil War.

Prince Rupert detested Lord Goring, who was to become the King's commander in the west. The young Prince succeeded in persuading Charles to order Goring to be sent back with his cavalry to help the Royalist cause in the west country, rather than remaining with the Oxford Army.

Subsequent events caused Charles to alter the orders in an attempt to head off a suspected thrust by Fairfax in the direction of Oxford.

While there is little doubt that the western Royalists needed relief, the presence of two thousand cavalry was much more crucial to the King's Army, which was already outnumbered by a powerful foe who would need no excuse to give battle at the first opportunity.

Moreover, there is certainly very little that such a meagre force could have achieved against Fairfax.

Nonetheless, Prince Rupert's counsel prevailed, and Goring with two thousand precious cavalrymen was sent into the west on his ambitious mission.

For his part, Goring disliked Rupert and relished the opportunity for independent command. In reality, he probably had little intention of being drawn back to Oxford or into the sphere of the Prince and it was that self interest that was to undermine the King's cause at its most crucial juncture.

Given Goring's yearning for the freedom of the west, it probably came as no surprise to Charles to find that, no sooner had he left Oxford on his march north, than the New Model Army arrived and laid siege to the city.

Fairfax had easily eluded Goring, who had marched straight to Taunton, and the New Model Army grew in strength and confidence with every day that passed.

The King was now in a serious dilemma. If Oxford was lost, the Royalist cause would suffer a huge blow to its already faltering morale. On the other hand, if the city could hold out for six or eight weeks it would give him time to effect his meeting with Montrose largely unhindered.

For his strategy to succeed, the King therefore needed to draw the Parliamentarians away from the city by a bold action. In this he was to prove entirely successful, though more by chance than design.

Rupert suggested that they make a pre-emptive strike against a Parliamentarian town. Charles still recalled with horror the scenes he had witnessed at the storming of Bristol in 1643 and he was at first reluctant to sanction the action now proposed by Rupert. The persistence of the Prince ultimately paid off, however, and Rupert was able to persuade the reluctant King of the wisdom of his plan to storm the Parliamentarian town of Leicester.

And so it was that the Royalist Army came to storm Leicester – but it was not to be the simple affair which Rupert had promised. Prince Rupert supervised the placing of the artillery batteries himself and much to the King's horror the town was stormed amidst great slaughter.

A portion of the defenders were Scots and no quarter was offered to them, as the contemporary diarist, Richard Symonds, later recalled in his memoirs:

"The Earl of Northampton's horse, about one of the clock were let in at the ports, and they scoured the towne. In the meane time the foot gott in and fell to plunder, so that ere day fully open scarse a cottage unplundered. There were many Scotts in this towne, and no quarter was given to any in the heat of battle."

In this nightmare situation the defenders of the town fought on. The surviving defenders of the East Gate were surrounded in Saint Martin's churchyard. Some of those who had defended the Newarke breach continued the struggle about the high cross where a handful of Scots dragoons held out. For this, they and the many other occupants of the town paid with their lives.

The actions of the New Model Army were controlled from Parliament by the Committee of both Kingdoms.

The news of the storming of Leicester provoked a panic in the house and among some members of the committee. Drastic action was now required.

Accordingly, Fairfax was instructed to abandon the siege of Oxford and march with all speed to oppose the King. So unsettled were the

Parliamentarians that they even began seriously to consider new terms for a peace with the King.

It seems that the doubts harboured by those such as the Earl of Manchester were once more at the forefront of the Parliamentary debate.

Once before, Cromwell had prevailed over Manchester and the advocates of a peaceful settlement with the King, yet it seemed that every time Parliament suffered a setback the peace party came to the fore. Men of iron like Cromwell ultimately triumphed over the doubters and waverers, but sometimes they were run close. The early summer of 1645 was just one such time.

Posterity tends to present the Civil War in terms of two very easily identified sides. Nothing could be further from the truth. In the case of the Parliamentarian side, there was always a great rift between two broad tendencies within the Parliamentary Party. There are those who were dubbed the War Party, and those who were dubbed the Peace Party.

The main difference between the two was that people like Cromwell, who was of the War Party, wanted to prosecute the war as a war and bring it to a successful conclusion. The Peace Party were always a lot more equivocal about that as an objective, and they felt that they were still, properly speaking, the King's subjects and wanted to make a point to the King. They did not necessarily want to defeat the King.

These tensions were often buried when the war itself needed the attention of, particularly, the Commons. But whenever an opportunity arose to try and to appease or to come to terms with the King, then the rift began to widen. Later on, this division in the Parliamentary side became a fight between the Presbyterians and the Independents. The Presbyterians, dominated the Commons and they tended most vigorously to pursue the Peace Party line.

On the other hand, the Independents, who were dominant in the army, were deeply suspicious of

This contemporary puritan pamphlet shows the Ship of State sailing through choppy seas with dangerous Royalists all around. The portraits are of the men responsible for the safe passage of that ship.

THE CAVALIERS

George Lord Goring. His cool relations with Prince Rupert played a decisive part in the Naseby campaign.

GEORGE LORD GORING

Probably the best cavalry commander on the Royalist side during the Civil Wars. Goring was a brave and daring commander, but he also lived up to the cavalier stereotype of a frivolous and irresponsible drinker and hellraiser. Nonetheless, he was steadfastly loyal to the cause he served and did sterling service throughout the Civil War.

Born in 1608, he was the heir to a comfortable fortune, but thanks to his spendthrift ways he was always short of money. Chasing his fortune overseas, he was wounded in the ankle at the Siege of Breda and walked with a limp for the rest of his life. Back home, he fought in both of the Bishops' Wars and gained the unusual distinction of being an Englishman who came out of that campaign with honour and credit.

With the outbreak of full scale war, he became General of Horse to Newcastle but was captured at Wakefield in 1644.

On his release he served Prince Rupert faithfully and ended the war as the Royalist Commander in the south-west. He died in exile in Madrid in 1657.

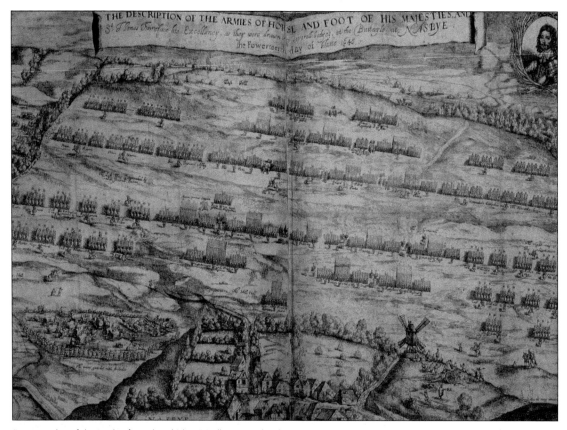

Streater's plan of the Battle of Naseby which originally accepted Joshua Sprigge's account of the campaign and field battles in the west.

Royalist intentions, deeply suspicious of the Catholic Queen, Henrietta Maria, and were vigorous Protestants; they were minded to bring the war to a successful conclusion.

It was for precisely this reason that the army was seen as an instrument of the Independents and therefore the War Party by the Commons. The Presbyterians in the Commons were deeply frightened by that.

Whatever the complexities of the political scene, the men of action triumphed over the Peace Party and Fairfax headed north with his New Model Army ready to face the King in what was to become a final reckoning.

As fate would have it, the King now changed his plans once more. Believing Oxford to be in great danger, the King abandoned his move north to link with Montrose and instead began to move south to the relief of Oxford. Urgent messages were sent to the west in a desperate attempt to recall Goring with his precious cavalry.

Charles believed the city to be hard pressed. But unbeknown to him, Oxford was already freed by Fairfax's move north to confront the King. This fateful coincidence placed the two armies on a collision course; the result was the Battle of Naseby.

The "Fog of War" now came into play. Inexplicable as it may seem to our modern minds, it seems both armies lost sight of exactly where the other was. But after some jockeying for position in the Midlands, the two armies finally came face to face with each other near the tiny village of Naseby on the morning of June 14th 1645.

Looking back more than three hundred years, from the point of view of the twenty-first century, we have a very distorted view of communications and logistics. In the seventeenth century, communications were very poor indeed; what roads existed were simply cart tracks which turned to rivers of mud at the first sign of rain. The distances between the inhabited centres were much larger and armies of the day travelled on foot.

In these circumstances, it was very easy to lose contact with an army. It was quite possible for armies to march past each other without being aware that their enemies were just over the next hill.

Reconnaissance in the seventeenth century was absolutely critical, but the means to achieve this were therefore limited. Without a good intelligence gathering operation, the army was blind. In the Naseby campaign the consequences of this were to have a profound effect on the Royalist fortunes.

Prior to the armies forming up ready for battle, Rupert sent his scout master, Russe, out to look for the Parliamentary Army. Russe, it would appear, was somewhat lackadaisical in his duty. He went out for a ride, did not find the Parliamentarians, came back and said that they were nowhere to be

seen. Rupert later rode out himself to see if he could find the Parliamentarians, found them, and thought they were retreating; in fact, they were busily choosing the ground on which to fight.

By contrast, the Parliamentarians had very good intelligence gathering; their scouts knew exactly the movements of the Royalist Army. This gave them an inestimable advantage in the fight that was to come.

Estimates as to the actual strengths of the two armies vary. Fairfax's force is reasonably thought to have amounted to between fourteen and fifteen thousand on the field that day.

Estimates of the King's strength vary, but passing of time and the romanticising of King Charles' lost cause has led to the inadvertent, or sometimes deliberate, exaggeration of the numbers he faced. As the legends have grown, so have the odds stacked against him. Some serious historians have placed the Royalist strength as low as seven thou-

A continental engraving of camp followers and soldiers at rest in a makeshift camp.

sand five hundred, which would have placed the King at a near 2:1 disadvantage.

At those odds there can be little doubt that even the ever-optimistic King Charles would have refused battle and the fact that Prince Rupert was against fighting that day is often cited as evidence for the lack of number on the Royalist side. In his memoirs, however, Lord Belayse, who fought at Naseby on the King's side, leaves us in no doubt. He recalls:

"The army of Fairfax as we conceive it was about fifteen thousand men, while the King's army was not exceeding twelve thousand horse and foot."

Based on Belayse's account, a fair estimate of the Royalist strength would appear to be between

Lord Clarendon, Secretary of State to Charles, who later wrote a comprehensive account of the war from the Royalist viewpoint.

eleven and twelve thousand men; a significant but not insurmountable disadvantage.

Whatever his actual strength, King Charles could certainly have used the support of Goring and his two thousand cavalrymen who had been sent into the west and who could not now reach him in time.

As Edward Walker makes clear, the advance of the Royalist army was caused by Prince Rupert's impatience. Lacking good intelligence of the enemy's movements, he had drawn out a party of horse and musketeers to discover their where-abouts. Catching sight of the van of the New Model Army, he called the rest of his army forward to join him:

"This made us quit our ground of advantage, and in reasonable order to advance. Having marched about a mile and half, we could perceive their Horse in the high ground about Naseby, but we could not judge of their number of intentions. To be short, the manner of our march being in full compania, gave them the means of disposing them-selves to the best advantage, and the heat of Prince Rupert, and his opinion they durst not stand him, engaged us before we had either turned our cannon or chosen fit ground to fight on.

About ten of the clock the battle began, the first charge being given by Prince Rupert with his own and Prince Maurice's troops; who did so well, and were so well seconded, as that they bore all down before them, and were (as 'tis said) masters of six pieces of the rebels' cannon. Presently, our forces advanced up the hill, the rebels only discharging five pieces at them, but overshot them and so did their musketeers. The foot on either side hardly saw each other until they were within carbine shot, and so only made one volley, ours falling in with sword and butt end of the muskets did notable execution so much as I saw their colours fall and their foot in great disorder. And had our left wing but at this time done half so well as either the foot or the right wing, we had got in a few minutes a glorious victory."

Contemporary plans drawn by staff officers are often the only surviving visual references to the disposition of armies on civil war battlefields. Fortunately, one such example survives on the subject of Naseby. It was drawn by Robert

Streater and was published with Joshua Sprigge's book "Anglia Rediviva", first printed in 1647. From Streater's work we can clearly see that the armies were arranged in the traditional manner of the day, following the strict practice of warfare at the time.

As Sprigge was Fairfax's chaplain, Streater's map is naturally drawn from the Parliamentarian position. That is, looking north from where the Roundheads were placed on Mill Hill towards the Royalist positions on Dust Hill. To the rear of the Roundhead Army is the Parliamentarian baggage train which was to play a key role in the ensuing battle.

Probably due to their superiority in numbers, the Parliamentarian left wing was able to overlap the Royalist right wing unopposed. One important detail on that wing is the presence of a large body of Dragoons under Colonel Okey. They dismounted and lined the hedgerows which masked the right flank of the Royalist cavalry. These musket-armed horsemen were now in a position where they could pour devastating fire into the ranks of the Royalist Horse as they charged home across the front.

The much-vaunted Royalist cavalry formed the bulk of the King's army. By this late stage of the war as many as two thirds of his force may have been horsemen. Prince Rupert commanded the right wing and Langdale led the left.

Joshua Sprigge described the battle in detail in his "Anglia Rediviva":

"The enemy this while marched up in good order, a swift march, with a great deal of gallantry and resolution.... It is hard to say whether wing of our horse charged first; but the Lieutenant-General not thinking it fit to stand and receive the enemy's charge, advanced forward with the right wing of the horse, in the same order wherein it was placed. Our word that day was, God our strength; their word was Queen Mary.

Colonel Whalley being the left hand on the right wing, charged first two divisions of Langdale's horse, who made a very gallant resistance, and firing at a very close charge, they came to the sword; wherein Colonel Whalley's division routed those two divisions of Langdale's bringing them

The Battle of Naseby from an eighteenth century source.

back to Prince Rupert's regiment, being the reserve of the enemy's foot, wither indeed they fled for shelter and rallied. The reserves to Colonel Whalley were ordered to second him, which they performed with a great deal of resolution. In the meantime, the rest of the divisions of the right wing being straitened by furzes on the right hand, advanced with great difficulty, as also by reason of the unevenness of the ground and a cony-warren over which they were to march, which put them somewhat out of their order in their advance. Notwithstanding which difficulty, they came up to the engaging the residue of the enemy's horse on the left wing, whom they routed and put into great confusion; not one body of the enemy's horse which they charged but they routed, and forced to fly beyond all their foot, except some that were for a time sheltered by the brigade of foot before mentioned.

The horse of the enemy's left wing being this beaten from their foot, retreated back about a quarter of a mile beyond the place where the battle was fought. The success of our main battle was not answerable, the right hand of the foot, being the General's regiment, stood, not being much pressed upon. Almost all the rest of the main battle being overpressed, gave ground and went off in some disorder falling behind the reserves. But the

John Okey, the Colonel of his own regiment of dragoons who played a significant part in the battle of Naseby.

colonels and officers, doing the duty of very gallant men, in endeavouring to keep their men from disorder, and finding their attempt fruitless therein, fell into the reserves with their colours, choosing rather there to fight and die, than to quit the ground they stood on. The reserves advancing, commanded by Colonel Rainsborough, Colonel Hammond, and Lieutenant-Colonel Pride, repelled the enemy, forcing them to a disorderly retreat. Thus much being said of the right wing and the main battle it comes next in order that an account be given of the left wing of our horse.

Upon the approach of the enemy's right wing of horse, our left wing drawing down the brow of the hill to meet them, the enemy coming on fast suddenly made a stand, as if they had not expected us in so ready a posture; ours seeing them stand, made a little stand also, partly by reason of some

Lord Fairfax, the inspired military leader who was the principal force behind Parliament's success in the field in the early part of the war.

disadvantage of the ground, and until the rest of the divisions of horse might recover their stations. Upon that, the enemy advanced again, whereupon our left wing sounded a charge, and fell upon them. The three right-hand divisions of our left wing made the first onset, and those divisions of the enemy opposite to them received the charge. The two left-hand divisions of the left wing did not advance equally, but being more backward, the opposite divisions of the enemy advanced upon them. Of the three right-hand divisions (before mentioned) which advanced, the middlemost charged not home; the other two coming to a close charge, routed the two opposite divisions of the enemy (and the Commissary-General seeing one of the enemy's brigades of foot on his right hand pressing sore upon our foot, commanded the division that was with him to charge that body of foot, and for their better encouragement he himself with great resolution fell in amongst the musketeers, where his horse being shot under him, and himself run through the thigh with a pike, and into the face with an halberd, was taken prisoner by the enemy, until afterward when the battle turning and the enemy in great distraction he had a happy opportunity to offer his keeper his liberty if he would carry him off, which was performed on both parts accordingly).

That division of the enemy's which was between, which the other division of ours should have charged, was carried away in the disorder of the other two, the one of those right-hand division of our left wing that did rout the front of the enemy charged the reserve too, and broke them, the other reserves of the enemy came on, and broke those divisions of ours that charged them; the divisions of the left hand of the right wing were likewise overborne, having much disadvantage, by reason of pits of water, and other pieces of ditches that they expected not, which hindered them in their order to charge.

The enemy having thus worsted our left wing pursued their advantage, and Prince Rupert himself having prosecuted his success upon the left wing almost to Naseby town, in his return summoned the train, offering them quarter, which

(Continued on page 178)

THE FIELD ARMIES - PARLIAMENTARIAN

THE NEW MODEL ARMY

After the disaster at Lostwithiel and yet another inconclusive battle at the 2nd Newbury dissent and acrimony broke out in the ranks of the Parliamentarian Commanders. Despite their overwhelming advantages in men and material, clearly the Parliamentarian Army structure was not working and something needed to be done.

The Self-Denying Ordinance of 1644 brought together the degenerate armies of Parliament

and forged them into one centrally commanded army – the New Model Army.

It was never to be defeated in the field.

Its first commander was Fairfax, and starting with Naseby in 1645, the New Model was to be victorious from the outset. Further triumph came at Bridgewater, Devises, Winchester, Basing, Torrington, Preston, Dunbar, Drogheda and Worcester. Here was a force without equal.

The ultimate foundation of Parliament's success and the rock upon which Cromwell built his commonwealth and Protectorate, the New Model was often the scene of political upheaval and dissent but on the battlefield it was second to none.

The standard Redcoats were gradually issued to all New Model infantry regiments from 1645 onwards. They were to be associated with British soldiers right up to the Zulu wars, almost 250 years later.

Listed below is a selection of regiments who served at various times in the New Model Army:

Foot	Horse
• Waller	• Rich
• Pickering	• Fleetwood
• Montague	• Vermuyden
• Fairfax	• Butler
• Hammond	• Ireton
• Rainsborough	• Whalley
• Pride	• Cromwell

THE FIELD ARMIES - ROYALIST

THE ARMY OF THE MARQUIS OF MONTROSE

The army of Montrose was comprised of a number of regiments which managed to land in Scotland from Ireland, supplemented with an irregular supply of Scots Highlander Troops.

The victories which Montrose won over the better armed and equipped Covenanter Armies, have often been described as miraculous, considering just how unreliable his army could be. After a victory, his Highland levies were very likely to desert for home with any plunder they could carry. Nonetheless, Montrose was able to win victory over the Covenanters until his final surprising defeat at Philliphaugh.

Listed below is a selection of regiments who served at various times in the army of the Marquis of Montrose:

Foot
- Donald Farquharson of Monaltrie
- Lord Kilpont
- Strathbogie Regiment
- Alexander MacDonnell
- Col. Thos. Laghtnan
- Col. Mums O'Cahan

Horse
- Lord Gordon's Regiment
- Earl of Airlie's Regiment
- John Mortimer's troop
- Captain Blackadder's troop

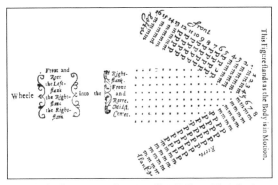

Typical wheel movement from Barriffe's 'Military Discipline'.

The Battle of Naseby as painted by Sir John Gilbert for the Royal Academy Exhibition in 1872.

(Continued from page 175)

being well defended with the firelocks, and a rear-guard left for that purpose, who fired with admirable courage on the Prince's horse, refusing to hearken to his offer, and the Prince probably perceiving by that time the success of our right wing of horse, he retreated in great haste to the rescue of the King's Army, which he found in such general distress, that instead of attempting anything in the rescue of them, (being close followed in the rear by some of Commissary-General's, Colonel Rich's, Colonel Fleetwood's, Major Huntington's, and Colonel Butler's horse), he made up further, until he came to the ground when the King was rallying the broken horse of his left wing and there joined with them, and made a stand.

To return again to our right wing, which, prosecuting their success, but this time had beaten all the enemy's horse quite behind their foot, which when they had accomplished, the remaining busi-

ness was with part of keep the enemy's horse from coming to the rescue of their foot, which were now all at mercy, except one tertia, which with the other part of the horse we endeavoured to break, but could not, they standing with incredible courage and resolution, although we attempted them in the flanks, front and rear, until such time as the General called up his own regiment of foot (the Lieutenant-General being likewise hastening of them) which immediately fell in with them, with butt-end of muskets, (the General had now nothing left in the field but his horse with whom was the King himself) which they had put again into as good order as the shortness of their time and our near pressing upon them would permit. The General (whom God preserved in many hazardous engagements of his person that day) seeing them in that order, and our whole army (saving some bodies of horse which faced the enemy) being busied in the execution upon the foot, and taking and securing

(Continued on page 182)

THE BATTLE OF NASEBY - MAY TO JULY 1645

The Battle of Naseby sealed the fate of the King's cause.

In the field, the New Model Army mustered some fifteen thousand men. Against this formidable foe, the King chose to concentrate only eleven thousand men, leaving the rest of his forces to hold garrisons in towns and castles scattered throughout the land. As the regiments left Oxford, the remaining garrison silently watched them march out. More than three hundred and fifty years on, opinion is divided as to what Charles hoped to achieve in this last campaign.

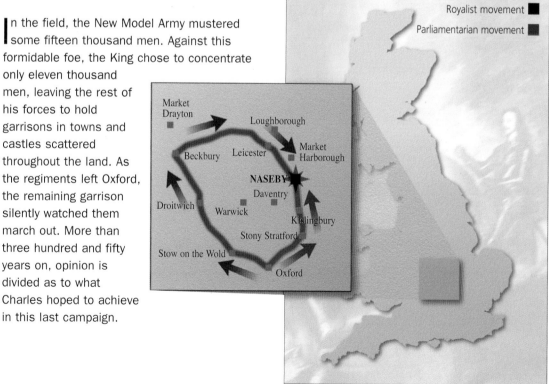

Royalist movements
Parliamentarian movements

1. Okey's dragoons are positioned behind hedges on the Parliamentarian left flank, where cavalry under Prince Rupert charge the Parliament-arian cavalry of Ireton.

2. The Roundheads are driven back and flee in disarray. Prince Rupert engages the Roundhead cavalry and pursues them off the field.

3. On the other flank however, Langdale and his Royalist cavalry flee the field leaving the Royalist left exposed.

4. Okey's dragoons mount and charge into the Royalist left flank exposed by the absence of Rupert.

5. The Roundhead threat is too great and the scattered Royalist cavalry and Foot break under preasure and run from the field.

6. Fairfax and his victorious New Model Army press home their advantage and the Royalist fugitives are cut down and killed. The remainder surrender to Rupert.

(Continued from page 178)

prisoners, endeavouring to put the army again into as good order as they could receive, to the perfecting of the work that remained."

The Royalist Cavalry, under Prince Rupert, were undoubtedly brave and courageous as they had proved on many battlefields, but they were also highly undisciplined as they had proved before.

Rupert's failure to rally his cavalry after the attack on the Parliamentary left wing is often cited as the reason why the Royalist Army lost the Battle of Naseby. In effect, the entire blame has been laid on Prince Rupert, but he was doing what cavalrymen throughout history have done. Cavalry tactics were essentially to break the cavalry opposite and then chase the stragglers from the field. It was at this point that most of the casualties occurred.

Casualties tended not to occur in the first clash. They occurred when the other side ran away. So in a sense, Rupert was following cavalry tactics as he knew them. It was almost universally accepted that cavalry were often given the opportunity for plunder so it is no surprise that Rupert's underpaid troops would not pass up such an opportunity.

What is more significant about Naseby is that Cromwell's cavalry did not break through and then pursue the stragglers. There were two reasons for that.

Firstly Cromwell's cavalry had more than enough men to be able to despatch a couple of regiments for the pursuit and kill. In addition, Cromwell's cavalry were superbly trained. They could, for instance, gallop knee to knee, which was quite a remarkable feat. They were also able to wheel and gallop and maintain that contact. So, the significant thing about Naseby is not that Rupert failed to rally, but that Cromwell was able to rally.

Facing Rupert and his cavalrymen drawn up on the right flank of the Royalist Army were the Parliamentarian troopers under Commissary General Henry Ireton. It was they who enjoyed the support of Okey's Dragoons.

After the defeat at Naseby, the hopes of King Charles rested with the Highland army of the Marquis of Montrose. This was to prove something of a forlorn hope as defeat was by now also imminent for Montrose. This Victorian view presents a rather melodramatic impression of Montrose's army, many of whom were, in fact, Irish.

Over on the other flank old Ironsides himself, Oliver Cromwell, led the Parliamentarian right wing against Sir Marmaduke Langdale and his northern horse.

The cavalry forces could be said to be roughly equal in terms of ability, but as a result of Goring's absence the Roundheads held the advantage in numbers. On Streater's plan it can clearly be seen how three ranks of Roundhead regiments are ranged against only two of Cavaliers.

The same situation also prevailed in the infantry. The Royalist strength had dwindled to such an extent that a mere four thousand five hundred Royalist infantry were expected to defeat some seven thousand Parliamentarian Foot.

At about 10 o'clock on the morning of 14th June, the Battle of Naseby commenced. Against all expectations, the battle began with a Royalist success.

On the right flank Rupert's Cavaliers clashed with Ireton's Roundheads, and after a fierce melee, Rupert's men sent them fleeing from the field. Unfortunately for the Royalist cause, the Prince could not stop his men from careering after them in hot-blooded pursuit.

In the centre, the Royalist Foot, encouraged by the success of their horsemen, launched a ferocious attack on the Parliamentarian Foot who also began to give way.

At this point the outnumbered Royalist infantry desperately needed the extra support which the victorious troopers of Prince Rupert's command could have given them. It was, however, not to be.

As he had done at Edgehill, Rupert and his victorious cavalry had charged on after the victory, furiously pursuing the beaten enemy. In so doing they charged right off the field and on to threaten the Parliamentarian baggage train, which lay some two miles to the rear.

As Rupert persisted with his unimportant efforts against the baggage train, things were going disastrously wrong back on the battlefield.

In marked contrast to the events on the Parliamentarian left, Cromwell on the right had succeeded in putting Langdale and his northern horse to flight.

But Cromwell was a far more able commander than Prince Rupert. While some of his command pursued the fleeing cavaliers, the others turned inwards to attack the Royalist Foot who were now being hard pressed by the second line of Parliamentarian Regiments.

It was now that the advantage of numbers really began to tell. Cromwell had the wisdom and the means to split his command; Langdale had no such luxury.

As the Royalist left veered towards disaster, over on the other flank things were also beginning to go wrong. Here Prince Rupert's continued absence allowed Colonel Okey to saddle up his dragoons and charge across the empty space into the exposed flank of the Royalist infantry regiments.

Now threatened on three sides, it was only a matter of time before the Royalist Foot was annihilated.

The hard pressed Royalists fought bravely but courage alone was not enough in the face of such odds. Ultimately, they were swept away by the force of the combined assault on three sides. The Royalist Army was now in a full scale rout.

As his Foot regiments fled from the field, King Charles made his famous decision to lead a last charge at the head of his own life guard.

It was typical of Charles that he allowed himself to be dissuaded from doing so. The aged and hitherto insignificant Earl of Carnwrath, using some choice Scots oaths, seized the King's bridle and turned his horse round and gave the order to march on the right.

With this, confusion and panic seems to have spread through the ranks and the King's life guard turned tail and fled the field. The battle was now totally lost.

Sprigge again...

"Our horse had the chase of them from that place, within two miles of Leicester (being the space of fourteen miles) took many prisoners, and had the execution of them all that way. The number of the slain we had not a certain account of by reason of the prosecution of our victory, and speedy advance to the reducing of Leicester. The prisoners taken in the field were about five thousand, whereof were six colonels, eight lieutenant-colonels, eighteen majors, seventy captains, eighty lieutenants, eighty ensigns, two hundred other inferior officers, besides the King's footmen and

household servants, the rest common soldiers, four thousand five hundred. The enemy lost very gallant men, and indeed their foot, commanded by the Lord Astley, were not wanting in courage. The whole booty of the field fell to the soldier, which was very rich and considerable, there being amongst it, besides the riches of the court and officers, the rich plunder of Leicester.

Their train of artillery was taken, all their ordnance, (being brass guns) whereof two were demi-cannon, besides two mortar-pieces (the enemy got away not one carriage), eight thousand arms and more, forty barrels of powder, two hundred horse, with their riders, the King's colours, the Duke of York's standard, and six of his colours, four of the Queen's white colours, with double crosses on each of them, and near one hundred other colours both of horse and foot; the King's cabinet, the King's sumpter, many coaches, with store of wealth in them. It was not the least mercy in this victory, that the cabinet letters, which discover so much to satisfy all honest men of the intention of the adverse party, fell likewise into our hands, and have been since published by the authority of the Parliament, to the view of the whole Kingdom."

For a Calvinist like Cromwell, the string of victories which Parliament enjoyed in the Civil War was proof of God's blessing upon the righteous. Time and time again his letters and speeches reflect the exaltation which came from the feeling that he was doing the Lord's work and that divine Providence was to be seen in everything he did. The best example of this feeling of spiritually

A Victorian view of the final defeat of the Marquis of Montrose at Philiphaugh in the Scottish borders. In the aftermath of the battle, Montrose was taken to Edinburgh for public execution. With him went the last hopes of King Charles.

Prisoners of war from an engraving of the Thirty Years War. Scenes like this would have been commonplace in civil war England. Although treatment was generally fair, there are numerous instances of barbaric acts, particularly against Irish troops brought over to assist the King's cause.

inspired self confidence comes from his letter of the Battle of Naseby fought in 1645.

"When I saw the enemy draw up and march in gallant order towards us, and we a company of poor ignorant men, I could not but smile out to God in praises, in assurance of victory, because God would, by things that are not, bring to naught things that are ... and God did it. O that men would therefore praise the Lord, and declare the wonders that He doth for the children of men!

Honest men served you faithfully in this action. They are trusty; I beseech you in the name of God, not to discourage them ... He that ventured his life for the liberty of his country, I wish he trust God for the liberty of his conscience, and you for the liberty he fights for."

The King himself escaped the carnage of Naseby field with a sizeable body of Cavalry and a much smaller body of Foot. He was later joined by Prince Rupert with his Cavaliers, who had escaped by a different route.

The King sought to use these men as the core of a new army. But the writing was now on the wall. His cause was all but lost. There would never again be a Royalist Field Army under the King's personal command.

1645

Royalist territory

Parliamentarian and allied territory

Royalist garrisons in
Parliamentarian territory

INVERNESS

ABERDEEN

PERTH

EDINBURGH

NEWCASTLE

CARLISLE

YORK

LINCOLN

CHESTER NEWARK

NOTTINGHAM

WORCESTER

PEMBROKE   COLCHESTER

GLOUCESTER   OXFORD

BRISTOL   LONDON

TAUNTON

PORTSMOUTH

PLYMOUTH

CHARLES IN DEFEAT

The flight of King Charles from Oxford in the wake of the final military collapse.

"Sir, this is none other but the hand of God, and to him alone belongs the glory...The General (Fairfax) served you with faithfulness and honour... honest men served you faithfully in this action...they are trusty, I beseech you in the name of God, not to discourage them...he that ventures his life for the liberty of his country, I wish he trust God for the liberty of his conscience, and you for the liberty he fights for."

Cromwell to Speaker of the Commons

After Naseby, the ordinary people thought the war was very close to a conclusion. Parliament wanted to bring it to a conclusion, and tried to do everything in its power to do so. At this juncture, the two main factions within the Parliamentarian forces appeared in disagreement, each offering one of two different solutions to the problem. On the one hand, there were the attempts to bring the King to the negotiating table, this route pursued most vigorously by the Presbyterian majority in the Commons, the Peace Party, led by Denzil Holles. On the other hand was the army, wanting to disable the King from prosecuting the war by military means and then to bring him to the negotiating table. This rift between the two parties became more and more virulent as time passed. Finally, the army mutinied because the commons themselves wanted to disband the army and were deliberately withholding pay.

With an increasingly small band of followers, Charles I travelled the country in the vain hope of raising more troops to his cause. He still hoped to join forces with Montrose, but in September came the crushing news that Montrose had been surprised and defeated at Philiphaugh in the borders of Scotland.

Charles was now the forlorn figure of legend who by his own duplicity would make his way inexorably to the scaffold.

Although defeated, he was King still, and after all, the Parliamentarians had taken up arms not against his Royal person but those advisers around the King who were now scattered or captured.

Given the sad events of the next few years, perhaps it might have been better had the unhappy monarch gone to a hero's death amidst the wreck of his last army.

The defeat of the King's Army at Naseby signalled the end of the last major Royalist Army. In a series of sieges and smaller affairs the war dragged on for another year.

One of the last Royalist strongholds to fall to the forces of Parliament was the seat of the Marquess of Winchester at Basing. The garrison had resisted numerous attempts by the Parliamentarians since 1643. With all hope of relief now gone, the garrison could have been forgiven for offering to surrender. Despite the hopelessness of the situation the Marquess refused their overtures to surrender

and Basing House was stormed by the forces of the New Model Army.

"In the several rooms, and about the house, there were slain seventy-four and only one woman, the daughter of Doctor Griffith, who by her railing provoked our soldiers (them in heat) into a further passion. There lay dead upon the ground, Major Cuffle (a man of great account amongst them, and a notorious papist) slain by the hands of Major Harrison (that godly and gallant gentlemen) and Robinson the player, who, a little before the storm, was known to her mocking and scorning the Parliament and our army. Eight or nine gentle women of rank, running forth together, were entertained by the common soldiers somewhat coarsely, yet not uncivilly, considering the action in hand.

The plunder of the soldiers continued till Tuesday night. One soldier had one hundred and twenty pieces in gold for his share, others plate, others jewels. Amongst the rest one got three bags of silver, which (he being not able to keep his own counsel) grew to be common pillage amongst the rest, and the

A rather melodramatic representation of the siege of Basing House. This highly stylised image is an example from the Victorian era depicting their passion for the Royalist cause.

fellow had not one half crown left for himself at last. Also the soldiers sold the wheat to country people, which they held up at good rates a while, but afterwards the market fell and there was some abatements for haste. After that they sold the household stuff, whereof there was a good store; and the country loaded away many carts and continued a great while fetching over all manner of household stuff, till they had fetched out all the stools, chairs and other lumber, all which they sold to the country people by piecemeal. In these great houses there was not one iron bar left in all the windows (save only what was in the fire) before night. And the last work of all was the lead, and by Thursday morning they had hardly left one gutter about the house. And what the soldiers left the fire took hold on; which made more than ordinary haste; leaving nothing but bare walls and chimneys in less than twenty hours, being occasioned by the neglect of the enemy in quenching a fireball of ours at first.

We know not how to give a just account of the number of persons that were within; for we have not three hundred prisoners and it may be an hundred

slain, whose bodies (some being covered with rubbish) came not to our view. Only riding to the house on Tuesday night, we heard divers crying in vaults for quarter, but our men could neither come to them nor they to us. But amongst those that we saw slain, one of their officers lying on the ground, seeming so exceeding tall, was measured, and from his great toe to his crown was nine foot in length.

The Marquess, being pressed by Mr Peters arguing with him, broke out, and said 'that if the King had no more ground in England but Basing House, he would adventure as he did, and so maintain it to his uttermost,' meaning with these papist; comforting himself in this disaster, that Basing House was called loyalty. But he was soon silenced in the question concerning the King and Parliament, only hoping that the King might have a day again."

The war dragged on for another year after the Battle of Naseby and ahead there was now only bad news for Charles. Word of the next catastrophe soon came in from Bristol, the last Royalist seaport and the centre of production for much of the Royalist arms manufactured during the war. The city, however, was surrendered by Prince Rupert who felt that he did not have a garrison of sufficient size to resist the Parliamentarian forces which had already captured some of the defences of the city. We can obtain a glimpse of a darker side of Charles' character when we survey the contents of the letter which was sent by the irate King dismissing the Prince into exile. A poor reward for a young man who had proved himself to be a loyal and brave servant of the last few years.

"Though the loss of Bristol be a great blow to me, yet your surrendering it as you did is of so much affliction to me, that it makes me forget not only the consideration of that place, but is likewise, the greatest trial of my constancy that be yet befallen me for what is to be done? After one that is so near me, as you are, both in blood and friendship submits himself to so mean an action (I give it the easiest terms) such - I have so much to say that I will say no more of it; only, lest rashness of judgment be laid to my charge. I must remember you of your letter of the 12 August, whereby you assured me (that if no mutiny happened) you would keep

(Continued on page 192)

NAVAL AFFAIRS

There were no great sea battles fought during the course of the English Civil War, but that is not to say that the events at sea did not play a major role in the course of the War. At the outset, the fleet which had been widely expected to declare for the King actually declared for Parliament. In order to offset this disadvantage in men and material, King Charles looked to bring in reinforcements from Ireland and from the continent to aid his cause.

The possibility of a regular supply of large scale reinforcements was effectively blocked by the Parliamentary navy who made the task of importing even small amounts of arms and supplies extremely difficult. The effectiveness of the naval blockade undoubtedly hampered the Royalist war effort throughout the first Civil War. Significant examples of naval intervention were the escape of the Earl of Essex from the wreck of his campaign at Lostwithiel, the

pursuit of Henrietta Maria as she escaped to England from the continent and the re-supplying of the besieged garrisons such as Lyme, which kept the Royalists from conquering the whole of the West Country. Under the steadfast leadership of the Earl of Warwick, the navy was to prove a vital instrument throughout the first civil war. It is ironic that the navy should have proved to be such a thorn in the flesh for Charles, for it was his decision to extend ship money tax to include towns in order to pay for the navy which was one of the chief causes of the war in the first place. After the war, the navy, under Admiral Blake, was to play a significant part in the Dutch wars, precipitated by Oliver Cromwell. The Civil War undoubtedly contributed to the growth of the Royal Navy and played a part in the development of this prominent force for the expansion of the British Empire.

The Sovereign of the Seas, Charles' flagship in the years prior to the Civil Wars.

THE ROYALIST FLEET

Despite the fact that the majority of the fleet took the side of Parliament, the Royalists were still very active. As the war progressed their fleet actually expanded, although it was composed mainly of smaller vessels used for privateering and limited runs to ferry troops from Ireland to England or Scotland. A Parliamentary estimate of Royalist strength in the spring of 1642 placed their strength at two hundred and fifty ships; a considerable force.

THE PARLIAMENTARIAN FLEET

Parliament launched and operated two fleets each year. One, the Summer Guard, operated from May until October. The other fleet operated from November to April, and was known as the Winter Guard.

Despite the stranglehold of the Parliamentarian navy, there was a gradual increase in Royalist activity at sea, so much so that in the spring of 1644, the Earl of Warwick demanded a further fifty ships and five thousand men to counter the Royalist activities. As a result, the Summer Guard was expanded from 1644 onwards.

The Sovereign of the Seas, with Peter Pett, the shipbuilder. This ship was launched in 1637 and was the finest the world had yet seen. The finance for it was raised by the highly unpopular Ship Money tax.

(Continued from page 189)

Bristol for four months. Did you keep it four days? Was there anything like a mutiny? More questions might be asked, but now, I confess to little purpose. My conclusion is to desire you to seek your subsistence (until it shall please God to determine of my condition) somewhere beyond seas, to which end I send you herewith a pass; and I pray God to make you sensible of your present condition, and give you means to redeem what you have lost, for I shall have no greater joy in a victory, than a just occasion without blushing to assure you of my being

Your loving uncle, and most faithful friend."

Charles R

Fairfax marched next into the West Country and cleared it of Royalists in a brisk campaign. Everywhere war-weariness was apparent; while many garrisons held out stubbornly, others surrendered with indecent haste. The King was now powerless – without the veteran infantry lost at Naseby, he could do nothing.

Scotland gave him some cause to hope for a while. The Marquis of Montrose led a Royalist uprising there which came tantalisingly close to victory but this brief spark too was extinguished. David Leslie utterly destroyed the army of Montrose at Philiphaugh near Selkirk on the 12th of September and the King's last hope was gone.

At length even Charles recognised his plight and surrendered himself to the Scots army besieging outside Newark on the 5th of May 1646. He seems to have had some thought of persuading them to support him, but their first act was to compel him to order the surrender of his remaining fortresses. With that the war should have been over, but the King even now refused to admit defeat and the Scots went home, leaving the King in Parliamentarian custody.

Two years of intrigue, plots and counter intrigue followed. Even though Charles was now effectively a prisoner of Parliament, a settlement was deferred time and time again as the King tried to play one faction off against the other.

The escape of Queen Henrietta Maria, a romantic view of the flight of the Queen from the pursuing Roundheads.

THE SECOND CIVIL WAR

In the early part of the Second Civil War an attempt was made to raise the London Apprentices for Charles. This move was soon suppressed by the Roundhead forces.

"The great misery and calamity of having an army of Scots without our country, that there will be war between us I fear is unavoidable. Your excellency will soon determine whether it is better to have this war in the bowels of another country or of our own, and that it will be one of them, I think it without scruple."

Cromwell to Fairfax, who refused to invade Scotland and resigned his commission. Cromwell became commander in chief. 1650

Richard Baxter described the new temper in the Army as he experienced it towards the end of the war:

"Naseby being not far from Coventry where I was, and the noise of the victory being loud in our ears, and I having two or three that of old had been my intimate friends in Cromwell's Army, whom I had not seen of above two years; I was desirous to go see whether they were dead or alive; and so to Naseby field I went two days after the fight and thence by the army's quarters before Leicester to seek my acquaintance. When I found them I stayed with them a night and I understood the state of the army much better than ever I had done before. We

that lived quietly in Coventry did keep to our old principles, and thought all others had done so too, except a very few inconsiderable persons. We were unfeignedly for King and Parliament. We believed that the war was only to save the Parliament and Kingdom from papists and delinquents and to remove the dividers, that the King might again return to his Parliament; and that no changes might be made in religion, but by the laws which had his free consent. We took the true happiness of King and people, church and state to be our end, and so we understood the Covenant, engaging both against papists and schismatics. And when the court newsbook told the world of the swarms of

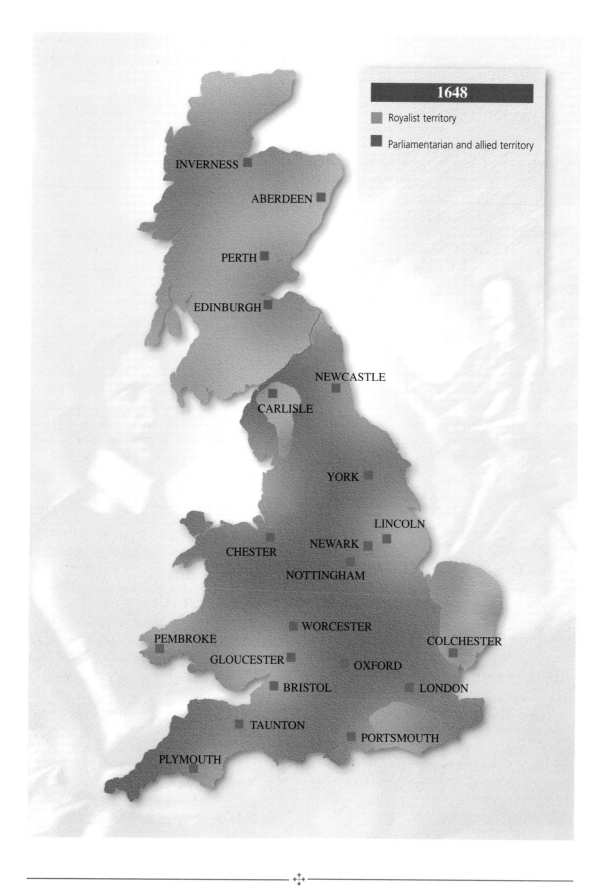

1648

◼ Royalist territory

◼ Parliamentarian and allied territory

INVERNESS

ABERDEEN

PERTH

EDINBURGH

NEWCASTLE

CARLISLE

YORK

LINCOLN

CHESTER   NEWARK

NOTTINGHAM

WORCESTER

PEMBROKE   COLCHESTER

GLOUCESTER   OXFORD

BRISTOL   LONDON

TAUNTON

PORTSMOUTH

PLYMOUTH

Anabaptists in our armies, we thought it had been a mere lie, because it was not so with us, nor in any of the garrison or county-forces about us. But when I came to the army among Cromwell's soldiers, I found a new face of things which intimated their intention to subvert both church and state. Independency and Anabaptistry were most prevalent. Antinomianism and Arminiarism were equally distributed and Thomas Moor's followers (as weaver of Wisbech and Lynn, of excellent parts) had made some shifts to join these two extremes together.

Abundance of the common troopers, and many of the officers, I found to be honest, sober, orthodox men, and others tractable ready to hear the truth, and of upright intentions. But a few proud, self-conceited, hot-headed sectaries had got into the highest places, and were Cromwell's chief favourites and by their very heat and activity bore down the rest, or carried them along with them, and were the soul of the Army, though much fewer in number than the rest (being indeed not one to twenty throughout the Army, their strength being in the generals and Whalley's and Rich's regiments of horse, and in the new-placed officers in many of the rest).

I perceived that they took the King for a tyrant and an enemy, and really intended absolutely to master him, or to ruin him, and that they thought if they might fight against him they might kill or conquer him, and if they might conquer, they were never more to trust him further than he was in their power, and that they thought it folly to irritate him either by wars or contradictions in Parliament, if so be they must needs take him for their King, and trust him with their lives when they had thus displeased him. They said: "They plainly showed me, that they thought God's providence would cast the trust of religion and the kingdom upon them as conquerors. They made nothing of all the most wise and godly in the armies and garrisons, that were not of their way. Per fas aut nefas, by law or without it they were resolved to take down, not only Bishops and liturgy and ceremonies but all that did withstand their way. They were far from thinking of a moderate episcopacy, or of any healing way between the episcopal and the Presbyterian's. They most honoured the Separitists, Anabaptists and Antinomians, but Cromwell and his council took on them to join themselves to no party, but to be for the liberty of all...

Surrender of Robert Lumsden to the forces of Parliament. A scene from the Second Civil War.

When I had informed myself to my sorrow of the state of the army, Captain Evanson (one of my orthodox informers) desired me yet to come to their regiment, telling me that it was the most religious most valiant most successful of all the Army, but in as much danger as any one whatsoever. I was loath to leave my studies and friends and quietness at Coventry to go into an army so contrary to my judgment. But I thought the public good commanded me, and so I gave him some encouragement. Whereupon he told his Colonel (Whalley) who also was orthodox in religion but engaged by kindred and interest to Cromwell. He invited me to be chaplain to his regiment and I told him I would take but a day's time to deliberate, and would send him an answer, or else come to him....

As soon as I came to the Army, Oliver Cromwell coldly bid me welcome, and never spoke one word to me more while I was there; not once all that time vouchsafed me an opportunity to come to the headquarters where the councils and meetings of the officers were, so that most of my design was thereby frustrated. And his secretary gave out that there was a reformer come to the army to undeceive them, and to save church and state, with some such other jeers."

Charles' army may have been defeated but he was King still, even though he was now effectively a prisoner. The Presbyterians were disposed to accommodate him but the Independents dominating the army became increasingly impatient with Charles. Concerned over its increasing power, Parliament tried to have the army disbanded, but the move failed. The army, along with its new champion, Oliver Cromwell, would have the last say.

The proof of this was that even in defeat they still recognised Charles as their rightful sovereign. They had taken the field because they wished merely to curb some of the arbitrary excess of his government, which they attributed to his wicked advisers. Now that the advisers had been dispensed with by force of arms, it was assumed by most Parliamentarians that it would now be possible to negotiate a new constitutional and religious settlement with the King which would be acceptable to all parties.

Cromwell was one of the many who believed this to be the case and he earnestly pursued the protracted negotiations with a defeated monarch who was nonetheless still head of state.

A fair, and to many, generous settlement which guaranteed religious toleration and curbed the Kings power, but still left him as de facto ruler, was rejected out of court by Charles in October 1647. It was Oliver Cromwell who, despite the reservations of his allies, persuaded the house to offer fresh terms to the King.

It must have come as a great disappointment to Cromwell to have had the proposals rejected but his disappointment was to turn to anger when early in 1648 he first realised that Charles had been negotiating in bad faith all along.

Trouble had been brewing in the New Model Army, still unpaid since the end of the war, and Charles had hoped to engineer a split between them and Parliament. Into this troubled arena he would bring a ten thousand strong Scots Army which was prepared to fight on his side, as the price of establishing Presbyterianism in England. This secret pact was

(Continued on page 202)

James, the first Duke of Hamilton, earned his nickname 'Captain Luckless' after the disastrous military performance of the armies which he brought into being on behalf of King Charles in the Second Civil War.

THE ROUNDHEADS

JOHN LILBURNE

Born in 1615 in Sunderland, John Lilburne has passed into legend as "Free Born John". He became a champion of political democracy and ended his days as a Quaker pacifist.

Contrary to the popular belief, he was in fact born as a minor gentleman, although he was apprenticed to a Puritan clothier. In December 1637, Lilburne was arrested for the first time and tried before the Star Chamber. Charged with smuggling and distributing illegal religious tracts and pamphlets, he was sentenced to be whipped and placed in the stocks. In addition he was fined £500, then a huge sum.

This was not to be his last taste of harsh treatment. From then on, Lilburne was to become a thorn in the side of King Charles. He played an active part in haranguing the crowds at Strafford's execution and during the war fought under the Earls of Essex and Manchester.

In 1645, Lilburne was arrested by order of Parliament for publishing and writing pamphlets without the consent of the censor.

In 1646, he was arrested for having committed contempt of the House of Lords for his attack on the Earl of Manchester. Even in prison he continued to write and smuggle out pamphlets. Needless to say, he was to incur the further wrath of Parliament.

As the controversy deepened between the Presbyterians and the Independents, Lilburne became a leading supporter of the Independents.

Throughout 1647, his pamphlets helped to inflame the already heated debate, and when the struggle between Parliament and the army threatened to get out of control, Lilburne's stream of pamphlets did not help matters.

In late 1647 he was allowed out of the Tower of London on bail but he used his new found freedom to cause further trouble by organising the Levellers. Not surprisingly, in 1648, he was again arrested and incarcerated in the Tower.

After the Second Civil War, Parliament hoped to gain supporters against Cromwell and released Lilburne from prison. In 1649 he was active against the new republican government, publishing a number of pamphlets.

Lilburne was accused of having incited the Leveller mutiny and again imprisoned in the Tower. He was released in 1649 but by 1652 he was once more in trouble. A pamphlet critical of Haselrigg caused him to flee into exile in 1652.

Foolishly, he returned to England in 1653 and was promptly arrested. He spent the remaining years of his life in and out of prison and died in the summer of 1657.

THE ROUNDHEADS

HENRY IRETON

Born in 1611 in Nottinghamshire, Henry Ireton rose to become one of the leading figures in the events of the Civil War.

Although he was only thirty when the war began, he quickly rose to a position of prominence and served under Oliver Cromwell in Lincolnshire in 1643 and at Marston Moor and 2nd Newbury in 1644.

He was a strong supporter of Cromwell in the debates of 1644 with Manchester and the other Presbyterians, which led directly to the overthrow of the Peace Party and the formation of the New Model Army.

He served with distinction throughout the war but gained real influence by his marriage to Oliver Cromwell's daughter, Bridget, in 1646. During the political conflict between the army and the Presbyterians in 1647, Ireton was Cromwell's greatest supporter and effectively became his right hand man.

At the outbreak of the Second Civil War he fought with Fairfax to suppress the Cavalier rising which ended with the siege of Colchester.

He then accompanied Cromwell in the expedition to Ireland in the summer of 1649.

Henry Ireton died at the Siege of Limerick in 1651 and was buried in Westminster Abbey.

After the Restoration, his body was disinterred and desecrated along with those of Cromwell and Bradshaw.

THE BATTLE OF PRESTON - 17TH AUGUST 1648

The Battle of Preston would prove to be one of the most complete victories won by Cromwell.

The Battle of Preston was fought as a direct consequence of the Scots intervention on behalf of King Charles under the terms of the engagement between them. While Fairfax dealt with the Royalist uprisings in the south, Oliver Cromwell swiftly crossed the Pennines and consolidated the Parliamentarian forces to oppose the Scots Army as it moved south. They were to meet in a decisive battle at Preston.

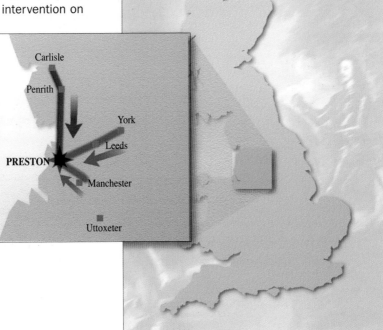

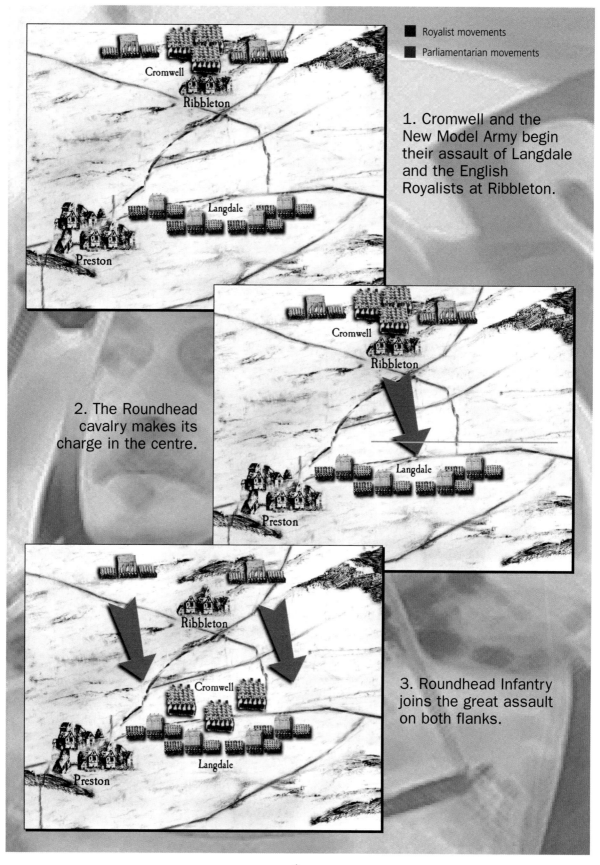

Royalist movements
Parliamentarian movements

1. Cromwell and the New Model Army begin their assault of Langdale and the English Royalists at Ribbleton.

2. The Roundhead cavalry makes its charge in the centre.

3. Roundhead Infantry joins the great assault on both flanks.

4. After a bloody fight the Royalists are driven back towards the town of Preston.

5. In panic and confusion, the Royalists break and run.

6. Cromwell presses home his advantage and captures four thousand prisoners.

(Continued from page 196)

known as the 'engagement'. All of this was to be supported by a popular Royalist uprising. Together these various actions would result in the Second Civil War. It was to be a war won once more by Cromwell.

Meanwhile, the King had concluded a secret alliance with some of the more moderate Scots. Royalist agents were also secretly prepared for a great uprising in England to coincide with another Scots invasion - this time on the side of the King.

On the 23rd of March 1648, the garrison of Pembroke declared for the King, in the rather naive belief that he would settle their arrears of pay.

Cromwell was at once sent to deal with them but a month later more Royalist rebels seized Berwick and Carlisle, opening the way for the arrival of the Scottish Army into England, now marching to the aid of the King.

Worse news was to come for Cromwell. At the end of May, a Royalist revolt broke out in Kent and the navy mutinied and declared for the King.

Although the Scots were to support the Royalist uprising and come to the aid of the King, they were delayed by fierce opposition at home until the beginning of July. By that time it was too late.

Fairfax had defeated the Kentish rebels at Maidstone in June 1648. He pursued the fugitives north across the Thames and besieged them in Colchester.

Pembroke surrendered to Cromwell on the 11th of August; only three days later the Scots at last crossed the border.

There was not a moment to lose. Marching hard, Cromwell joined General Lambert at Wetherby then turned westwards again across the Pennines to pursue the Scottish Army marching southwards on London. By this time the Scots had reached Preston, but on the 17th of August Cromwell's men defeated the English Royalist forces allied to the Scots outside the town.

CROMWELLS FOOT AT PRESTON

"They were drawn up very formidably. One Major Poundall and myself commanded the forlorn of foot, and being drawn up by the moor side (that scattering we had being not half the number we should have been) the general comes to us and commands to march. We not having half of our men come up, desired a little patience, he gives out the word "March!" and so we drew over a little common, where our horse was drawn up and came to a ditch, and the enemy let fly at us (a company of Langdale's men that was newly raised). They shot at the skies, which did so encourage our man, that they were willing to venture upon any attempt, and the major orders me to march to the next hedge, and I bid him order the men to follow me, and there drew out a small party, and we came up to the hedge end, and the enemy, many of them, threw down their arms, and run to their party, where was their stand of pikes, and a great body of colours. We drew up toward them, and on our right hand was a party of foot drawing off, that laid an ambuscade to hinder our horse, commanded by Major Smithson, from passing up the lane, and I seeing their officer, that over-run his soldiers, retreating by himself and the soldiers a great way behind him, bid the soldiers be in readiness, and stand still, and I leaped over the ditch, and made at the champion, which was one Colonel Carleton that afterwards I knew, but he over-run me on the plain-field, which caused a great shout in our army; in which time Major Smithson was advanced as forward as we were, and the enemy coming against us with a great body of colours, we had no way to shelter ourselves, but drew over a lane where Major Smithson was, and there we kept them in play so long as our ammunition lasted, and still kept our ground.

At last comes a party of Scots lancers, and charged Major Smithson in the lane, passing by us, and put him to retreat, but they were routed immediately, and one of their commanders was running away, and I being aware of him, stepped into the lane, and dismounted him, and clapped into the saddle, and our horse came up in pursuit. My captain sees me mounted and orders me to ride up to my colonel that was deeply engaged both in front and flank. And I did so, and there was nothing but fire and smoke and I met Major-General Lambert coming off on foot, who had been with his brother Bright; and coming to him, I told him

THE SCOTS HOLDING THEIR YOVNG KINGES NOSE TO Y̆ GRINSTO

Come to the Grinftone Charles tie now to late.
To Recolech tis prefbiterian fate.

You Couinant pretenders must See.
The fubiect of youer Tradgie Comedie

Jockie

George Charles

The Scots were very aggressive in their demands that Charles II adopt Presbyterianism as the price for their support in the Second Civil War. They had already been duped by the Parliamentarians in the first Civil War and in consequence they were determined to make their case very clear second time round. In this contemporary cartoon the Scots are depicted as holding the young Charles' nose to the grindstone in order to make him accept the Presbyterian religion.

where his danger lay, on his left wing chiefly. He ordered me to fetch up the Lancashire regiment, and God brought me off, both horse and myself. The bullets flew freely, then was the heat of the battle that day. I came down to the moor, where I met with Major Jackson, that belonged to Aston's regiment, and about three hundred men were come up, and I ordered him to march, but he said he would not till his men were come up. A sergeant, belonging to them, asked me where they should march? I showed him the party he was to fight and he like a true bred Englishman, marched, and I caused the soldiers to follow him; which presently fell upon the enemy and losing that wing, the whole army gave ground and fled. Such valiant acts were done by contemptible instruments! The major had been called to a council of war, but that he cried peccavi. The Lancashire Foot were as stout men as were in the world, and as brave firemen, I have often told them they were as good fighters and as great plunderers, as ever went to a field....It was to admiration to see what a spirit of courage and resolution there was amongst us, and how God hid from us the fears and dangers we were exposed to.... Such things did God for a handful of men!"

Over the next two days the Scots Army, now in considerable disorder, continued to push south in driving rain while Cromwell's men snapped at their heels. On the 19th, abandoned by their cavalry, the Scottish infantry turned at bay outside Warrington.

"We held them in some dispute," wrote Cromwell afterwards. "Till our army came up, they maintaining the pass with great resolution for many hours; ours and theirs coming to push of pike and very close charges."

Eventually the Scots ran out of ammunition and fell back into Warrington. There was some talk of fortifying the town but without ammunition it was hopeless. Next day they surrendered.

A week later Fairfax's men flaunted the banners taken from the Scot's army before the walls of Colchester. The defenders realised that no relief could now be expected, so they surrendered on the 28th of August 1648.

The Second Civil War was over and it was time for a reckoning with the King.

The events of Colchester and Preston proved to be Charles's final undoing. It was clear to all that with his various intrigues the King had played a significant part in plunging the country once more into Civil War. But it was "what to do now?", which was the unanswerable question.

Detail from a Victorian engraving: the execution of Charles Lucas and Sir George Lisle in the aftermath of the failure of the Royalist cause in the Second Civil War.

THE TRIAL OF THE KING

Coronet Joyce comes to arrest Charles, the starting point for the chain of events which would bring Charles to trial and eventual execution.

"We are not traitors, nor murderers, nor fanatics, but true Christians and good commonwealth men fixed and constant to the principles of sanctity, truth, justice and mercy, which Parliament and the Army declared and engaged for."

John Cook, regicide, before his execution, 1660

The role of the King lay at the very heart of the causes of the war and the dilemma was now greater than ever. The Parliamentary Party had embarked upon the Civil War earnestly believing that they fought for God and Parliament against the King's "evil councillors". They genuinely believed that they were at war, not with the King himself, but with the malignant party which advised him. Now the awful truth was becoming abundantly clear; his armies may have been defeated, but even in defeat Charles Stuart the man was still the King and he embodied all that went with that office.

King Charles was a man who would not yield his personal position. He still clung to principles which he had taken to the field to protect in 1642.

The great constitutional issues therefore still remained unsolved. No-one had intended that it should end this way, but among the victorious Roundheads the uncomfortable realisation gradually dawned that the only lasting solution lay in the drastic step of abolishing the monarchy and the execution of the sovereign. As yet no-one had dared to voice such a treacherous solution. It fell to Oliver Cromwell to grasp that poisoned chalice.

An engraving of the iron hat which was worn by King Charles underneath his ordinary hat during his trial as a guard against any attempt at assassination.

"We shall cut off the head of the King with the crown upon it."

But even Cromwell had supported all of the attempts to find a mutually acceptable way forward which would accommodate both the dignity of the King's position and the wishes of Parliament. The role of the King, however, in bringing about the Second Civil War convinced that God-fearing man there was no other solution.

Cromwell therefore decided that Charles would face trial for his life. Cromwell knew that no lasting peace could be found while Charles Stuart, "that man of blood", still lived. Even the most Puritan lawyers, however, declared the trial illegal. Of the one hundred and thirty five commissioners selected by Cromwell to try Charles, only sixty eight appeared when the trial opened.

CHARLES AND CROMWELL

Turning to consider the whole matter of the trial of King Charles I, we have to establish whether it was legal or not. There was certainly no precedent whatsoever, either in the unwritten or such written parts of the constitution that then existed, to allow a King to be killed by his subjects for supposed acts of treason against his own people. So King Charles I was perfectly in order, first of all, to deny the legality of the charges, and secondly to refuse to recognise the court which was sent to try him. But by now Cromwell was determined to try to solve the problem of the future of the whole country and he believed that he could not do so while the King still lived. Ironically, Oliver Cromwell was to become far more of a tyrant than Charles I. He had to rule through the army, the rule of the major generals which had a major effect, right down to the present day, on the constitutional position of the army within the British realm. Cromwell was later offered the crown twice and very wisely refused it, but as Lord Protector he had, in fact, far more power than Charles I had ever exerted.

All his life Charles had cut a rather reticent figure, not at all aided by his slight speech impediment. His trial was to be the finest hour of his life. His stammer miraculously left him and he won new admiration and respect from among even his most bitter opponents by his steadfast and dignified defence of his position.

After his first eloquent speech in his own defence, in which he refused to recognise the authority of the court, Charles was not allowed to speak again, and it was soon obvious that the trial was nothing more than a charade by which Cromwell hoped to give the dubious proceedings an air of legality.

"I would know by what authority and I mean lawful authority I am to be tried. There are many unlawful authorities in the world such as thieves and robbers on the highway which have the same authority as this assembly.

Do not forget that I am your sovereign King, ordained by God to rule his people. By that authority I stand more for the liberty of my people than any that come here to be my pretended judges. You have shown no lawful authority to satisfy any reasonable man. If I am not suffered to speak, what justice shall my people have?"

But however eloquent his defence may have been, as Cromwell had intended, Charles was sentenced to death by beheading. In order to prevent any public groundswell of support for

A Victorian engraving of the trial of King Charles I. Although he had a lifelong stammer this appears to have miraculously left him at the time of his trial where he was widely credited as having given a worthy performance.

Carnifex Maiestatis Regis Angliæ.

Fairfax is depicted as the real power behind the execution of King Charles in this contemporary engraving.

Charles bids fairwell to the Duke of Gloucester and the young Princess Elizabeth on the eve of his execution.

Charles, the sentence was to be carried out the day after the signature of his death warrant, on January 30th 1649.

Typically of Charles, that unhappy sovereign went to meet his cruel fate still espousing his unshakeable belief that it was the divine role of Kings to rule and that of his subjects to be governed.

It was his implacable adherence to this principle which had been at the root cause of the wars and Charles would carry that belief with him to the grave. In his last speech on earth, he once again returned to the principles for which he had fought and lost.

JOHN RUSHWORTH IN THE CROWD

"This day his Majesty was brought from St James's about ten in the morning, walking on foot through the Park, with a regiment of foot for his guard, with colours flying, drums beating, his private guard of partisans with some of his gentlemen before and some behind, bareheaded; Dr Juxon, late Bishop of London, next behind him and Colonel Tomlinson (who had charge of him) to the gallery in Whitehall and so into the cabinet chamber where he used to lie, where he continued at his devotion, refusing to dine (having before taken the Sacrament) only at about twelve at noon he drank a glass of claret wine and ate a piece of bread.

From thence he was accompanied by Dr Juxon, Colonel Tomlinson, Colonel Hacker and the guards before-mentioned through the Banqueting House, adjoining to which the scaffold was erected, between Whitehall Gate and the gate leading into the Gallery from St James's. The scaffold was hung round with black, and the floor covered with black, and the axe and block laid in the middle of the scaffold, and the multitudes of people that came to be spectators were very great.

The King, making a pass upon the scaffold, looked very earnestly on the block and asked Colonel Hacker if there were no higher and then spoke thus, directing his speech to the gentlemen on the scaffold..

'I shall be very little heard of anybody here,' began the King speaking from notes on a small piece of paper he had taken from his pocket, 'I shall therefore speak a word unto you here. Indeed, I could hold my peace very well, if I did not submit to the guilt as well as to the punishment.' He protested his innocence of beginning the war against the two Houses of Parliament and of any intention to encroach upon their privileges. 'They began upon me. It is the militia they began upon. They confessed the militia was mine, but they thought it fit to have it from me. And to be short, if anybody will look upon the dates of the commissions, their commission and mine, and likewise to the declarations will see clearly that they began these unhappy troubles, not I.' But he did not lay the guilt on Parliament, 'for I believe that ill instruments between them and me has been the chief cause of all this bloodshed.' Yet he

accepted God's justice in this unjust sentence as a punishment, alluding to his part in Strafford's death. He professed his forgiveness now for all men, even the chief causes of his death.

'Now Sirs, I must show you both how you are out of your way and I will put you in that way.' Conquest in an unjust cause would avail them nothing. 'You will never do right, nor God will never prosper you, until you give God his due, the King his due (that is, my successors) and the people their due, I am as much for them as any of you. You must give God his due by regulating rightly his Church (according to his Scriptures) which is now out of order.... A national synod, freely called, freely debating among yourselves must settle this, when that every opinion is freely and clearly heard. For the King indeed I will not.'

Charles suddenly stopped and turning to a gentleman who was fingering the axe he said, 'Hurt not the axe that may hurt me.' Then he continued. The laws of the land would clearly instruct them as to their duty to the King. 'For the people truly I desire their liberty and freedom as much as anybody whatsoever, but I must tell you their liberty

The Death Warrant for the execution of King Charles I. Oliver Cromwell's signature is third down on the extreme left of the document.

CROMWELL COMES OF AGE

Cromwell is depicted here in the act of dissolving the long Parliament. He had fought hard against the excesses of the King, and had himself refused the title, although it is arguable that he had become King in all but name.

With the King gone, Cromwell at last began to wield some real political authority. He was elected as the first Chairman of the New Council of State first convened in February 1649.

With the King gone, Cromwell at last began to wield some real political authority. He was elected as the first Chairman of the New Council of State first convened in February 1649. Up to this point, Cromwell had achieved his ambitions through the power of his personality and the force of his fiery oratory - now he had genuine political authority, surely he could assist in the Godly work of establishing the new Jerusalem in England.

Sadly, it was not to be, for once more, military matters would require the urgent attention of Oliver Cromwell. England may have been pacified, but Ireland and Scotland were still host to Royalist sympathies and both harboured Royalist forces in arms. Cromwell viewed these extended threats as even more dangerous than a return of his English Royalist enemies.

"There is more cause of danger from disunion among ourselves than by anything from our enemies, but I had rather be overrun with a Cavalierish interest than a Scotch interest; I had rather be overrun with a Scotch interest than an Irish interest; and I think of all this is the most dangerous. Now that should awaken all Englishmen."

So it was that Cromwell turned his attention first to Ireland. Selected as Lord General of Parliament's forces in Ireland in March 1649, he set about the task of subduing the rebellious Irish forces with his usual vigour and confident expectations of victory.

It was this phase of his career which was to bring infamy to the name of Cromwell.

On 4th September 1649, Cromwell's fearsome New Model Army made its assault on the Royalist held town of Drogheda in Southern Ireland.

The rules of war required the garrison of a town to accept an offer of surrender once its walls had been breached by cannon fire. If the offer of surrender was rejected and the town had to be taken by the bloody process of a contested attack, then no quarter was to be offered to the garrison or inhabitants. In most cases the garrison surrendered at this stage and the unnecessary spillage of blood was avoided.

For such a policy to be effective, however, the threat of such slaughter had to be carried through. Cromwell had shown himself resolute in pursuing this harsh policy. In England his men had been responsible for the storming and slaughter of the Royalist garrison at Basing House, after they had refused an invitation to surrender.

Drogheda was to prove no exception.

By refusing Cromwell's summons to surrender, the garrison and the townsfolk had effectively signed their own death warrants.

Two assaults were thrown back before a third, led by Cromwell in person, succeeded in breaking into the town - and now he was in a savage mood.

"The enemy retreated, divers of them, into the Mill Mount; a place very strong and of difficult access, being exceedingly high, having a good graft, and strongly palisaded. The Governor, Sir Arthur Aston, and divers considerable officers being there, our men, getting up to them, were ordered by me to put them all to the sword. And indeed, being in the heat of action, I forbade them to spare any that were in arms in the town, and I think that night they put to sword about two thousand men.

These atrocities, they were done in the heat of action, but the slaughter will tend to prevent the

When wielded by musketeers in close combat, the butt end of a musket was a vicious weapon.

The Parliamentarian forces lead the attack on fleeing Scots after the successful Battle of Dunbar.

effusion of blood for the future, which are the only satisfactory grounds to such actions, which otherwise cannot but work remorse and regret."

At Wexford, a similar tragic sequence of events to Drogheda was played out. This time two thousand soldiers and civilians were massacred.

Despite some later Royalist success, the backbone of resistance in Ireland was effectively broken by these horrific actions and Cromwell could turn his attention to Scotland. But the savagery of the subjections of Drogheda and Wexford was to produce a lasting legacy of bitterness in Ireland, which caused Oliver's name to be forever reviled as the "Curse of Cromwell". He himself felt he had done an unpleasant job to the best of his ability. But ultimately they were to prove hollow victories - as the noted historian Charles Firth observed:

"In truth Cromwell did much harm and little good in Ireland, of Drogheda and Wexford their memory still helps to separate the two races Cromwell wished to unite."

Fresh from his triumphs in Catholic Ireland, Cromwell now moved to confront the Protestant Scots. Ironically, Scotland was now the sworn enemy of the Parliamentary forces together with whom they had helped to defeat Charles I in the Civil War fought only three years before.

The reasons for this sudden about turn were fairly straightforward. Charles Stuart had been a Scotsman and like Parliament, the Scots armies of the Civil War had fought in the genuine belief that they were fighting for King and Parliament against the King's evil advisers, not against the King himself. There was genuine outrage in Scotland when Charles was executed by that same Parliament.

The Scots had also been fooled by Parliament into believing that the Scots' Presbyterian religion would be established as the official state religion in England as the price of their support in the Civil War. By 1650, the hollowness of that promise was clear to all.

To the fury of Cromwell, the Scots now proclaimed Charles II King of Scotland and England, with a view to establishing him as the sovereign of both Kingdoms, and with him, the Presbyterian religion. War was once again inevitable.

Almost as inevitable as the act of war, it seemed, was the assurance of victory for Oliver Cromwell. With his usual tireless energy he invaded Scotland and defeated a large Scots army at Dunbar on 3rd September 1650.

Another army of Scots and English Royalists combined at the Battle of Worcester exactly one year later.

The fight, in and around the streets of Worcester, was to prove the last great battle of the Civil Wars and for many it should have remained as Cromwell's crowning glory.

His political career was to prove far less inspired than his proud military record.

In 1651 there was a feeling in England that, with the years of military combat behind him, Cromwell was the man who would now set about the task of the great reformation of Church and State. They were to be disappointed. What lay ahead after the years of military struggle for Cromwell were more years of political turmoil.

Since 1648 the country had been governed by what was known as the Rump Parliament. These sixty odd men were the remains of the Long Parliament of 1640 who had survived the various coups, plots, fighting and changes of allegiance in the intervening eleven years. They were guided by the Council of State, of which Cromwell was once again elected to membership in November 1651.

A cloak for Knavery, 1648.

It was clear to all that it was high time this Parliament was dissolved and a new body elected. But the Rump, with its own financial interests in mind, proved to be in no hurry to dissolve itself.

Finally, in April 1653, Cromwell lost patience. Forewarned of a plot to relieve him of his command of the army, Cromwell prepared for the coming debate by placing a body of his trusted musketeers in the lobby of the house.

As the bill was read out Cromwell said nothing, but as the speaker proposed the motion that the bill be passed, Cromwell rose to his feet and began to speak:

"I thank the members of this noble house for the great care and pains it has formerly taken with regard to the public good in the early years of its sitting.

In recent years, however, your love of good works hath turned to a love of injustice, delays of justice, self-interest, and other faults. Do you have a heart to do anything for public good? You have espoused the corrupt interest of Presbytery and lawyers who were the supporters of tyranny and oppression. Perhaps you think this is not Parliamentary language. I confess it is not, neither are you to expect any such from me. It is not fit that you should sit as a Parliament any longer. You have sat long enough, unless you had done more good.

Come, come, I will put an end to your prating. You are no Parliament. I say you are no Parliament. I will put an end to your sitting. Call them in; call them in.

"O Sir Henry Vane! Sir Henry Vane! The Lord Deliver me from Sir Henry Vane! It is you that have forced me to this, for I have sought the Lord night and day, that He would rather slay me than put me upon the doing this work."

Despite his dissolution of Parliament, Cromwell had no intention of setting himself up as Dictator. As quickly as possible an interim Parliament of Puritan representatives known as the "Barebone Parliament" was nominated and commenced sitting in July 1653.

As an exercise in Parliamentary government, this too was to prove a failure. The Barebone Parliament soon made it clear that they wished Cromwell to accept the title of King of England. When he refused to do so, they simply resigned en-mass, leaving him to rule alone as a reluctant dictator. Cromwell was now back in the same lonely position he had been when he dissolved the Rump Parliament.

"My power was again by this resignation as boundless and unlimited as before, all things being subject to arbitrariness and myself a person having power over the three nations without bound or limit set. A story of my own weakness and folly. And yet it was done in my simplicity. I had thought that men of our own judgement, who had fought in the wars, would work with me in harmony but it was not to be."

With only the other army Generals alongside him, reluctantly Cromwell now accepted the written constitution which the Barebone Parliament had proposed before it dissolved itself. He flatly refused, however, to become King and was loath to accept any other title than "Protector", which he felt signalled his good intentions towards the populace. These good intentions were also made clear in the oath he swore accepting the new constitution. His abiding commitment to Parliament meant new elections would be held for Parliament in 1654; in the meantime Cromwell and his Major Generals

Oliver Cromwell at the Battle of Dunbar, a detail from one of Ernest Crofts' enduring series of Civil War scenes.

Oliver Cromwell.

Protestant Holland, which was draining the country's exchequer, his Jamaica expedition was seen as a disastrous failure and there was again domestic trouble both with his own army and the Royalists. A naval war with Spain proved to be the straw which broke the camel's back.

In the summer of 1656, Cromwell was forced to recall Parliament in order to pay for the Spanish war. This was the supreme irony. In 1640 it had been King Charles' need to pay for the wars with the Scots which had caused him to have to call the Long Parliament of 1640 which became both his enemy and executioner. Cromwell had been a member of that Parliament. Now a Parliament summoned by Cromwell was about to cause another major constitutional crisis.

At first things looked promising. Once again the new Parliament urged the office of King on Cromwell; once again he refused. But by changing the title from King to Protector, Parliament forced Cromwell to accept a new constitution which allowed him to appoint his own successor and recall an upper chamber in Parliament - effectively a House of Lords.

The wheel had now come full circle. In all but name, Cromwell had effectively become the King that he had helped to remove. Like Charles, however, he was to have more trouble with his Parliament. He quarrelled constantly with them on key issues and he angrily dissolved the second Parliament of the Protectorate in 1648 telling them that "God would judge between you and me".

This time God would appear to judge against Cromwell.

On the 3rd of September 1658, by an eerie coincidence the same day as the anniversary of his great victories at Dunbar and Worcester, Oliver Cromwell breathed his last. He died of a fever akin to malaria after an illness lasting about one month.

His much hoped for Constitutional and Religious Settlement had not been achieved. In fact, in the uncertain hands of his son Richard, his Protectorate would survive for only twenty months before a joyful populace proclaimed the restoration of Charles II and the return of the monarchy.

Although Cromwell was an undoubted genius as a military commander, on the surface it would

would rule alone. If Cromwell was to become a dictator he did so unwillingly. What follows are clearly not the words of a Hitler or Mussolini.

"I do promise in the presence of God that I will not violate or infringe the matters and things contained therein; but, to my power, observe the same, and cause them to be observed; and shall in all other things, to the best of my understanding, govern these nations according to the laws, statutes, and customs thereof; seeking their peace, and causing justice and law to be equally administered."

Despite his emotional commitment to Parliament, the seductive allure of the unrestricted power he enjoyed while ruling alone left its mark on Cromwell and he was never again able to work with a Parliament.

Although the elections had been held as promised, in 1655 he personally dissolved the troublesome group who had been elected as the first Parliament of the Protectorate. Cromwell had been unable to agree with them on key religious and constitutional issues, so once more he ruled alone, this time by choice.

The periods of rule by Cromwell and his Major Generals were not happy ones; his foreign policy had embroiled him in an unlooked for war with

Cromwell refusing the crown.

Charles is now depicted as the Royal Martyr.

appear that his military gifts greatly outweighed his political skills. In peace it seemed Cromwell's rule brought little but confusion and anarchy. While this simple analysis might be outwardly true, there was to be a Cromwellian political legacy which, it has been argued, was pivotal in establishing Britain as a major power.

The restoration of the Stuarts was itself to prove merely an interlude and the Glorious Revolution of 1688 restored many of the values of the Protectorate. Thanks to Cromwell and the Puritan revolution, by 1688 Britain was poised on the verge of greatness. Britain was the only European country without a peasant class; Cromwell's policy of naval expansion, particularly in the Caribbean, laid the seeds of empire. Trade, the basis of Britain's greatness, was expanded and encouraged beyond measure by the Puritan revolution. The advancement of science, which was to breed Britain's success in the industrial revolution, was another of the fruits of Cromwell's rule. The Royal Society was his creation.

Could Cromwell have foreseen all of this? Probably not, but he certainly believed that his God did, and as for the man, Cromwell himself was right to observe:

"None climbs so high as he who knows not wither he is going."

SELECT BIBLIOGRAPHY

Ashley, Maurice. **The English Civil War.** A Concise History. Book Club Associates, London. 1974.

Asquith, Stuart A. Peter, Gilder. **The Campaign of Naseby 1645.** Osprey Publishing, London. 1979.

Asquith, Stuart A. **New Model Army 1645-60.** Osprey Publishing, London. 1981.

Baker, Anthony. **A Battlefield Atlas of the English Civil War.** Ian Allan Publishing, London. 1986.

Barratt, John. **The English Civil War. By the Sword Divided.** Partizan Press, London. 1992.

Barriffe, William. **Military Discipline or the Young Artilleryman.** 1635

Bence-Jones, Mark. **The Cavaliers.** Constable and Company, London. 1976.

Carlton, Charles. **Going to the Wars. The Experience of the British Civil Wars 1638-1651.** Routledge, London. 1992.

Corbett, M. Norton, M. **Engravings in England.** Cambridge University Press, London. 1964.

Cowan, A. W. **Cassell's History of England.** Cassell and Co., London.

Douglas, Hugh. **Charles Edward Stuart.** Robert Hale and Co., London. 1975.

Drinkwater, John. **Oliver Cromwell. A Character Study.** Doubleday, Doran and Company, New York. 1927.

Emberton, W. Young, P. **Sieges of the Great Civil War.** Bell and Hyman, London. 1978.

English Civil War Notes and Queries. Partizan Press, London.

Gardiner, S.R. **The History of the Great Civil War 1642 - 1649.** Longmans, Green and Co.

Gaunt, Peter. **The Cromwellian Gazetteer.** Alan Sutton Publishing, Gloucester. 1987.

Green, R.J. **A Short History of the English People.** George Newnes. London, 1907.

Haythornthwaite, Philip. **The English Civil War 1642-1651.** Blandford Press, London. 1983.

Maurice, Ashley. **Rupert of the Rhine.** Purnell Book Services, Oxford. 1976.

Milford, Anna. **Eye and Ear Witnesses.** Partizan Press, London. 1992.

Oman, Charles. **A History of England.** Edward Arnold Publishing, London. 1905.

Reid, Stuart. **Scots Armies of the Civil War.** Partizan Press, London. 1982.

Ridley, Jasper. **The Roundheads.** Constable and Company, London. 1976.

Smurthwaite, David. **Battlefields of Britain.** Penguin Books, London. 1984.

Tincey, John. **Soldiers of the English Civil War (2): Cavalry.** Osprey Publishing, London. 1990.

Wedgewood, C.V. **The King's Peace 1637-1641.** Penguin Books, London. 1983.

Wedgewood, C.V. **The King's War 1641-1647.** Penguin Books, London. 1983.

Worden, Blair. **Stuart England.** Phaidon Press, Oxford. 1986.

INDEX

A

Adwalton Moor 99, 125–126, 128–129, 132
Alford, Battle of 165
Alton, Battle of 111, 113
Anglicanism 15
Artillery 59, 70, 76, 113, 136, 142, 157, 167, 184
Astly, Sir Jacob 58, 63, 184
Aston, Sir Arthur 74, 137, 203, 214
Atkyns, Richard 77, 81–82, 88–89
Auldearn, Battle of 165

B

Baillie, Robert 120
Baillie, William 142, 151
Balfour, Sir William 60, 64
Bard, Sir Henry 61
Barriffe, William 91, 96, 111, 128, 145, 165, 177
Basing House 110, 113, 176, 188–189, 214
Bath 29, 35, 89, 93, 97
Batten, Admiral 191
Berwick 120, 202
Birch, Hall 118
Blake, Admiral 190
Braddock Down 44, 90
Breda, Treaty of 169
Brentford 70, 156
Brereton, Sir William 137, 145
Bridgewater 176
Bridlington 74
Bristol 54, 57, 72, 89, 97–99, 127, 137, 139, 152, 167, 186, 189, 192, 194
Brooke, Lord 44, 51, 114
Broughton 145
Brown, Sir John 144
Byron, Lord 44, 82, 94, 104, 114, 122, 140, 145
Byron, Sir Nicholas 137
Byron, Richard 138
Byron, Sir Thomas 64

C

Cambridge, Owen 50
Carlisle 27, 148, 152, 186, 194, 199, 202
Catholicism 13, 18, 21, 23, 26, 123
Cavendish, William 125, 126, 129, 131, 137
Chalgrove Field, Battle of 57, 75, 78
Charles I 7, 9–11, 13–17, 21, 23, 25–31, 32, 61, 71, 104, 126, 132, 136, 138, 166, 167, 187, 196, 205–212, 215, 218, 220,
Charles II 17, 57, 71, 83, 126, 132, 203, 215, 218

Cheriton, Battle of 90, 131
Chester 54, 72, 127, 137, 152, 186, 194
Church of England 15, 54, 154, 212
Cirencester 57, 63– 64, 70, 105
Colchester 68, 72, 127, 152, 186, 194, 198, 202, 204
Colours 47–50, 98, 103, 114, 147, 154, 172, 175, 184, 202
Commissioners 120, 122, 204
Commonwealth 54, 132, 176, 205
Copley, General 54, 128
Council of State 63–64, 70, 213, 216
Covenanters 25, 50, 68, 177
Crawford, Lord 94, 115, 140, 141, 147, 150–151
Cromwell, Oliver 13, 16–17, 20, 44, 64, 68, 71, 73, 83, 89, 97, 112, 121, 132, 139–143, 147–148, 150–151, 154, 159, 161, 163, 168, 176, 181–184, 187, 190, 193, 195–196, 198–206, 210, 213–220
Cropredy, Battle of 41, 43, 61, 76, 134, 154–157
Cuirassiers 38, 39, 82

D

Derby, Countess of 138
Digby, Lord 163, 166
Donnington Castle 138
Dragoons 33, 58, 62, 86, 98, 142, 167, 173–174, 180–181, 183
Drogheda 71, 176, 214–215
Dunbar 176, 215, 217–218
Durham 73

E

Eastern Association 32, 73, 96, 126, 129, 140, 148–149, 159
Edgehill, Battle of 42, 51, 53, 55–57, 59–61, 63–65, 68–71, 74, 81, 116, 183
Edinburgh 17, 27, 30, 54, 72, 127, 152, 186, 194
Essex's Army 55, 58, 60, 62
Essex, Robert Devereux, Earl of 32–33, 45, 52, 55–56, 59–60, 63–65, 67–70, 74, 102–103, 105, 107, 109, 111, 131, 137, 153–154, 160, 163, 190, 197
Exeter 159
Eythin, Lord 134–135, 148

F

Fairfax, Ferdinando 137
Fairfax, Sir Thomas 74, 125–126, 128–133, 137, 140–141, 147, 153, 161–163, 167, 168, 170, 172–176, 208
Fairfax, William 62, 145, 149–151, 187, 192–193, 198–199, 202, 204